Reading the I Ching
(Book of Changes)

Also available from Bloomsbury

The I Ching (Book of Changes), by Geoffrey Redmond
A Spiritual Geography of Early Chinese Thought, by Kelly James Clark
and Justin Winslett
Chinese Philosophy and Philosophers, by Ronnie L. Littlejohn
Interpreting Chinese Philosophy, by Jana S. Rošker
Readings in Chinese Women's Philosophical and Feminist Thought,
edited and translated by Ann A. Pang-White

Reading the I Ching (Book of Changes)

Themes, Imagery, Expressions, and Rhetoric

Geoffrey Redmond

BLOOMSBURY ACADEMIC
LONDON • NEW YORK • OXFORD • NEW DELHI • SYDNEY

BLOOMSBURY ACADEMIC
Bloomsbury Publishing Plc, 50 Bedford Square, London, WC1B 3DP, UK
Bloomsbury Publishing Inc, 1359 Broadway, 12th Floor, New York, NY 10018, USA
Bloomsbury Publishing Ireland, 29 Earlsfort Terrace, Dublin 2, D02 AY28, Ireland

BLOOMSBURY, BLOOMSBURY ACADEMIC and the Diana logo are trademarks of Bloomsbury Publishing Plc

First published in Great Britain 2024
This paperback edition published 2026

Copyright © Geoffrey Redmond, 2024

Geoffrey Redmond has asserted his right under the Copyright, Designs and Patents Act, 1988, to be identified as Author of this work.

For legal purposes the Acknowledgements on p. xvii constitute an extension of this copyright page.

Cover illustration by Mingmei Yip

All rights reserved. No part of this publication may be: i) reproduced or transmitted |in any form, electronic or mechanical, including photocopying, recording or by means of any information storage or retrieval system without prior permission in writing from the publishers; or ii) used or reproduced in any way for the training, development or operation of artificial intelligence (AI) technologies, including generative AI technologies. The rights holders expressly reserve this publication from the text and data mining exception as per Article 4(3) of the Digital Single Market Directive (EU) 2019/790.

Bloomsbury Publishing Inc does not have any control over, or responsibility for, any third-party websites referred to or in this book. All internet addresses given in this book were correct at the time of going to press. The author and publisher regret any inconvenience caused if addresses have changed or sites have ceased to exist, but can accept no responsibility for any such changes.

A catalogue record for this book is available from the British Library.

ISBN: HB: 978-1-3500-7817-8
PB: 978-1-3504-4353-2
ePDF: 978-1-3500-7818-5
eBook: 978-1-3500-7819-2

Typeset by RefineCatch Limited, Bungay, Suffolk

For product safety related questions contact productsafety@bloomsbury.com.

To find out more about our authors and books visit www.bloomsbury.com and sign up for our newsletters.

For my untiringly affectionate wife 葉明媚 *(Yip Mingmei), renowned guqin player, creator of amusing paintings, and much admired calligrapher, as well as endlessly inventive story teller. Thank you for our wonderful years together.*

Contents

List of Illustrations	ix
Preface	x
Note to the Reader	xv
Acknowledgments	xvii

Part I. Background

	Introduction: Starting to Read a 3,000-Year-Old Book	3
1	Engaging with the Archaic Text	19
2	Divination: Managing Uncertainty	35
3	Is the *Book of Changes* Esoteric?	45

Part II. Grammar and Structure

4	Divinatory Prognostic Terms	55
5	The Grammar of the *Zhouyi*	71
6	Rhetoric and Forms of Expression	87

Part III. Imagery

7	The Nature of Omens	97
8	Divining About Numbers and Durations	103
9	Joys and Hazards of Daily Life	109
10	Women's Lives	117
11	Emotions and the Body	129
12	Hierarchy: Kings, Nobles, Commoners	145
13	Travel and Its Hazards	155

14	Human Sacrifice: Ritual Cruelty	159
15	Animals in Early China	175
16	Warfare	201
17	Optical Imagery: The Diagrams	207

Part IV

Final Reflections	217
Appendix	219
Zhouyi Prognostic Terms	220
Glossary of Names and Specialized Terms	221
Hexagram Chart	229
Hexagram Finder	233

Notes	235
Bibliography	243
Index	253

Illustrations

Figures

1. The *Luo Shu* or River Diagram. Public domain via Wikimedia Commons.   13
2. The most frequent yin-yang diagram. Public domain via Wikimedia Commons.   209
3. The Supreme Ultimate in one of its many variants. Public domain via Wikimedia Commons.   210
4. A Tibetan assemblage of symbols both Chinese and Vajrayana Buddhist. From Waddell (1865) *Buddhism of Tibet or Lamaism*. Public domain via Wikimedia Commons.   212
5. The diagram of Shao Yong that introduced hexagram arrays to the West. Public domain via Wikimedia Commons.   213

Table

1. *Zhouyi* prognostic terms © Geoffrey Redmond   219

Preface

Exploring Ancient China with the *Book of Changes*

During its first 3,000 years, the *Book of Changes*, also known variously as the *I Ching*, *Yijing*, and *Zhouyi*, has been read by untold millions, who variously have regarded it as a divination manual, a work of ethics and philosophy, a guide to overcoming the ego, a prefiguration of quantum physics, and, by some of the first non-Chinese trying to make sense of it, a collection of magic spells and a depiction of early Babylonian sex magic. It is usually held in high esteem, even by those who know it only by reputation; a few disdain it as superstitious, while some scholars dismiss it as unintelligible. In the pithy words of Richard J. Smith, one of the most distinguished Western scholars of the work:

> There is probably no work circulating in the modern world that is at once as instantly recognized and as stupendously misunderstood as the *Yijing* ... To some the *Yijing* is a sacred scripture ... to others it is a work of "awesome obscurity," teetering on the brink between *a profound awareness of the human mind's capacities* and superficial incoherency. (Smith 2008: 1; italics added)

Over my decades of engagement with the ancient classic, my view has fluctuated within these extremes, before finally coming to see it, not fancifully, but as one of the best objective sources we have for the workings of the human mind of 3,000 years ago, my focus being on the reconstructed early meanings. Because ancient life was quite different from that of our own time, thought was also different, yet it evolved into how we think today, in both positive and negative ways. Despite its skeptical critics, divination has been practiced at all times in all places, including our own, because making decisions is a fraught aspect of human life. In spite of being "alternative" in the West, divination continues to be widely practiced, if not always seriously, with a variety of methods, now including electronic. Originally an anthology of divination responses, the *Changes* is now most constructively viewed as an invaluable source for the history of human decision making. It shows us what sorts of decisions had to be made in the ancient past, how they were made, and, sometimes, how they worked out.

As part of the new openness to non-Western religion and philosophy that arose in the 1960s, the *I Ching* became widely popular even to the point of becoming a world classic. While many sought wisdom in the ancient Chinese book, divination remains essential to its appeal, serving to open the mind to new possibilities, while also providing entertainment. It is best performed in the spirit of experimentation, maintaining healthy skepticism about the results. Any divination method can be used to defraud; caution should be maintained.

As an American who came of age during the 1960s, it was the countercultural status of the *I Ching* that initially attracted me. It was not so much its occult aspects that stirred my curiosity, but its interest from the perspectives of philology and a philosophy quite different from the Western traditions I had been taught. A decade before I took up the *I Ching*, I had already become fascinated with Chinese culture; idly browsing in a bookstore, I happened to pull out a book on Chinese landscape painting and was instantly enthralled by the expansive space and tall mountains, balanced with waterfalls and flowing rivers. Coming at a difficult time of my life, the serenity I found in the art inspired me to further explore Chinese culture and philosophy. Fortunately, many of the classics were newly becoming available in reasonable translations. Beginning with the *Dao De Jing*, I read the *Zhuangzi*, and later the *Lunyu*. I deferred engagement with the *I Ching* until somewhat later because I could not afford the hardcover Wilhelm-Baynes translation.

When I finally shelled out for the famous gray-and-yellow compact volume with its elegant typography, I was intrigued, but found its prose frustratingly nebulous. My main problem with Wilhelm-Baynes was that it is a *gemish* גמיש, a Yiddish word used by biochemists to designate a somewhat suspect mixture of indeterminate ingredients. Just as some used to claim not to like Chinese food because they want to know what they are eating, my academic background in literature had made me want to know what I am reading. The first reasonably sound English translations were those of James Legge, followed by that of Richard Wilhelm and Cary F. Baynes. Unfortunately, in their enthusiasm to explicate, they interlarded the primary text with passages from other material including bits of the canonical *Ten Wings* and their own prolix commentary. Legge's more literal version intimidated by its dense prose interrupted by numerous bracketed insertions as well as voluminous footnotes.

Legge and Wilhelm acknowledged working with Chinese informants but, as was the practice at the time, did not grant them the recognition of being co-authors. Wilhelm wrote in German, which Cary F. Baynes translated into English. (Baynes was an American woman, although the first review of the book mistakenly referred to her in male gender.) Both were part of Carl Jung's coterie in Switzerland; while it has been suggested that Baynes might have added Jungian ideas to the *I Ching*, this was really the contribution of the celebrated Swiss psychiatrist himself in his highly influential Foreword. By redefining *I Ching* consultation as a technique for accessing the unconscious mind, Jung facilitated its adoption into Western culture, with the result that most Western writing about the *Changes* explains it using the vocabulary of psychology. With Wilhelm and Baynes, some Christian concepts, such as grace, make their appearance. The use of such language makes the *Changes* seem easier to understand but also tends to occlude the otherness of the ancient work.

Despite these limitations, the Wilhelm-Baynes edition, including Jung's contribution, well merits the praise it has received. It is no less than a major work of literature; but it is not quite the *Chinese Book of Changes*. For many Anglosphere readers, the Wilhelm-Baynes version *is* the *Book of Changes* to the point that other, more accurate translations are rejected, sometimes angrily.

It was not until I discovered the version of Richard Rutt that I was able to make progress in understanding the *Book of Changes*. I fortuitously encountered his book more than two decades ago when I walked into the book exhibit at the Association for Asian Studies, spotted the green cover of his new version entitled *Zhouyi* and immediately purchased it, recording the date, March 19, 1997, on the flyleaf. Rutt based his translation and analysis on the reconstructed early Western Zhou meanings; on my first reading of his version, although I still did not understand the ancient book, I somehow sensed that it *could be understood*. A necessary step was recognizing that the *Changes* was not a unified creation by one or a few authors, but was the work of many hands over a long duration. It is thought to have been first set into writing about 3,000 years ago, but included much material of earlier origin. The work of composing the *Book of Changes* must have been long and arduous, considering its diverse sources and that literacy was still fairly new.

Essential for me was the work on the nature of oral transmission by Milman Parry, Arthur Lord, Jack Goody, and particularly Walter Ong, which helped me greatly in understanding the syntax and rhetoric of the *Zhouyi*, derived as they were from oral usage. From my prior study of literature I was able to recognize that the ancient work was not a systematic discourse or narrative, but a collection of simple images, together with terse explanatory phrases, and standardized prognostic terms. The beguiling hexagrams, although lacking inherent meanings, added an aura of numinosity; they were later imagined to be the expedient by which the ancient sages were able to record their deep wisdom before the development of writing. The texts and diagrams became a template upon which were overlaid more than two further millennia of Chinese thought, topped off with two centuries of Western efforts to figure it out. The result is a multilayered compilation that grew to encompass very diverse meanings.

Although I appreciated Rutt's translation, I soon realized that to further pursue my quest to understand the *Changes*, I would need to learn to read the Western Zhou language as reconstructed by Chinese literati and Western linguists. My reward for this onerous task was that the ancient book gradually came to make sense to me. It helped that the vocabulary of the *Zhouyi* is limited and mostly concrete, in contrast to the abstractions in some parts of the *Ten Wings*. Grammatical clues are limited, but the brevity of the texts narrows the possibilities when parsing.

As I came (very gradually) to understand the grammar and vocabulary of the early text, I began to see how the *Zhouyi* preserved for us the thoughts and behavior of people at a time quite early in the development of literacy in China. On a deeper level, it provides glimpses of an early stage of human consciousness. (Consciousness long preceded literacy, but our evidence for it can only be inferred from writings and material culture.) Of particular interest is how language functioned near the dawn of literacy; that is, how people used the limited available vocabulary to express what was important to them.

As it happened, I was fortunate to have taken up the study of the linguistic patterns of the *Book of Changes* when it was being explicated by newly rigorous modes of scholarship. This trend had developed slowly, beginning in Qing dynasty China with the evidentiary scholarship movement *kaojuxue* 考據學, followed by the Doubting Antiquity movement *Yigupai* 疑古派 of the early twentieth century. The latter initiated the process of reconstructing ancient meanings of the classics, but often substituted ones even more fanciful. Despite numerous errors, particularly in its revision of early chronology (Wilkinson 2013: 675 f), it initiated critical study of the *Yijing*. The early Chinese texts are now usually studied from the perspectives of language and historical change. The reconstruction of the early Western Zhou meanings resulted in a *Book of Changes*, now referred to as the *Zhouyi*, radically unlike the Ruist (Confucianized) version that had supplanted it at least as early as some bits of Guodian manuscripts *c.* 300 BCE. As with any reconfiguring of an esteemed ancient work, that of the *Zhouyi* remains contentious. In the West, practitioners have ignored or rejected newer research, the Wilhelm-Baynes edition, including Jung's Foreword, being the true *I Ching* for them. Many find spiritual value in it; Cary F. Baynes summed it up well:

> If the reader is drawn out of the accustomed framework of his thought to view the world in a new perspective, if his imagination is stimulated and his psychological insight deepened, he will know that Wilhelm's *I Ching* has been faithfully reproduced. (1967: xliii)

This seems to me a reasonable way to view the great gray-and-yellow volume—as a source of new perspectives and insights; not the Chinese classic, but inspired by it.

Scholarly study has mostly avoided the divinatory function of the *Book of Changes*, but I felt it necessary to understand divination to fully understand how the book actually worked. Since divination is widely practiced today, including in the United States, I have done what is in effect field work—attending conferences for practitioners of *I Ching*, Tarot, and astrology, as well as several Spiritualist seances. I have learned much from observing actual divinations and conversations with attendees, providing insights on how divination functions in actual people's lives. It was clear that divination continues to be widely practiced by a diverse assortment of people, many of whom are articulate and some possessing advanced degrees. Many were quite facile: at lunch I sat next to someone I did not know; he quickly pulled out his phone, asked me for my time and place of birth and immediately provided me with a detailed horoscope reading. This illustrates another aspect of divination—it can serve as entertainment, although in early China it seems to have been quite solemn.

Note to the Reader

What This Book is *Not* About

Having paid my respects to Wilhelm-Baynes, I need to emphasize that the present book is something quite different; indeed, with respect to its goals as described by Baynes, their work cannot be improved upon. Instead, my goal was to reconstruct as closely as possible what the *Zhouyi* meant in Bronze Age China. I have based this on my own translation, for which I am indebted to many other scholars, particularly Richard Kunst, Edward Shaughnessy, Richard Rutt, and Richard J. Smith, but who are not to be blamed for whatever errors I have made. Also, it must be kept in mind that the reconstruction of the early meanings, although evidence-based, it is still a reconstruction, and thus a product of modern scholarship. As the study of recently excavated texts continues, a very laborious process, revisions are almost certain.

To forewarn the reader, there are several subjects the present work is not about, particularly the complex development of *Yijing* interpretation over the ensuing millennia of Chinese intellectual history. This is a fascinating story with many twists and turns; those interested are fortunate in having available a comprehensive account in Richard J. Smith's magnum opus *Fathoming the Cosmos and Ordering the World* (2008), which noted, "One of the principal arguments of this book is that the *Yijing* mirrors the mentality of its adherents" (2008: 1). Put another way, the historical meanings of the *Yijing*, though inspired by it, are mainly in the writings of the commentators, as is true of scriptural texts generally. Ruism (what is called Confucianism in the West) has been the major interpretative perspective, but Daoism and Buddhism have shaped understanding as well. Thus the study of the *Yijing* in traditional China is mainly the study of its commentaries, which are often more obscure than the primary text itself. Those of Wang Bi, Cheng Yi, Zhu Xi, and Shao Yong have been particularly influential, but there are many others. Appreciating the subtleties of their views requires knowledge of their often slippery philosophical language. Wilhelm-Baynes, despite their best efforts to convey the late Qing views of the classic, could not avoid leaving many readers perplexed. In all fairness, however, if it were not perplexing it would not be the *Book of Changes*.

The *Changes* can be a different book for different readers. The most basic difference is between scholars who conceive it as an historical document of great importance in Chinese intellectual history, and practitioners who use it for personal consultation and/or divination—those described by Baynes. Both sorts of interest exist among Chinese as well. Because of a cultural gulf, scholars and practitioners rarely meet; as a result, few interested in the *Changes* have both academic and experiential knowledge. There is also a divide between those who consider it a book of wisdom and those who also use it for divination.

In the controversies I have described, each view captures only part of the phenomenon that is the *Book of Changes*. Academics know the history and subtleties of language, while practitioners experience it in actual use. In traditional China, use of the book for wisdom and divination were not distinct because the wisdom of the *Changes* emerged during consultation about a specific situation. As a way to experience this process I suggest asking the book a question, then pondering its responses, as did Zhu Xi and other Chinese literati. This is not unlike looking on the internet for help with a personal problem; with both methods you have no idea what the response will be and must decide for yourself if the advice is correct.

On first encounter with the *Book of Changes*, modern readers, even Chinese native speakers, find it bewildering. There are two reasons for this. First, the customs of the time, such as omen interpretation and, most strikingly, human sacrifice, seem peculiar in a culture that tries to suppress the irrational. Second, Chinese is what is termed an isolating language with a paucity of grammatical clues; there are no inflections to indicate tense or case, few conjunctions, and no punctuation. The reader must therefore divide the strings of words into phrases and determine the grammatical function of each word. In the present work I explain how this can be done with the result, I hope, of making the *Zhouyi* readable, and thereby opening up the ways of thought and life of its ancient culture.

Acknowledgments

I want to begin by expressing my gratitude to Colleen Coalter, editor and now publisher at Bloomsbury Academic, who accepted my plan for a new translation and guided me through critical decisions about the best ways to present the 3,000-year-old text. I could not have completed the translation of this complex work, so remote from us in time and consciousness, without her support and encouragement. More recently, I have had the pleasure of working with assistant editor Suzie Nash, who cheerfully granted me numerous extensions, while patiently awaiting my manuscript.

Understanding of the *Book of Changes* has been transformed by recognition that the early meanings differed substantially from those imposed upon it later with the rise of Confucianism. The project of reconstructing the early meanings of the classics began in the early twentieth century as part of the New Thought Movement, through which China began critical re-examination of the mythology of its ancient past based on advances in archaeology and historical linguistics.

This new approach to study of the *Changes* was introduced to English language Sinological scholarship in the form of two doctoral dissertations, those of Richard Kunst (1985), who translated the ancient text, and Edward L. Shaughnessy (1983), who explicated the reconstructed early meanings in the Western Zhou historical context. Their work has transformed Western language scholarship of the ancient text; Shaughnessy has continued to add to our knowledge of the Zhouyi, especially with his recent publication of the major excavated texts (2014). Without the efforts of these scholars the present volume would not have been possible.

I had the pleasure of collaborating with the distinguished scholar Hon Tze-ki on my first book on the *Changes*, and continue to benefit greatly from our numerous discussions about the classic.

My translation of the *Zhouyi* took me four years, but I had already been studying it for almost two decades. In the present work I describe the methods I developed to make sense of this peculiar text in the hope that these will aid others in making sense of the archaic language and world of the *Changes*. To the extent I have been able to offer any fresh insights, these have been possible because of the work of numerous other scholars. Sarah Allan, Dennis Cheng, Keith Knapp, Ng On-cho, and Richard J. Smith were particularly supportive.

Additionally, I benefited from the lectures and publications and sometimes conversations with Constance Cook, Dennis Cheng, Catherine Despeux, Li Feng, Stephen Field, Norman Girardot, Paul Goldin, Marc Kalinowski, Michael Loewe, Ng On-cho, Michael Nylan, David Pankenier, and Robin Yates. Robin R. Wang's detailed treatise on yin-yang was particularly informative. For me to gain a sense of the way of thought of *Xiangshu*, Bent Nielsen's comprehensive work was essential, as was the immense compendium of diagrams compiled by Li Shen 李申 and Guo Yu 郭彧 (2004).

Because the early *Zhouyi* appears to have been solely for divination, understanding it requires some knowledge of these ancient practices. Publications that were useful to me for this background include those of Joseph Adler, Richard Gotshalk, Mark Edward Lewis, Liu Dajun, Ming Dong Gu, Bent Nielsen, Lisa Raphals, Frank J. Swetz, Yau Shun-chin, and Chrystelle Marechal.

The *Zhouyi* was composed in an era when oral transmission still predominated; accordingly much of the text retains oral characteristics. To make sense of the texts, it is helpful to recognize the linguistic patterns of originally oral material. This facilitates discerning patterns of imagery and syntax underlying the apparent "word salad" of the *Changes*. These patterns were first clearly described by the work of a group of philologists who spent at least some of their careers at Harvard and/or the University of Toronto, including Milman Parry, Arthur Lord, Eric Havelock, and Walter Ong, SJ, and also Marshall McLuhan, who compared the effects of printing to the much earlier oral-to-written transformation. At Cambridge University Jack Goody further contributed by approaching these issues from an anthropological rather than philological perspective.

The materials these scholars analyzed with were culturally diverse, but none can be said to resemble the *Book of Changes*. There are, however, commonalities in modes of expression used by early literate societies, including China. Within this framework, the reconstructed *Zhouyi* can be understood as representative of early written composition, rather than as a defective version of more fully developed literacy.

Translating requires facility with both the source and target languages. To be legitimate, a translation must be literally accurate, as well as readable and, ideally, interesting. Accordingly, I am indebted to several of my teachers early in my graduate study who introduced me to the complex idioms and tortuous syntax of pre-modern literature. I had the privilege of studying with the late Fredson Bowers, considered the leading English language philologist of his day (and one-time U.S. Navy code breaker), and also with Lester A. Beaurline, whose invaluable course unveiled the mysteries of scholarly methodology.

Without the electronic resources that allow almost instantaneously collating related images and vocabulary, the present work would have taken at least a decade longer. Particularly valuable were biroco.com/Yijing; ctext.org; and Pleco.com; the latter includes the multivolume French *Grand Ricci*, the most useful Western language dictionary for archaic Chinese.

In recent decades, our understanding of early China has been transformed by the work of the scholars such as those whom I list above, to whom I am deeply grateful for their stimulating contributions.

Part One

Background

Introduction

Starting to Read a 3,000-Year-Old Book

To begin, we cannot avoid the question of why we should study an obscure 3,000-year-old text. The answer is that texts from so long ago are a particularly precious part of the human legacy. Without our history, our humanity is diminished. The *Book of Changes* was created about 3,000 years ago (traditionally in 1046 BCE), not long, in relative terms, after the first evidence of Chinese literacy, the oracle bone inscriptions. Life and thought in early China were very different, sometimes shockingly so, yet we can recognize many of the same concerns present in the modern world. Still, the need for a long book to explain a very short one needs some justification. Even though the *Book of Changes* is still read after 3,000 years, its language, even in accurate translation, presents considerable difficulties on first encounter. Once the archaic grammar and metaphorical means of expression are clarified, and some of the historical context is supplied, the texts begin to make sense. Some ancient ways may still seem peculiar, even repellent, but this is not the fault of the text, which was created to help the people of its time navigate their dangerous world.

The mind of the Western Zhou was almost unimaginably different from that of the modern era. This radical otherness, I suspect, is why some scholars are attracted to this period and also why others avoid it. Much of the seeming obscurity of the *Changes* results from modern assumptions about how texts and the mind work that do not apply to the *Zhouyi*. Recognizing these assumptions and how different was the culture of the Western Zhou is the key to making sense of the *Zhouyi*.

In this introduction, I will try to clarify the nature of the *Book of Changes*, and address some of the basic questions that arise when reading it—whether for the first time, or even after years of study.

A different kind of scriptural text

The *Zhouyi* shares with the Hebrew Bible the distinction of three millennia of continuous use, although both have changed considerably over this long time span. Both have been foundational for their cultures, but are otherwise very different. While I do not find broad comparisons of scriptures to be necessarily productive, I will indulge in a brief comparison mainly to show how a text can have the role of scripture and yet be quite unlike those of the West. The Hebrew Bible was the central scripture core of an organized religion of a relatively small ethnic group. Membership in this group was to some degree hereditary until modern times; cohesion was provided by the scripture, the diverse content of which included many stories of the Jewish peoples including their communications with God. It provided explicit moral teachings, precepts, and rules, not only the Ten Commandments, but other detailed instructions for ritual and personal behavior.

The very concise *Book of Changes* became the common heritage of a civilization that was much larger and more diverse ethnically, culturally, and linguistically. Although many of the literati considered the *Changes* to be the greatest of their ancient texts, in contrast to the Bible, it was one of several canonical classics. It was considered to represent everything in heaven and earth, but with abstract diagrams, not divine pronouncements. The core text contains no myth of its creation. While it refers to rituals, the abstract high god *di* 帝 of the Shang is mentioned only once, being mostly replaced in the Zhou by the impersonal Heaven 天 *Tian*. Heaven had no attributes of a god, but did judge humans, especially rulers, whose reign was justified by the mandate of heaven 天命 *tian ming*.

Some of the early Jesuit missionaries advanced a view know as figurism, which attempted to reconcile the *Yijing* with their faith as prefiguring the Christian revelation. This had no significant influence within China and was eventually rejected by the Christian authorities back in Europe. In retrospect, this was at best wishful thinking as the *Book of Changes* has nothing in any way analogous to Christian doctrines. The early Christian missionaries were traumatized to discover a large and thriving civilization that knew nothing of the Christian revelation. (The Chinese, on the other hand, were confused by the discovery that their country was not in fact the center of the world.)

The problem for the Christians was not that the *Changes* contravened Christian doctrines or practices, but that it assumed a very different worldview. In contrast to the Hebrew Bible which is rich in stories, to the extent that the *Changes* contains stories at all, they consist of only a few phrases. While it advises on correct behavior in specific circumstances, it does not provide codified moral injunctions. Rather it indicates the appropriate behavior in the specific situation being divined about, although its moral admonitions lack the generality of the Ten Commandments. The *Changes*, together with the much later *Lunyu* (*Analects of Confucius*) was, like the Bible, considered to improve a person's character, yet in very different ways. (While Confucius in the *Lunyu* states, "What you do not want others to do to you, do not do to others" (15.24; Watson 109), this principle is found in most religions and so does not suggest Christian influence.

The earliest known textual layer, referred to as the *Zhouyi*, is more practical than ethical. Only later did it become part of the mythology of the beginning of virtuous government in China, attributed to the Western Zhou replacing the supposedly wicked Shang. The judgment and line texts were mythically attributed to the culture heroes of this time: King Wen, King Wu, and the Duke of Zhou. The actual *Zhouyi* text does not contain any mention of the Zhou defeat of Shang, or the historical figures who supposedly brought it about. It became a symbol of virtue, but this was more based on myth than actual content. The *Zhouyi* has occasionally been read as if recording the Zhou replacement of Shang. Stephen Field's recent translation is in this tradition. It rearranges the texts in an interesting way, but I question his claim that "it is as close to the original intent of the ancient Zhou diviners as has ever been possible in the West" (2015: 2). While it makes for interesting reading, it goes far beyond what I, at least, can find in the actual text. There have been other attempts to systematize the early classics, such as that of Qian Ning of the *Lunyu*, who justified this because "the Analects as we know them now have been assembled from various lecture notes made by different disciples of Kongzi at different times" (2011: 10).

I mention these because I feel they exemplify what is the wrong approach to understanding the ancient classics—rewriting them as the translator thinks they should have been by rearranging the texts in accordance with more modern notions of organization. Regarding Field's claim, we do not know the intent of the early diviners beyond what we can infer from the text as it has been transmitted, with the meanings reconstructed based on linguistic evidence. It seems to me better to work with the text we have rather than create one that never existed.

Can the ancient *Zhouyi* be understood in translation?

It is a commonplace that texts, especially ancient ones, or those in non-European languages, cannot be truly translated into another language. On a trivial level this is correct—the translation is not the original. Given the impracticality of learning the original language of every book one wants to read, translations can bring us close to their meanings, despite the nuances that are lost. Translations of works in many languages are published every year, more than a few become best-sellers, demonstrating that readers find them of value.

My maxim in reading or translating ancient texts is that if a work could be understood when it was created (3,000 years ago in this case) it can be made understandable today. There are, of course, passages in some works that resist complete understanding, but with enough effort by the translator, these should be few. I strived to reproduce not only the meanings, but also the matter-of-fact tone of the early text, to the extent possible in contemporary English . Chinese, especially the ancient form, is highly polysemous; that is, many words have numerous possible meanings. The translator must pick one, while a Chinese reader will be aware of several meanings that fit the context.

This approach is unavoidably philological, in the sense well described by Islam Dayeh:

> Philology deals with the unraveling of linguistic difficulties and obscurities, with textual fragmentation, cultural loss and alterity. Philological projects are revivalist in essence; they seek to make the unavailable available, to preserve and to bring back to life. (2016: 403)

With the *Zhouyi* one could suggest that the text has needed not just revival, but resuscitation. This was achieved with great effort, based on advances in historical phonology and the unearthing of Chinese texts of comparable antiquity. Once the tedious work of restoring the inscriptions has been carried out, literary intuition is needed to bring the text to life. As much attention must be paid to the target language as to the source. As stated by Steve G. Lofts regarding his translation of Ernst Cassirer's difficult *Philosophy of Symbolic Forms*:

> The goal of a translation should not be to interpret for the reader but rather to facilitate the reader in undertaking their own interpretation. That said, there is always a degree of interpretation that cannot be avoided. (2021: xvii)

The contrary of this—paraphrasing rather than translating—was the method of some of the early great Chinese-to-English translators, such as D. C. Lau and Arthur Waley. This can no longer be excused by the canard that a translation can be both literal or readable, but not both. With all due respect to their achievements, their method unintentionally assumes the stereotype of the inscrutable East, which Westerners would not be able to understand directly. There is nothing wrong with creating an adaptation, which is what Wilhelm-Baynes actually is, but it should be labeled as such. Some translators, appropriately preoccupied with the source language, seem to have given the target language less attention. An example is James Legge, arguably the first British sinologist, who became the first Professor of Chinese at Oxford, but, unfortunately, a less than felicitous translator.

Philology has a reputation, not entirely undeserved, of pedantically missing the forest for the trees. But philology, delicately applied, is needed to illuminate texts obscured by the darkness of time. Meaning begins on the level of the word, which then can be formed into phrases, and on to recognition of higher-level structures. Without fussing over the precise meanings of the words we cannot reach the ideas nor the aesthetics. The final result should, out of modesty, hide the strenuous work of restoring meanings in naturally flowing prose. In a text to be read as well as studied, glosses should be concise so as not to interrupt the flow of reading.

Regrettably, there are many pseudo-translations that substitute New Age or pop-psychological jargon for the actual meanings. There are worthwhile translations but they have to be sought out. In his list of "noteworthy" English translations, Joseph Adler, a leading American scholar of the *Changes*, lists those of James Legge, Richard Wilhelm and Cary F. Baynes, Richard John Lynn, Richard Rutt and, kindly, my own (Adler 2020: 19).

Why Chinese characters with the English translations?

The present work is intended primarily for English language readers who want a guide to lead them through a text that both fascinates and mystifies. Lest anglophone readers feel put off by the Chinese characters and pinyin Romanizations, they can be reassured that these are optional. They are for readers with some Chinese to help them connect with the original; they contain nothing not also stated in the English text.

The genre of the *Zhouyi*: Divination manual and more

To understand any text, it is necessary to recognize its genre. With modern material, this happens almost automatically; the book cover or online listing usually tells us what sort of book we are about to read and so there is no need to think consciously about its genre. With ancient works, however, such clues are often lacking, unless the genre has been explained by experts. Genre theory has become quite complex, but the point to be made here is straightforward.

Whether or not it is a book of wisdom, in the earliest forms we know of, the *Book of Changes* was used as a divination manual, as it continues to be. It is possible, however, that the intent of the compilers was slightly different—to assemble an anthology of important divinations. Most of the texts read as records of divinations, rather than as answers to questions. Translators, including myself, have considered it to be a source of divination responses and translated it accordingly. Given the lack of tense indications, many of the texts could be translated as records of prior divinations, rather than predictions or recommendations for future behavior. Here is one of many possible examples:

> 57.2 Kneeling at the low platform. Employ record keepers and shamans in large numbers. Auspicious, there will be no blame.
>
> 九二巽在牀下. 用史巫紛若. 吉, 无咎.

This could be:

> Having knelt at the low platform, and having employed record keepers and shamans in large numbers, it was auspicious in averting blame.

In a way, this makes more sense, because the description of this ritual event has the character of a record rather than a recommendation for a future ritual. Because for most of its history the *Changes* functioned as a divination manual, it has been translated as guidance for the future, rather than accounts of the past. Given the lack of tense indications, as well as the terse nature of the text, both ways of reading it are plausible. The presence of prognostic indicators suggests it was used for divination quite early; alternatively, some or most of the prognoses may have been added somewhat later to facilitate divinatory use. These two possible accounts of its origins—as a collection of divinations versus phrases to use for divination—are not necessarily incompatible. To compile a divination manual, compilers would have needed sources and prior events would have served this purpose. That the *Zhouyi* texts were put into writing indicates that they held potency, and so might have multiple uses.

Word magic

The *Zhouyi* does not contain much explicit word magic, although the invocation in 1.1 and other judgment texts could fit this category:

> 1.0 Begin with an offering; beneficial to divine
>
> 元亨利貞 *Yuan, Heng, Li, Zhen*

The oracle bone inscriptions began as divinations and later evolved into spells to bring about a desired outcome. I suspect something like this with the *Zhouyi* texts—not that they were intended to bring about the outcome they describe, but that they somehow had the power to make correct predictions and therefore could be used repeatedly. This explains why it seems to combine simple advice for present and future with historical references.

Although compiled from multiple sources, it is clear that the *Book of Changes* belongs to the genre of divination manuals. Once this is recognized, its sometimes specialized language and often peculiar modes of expression become mostly understandable. Although unfamiliar to most modern readers, divination manuals were widely disseminated in the premodern world, and still retain a niche readership, who find them in New Age sections of bookstores or online. Functionally, divination manuals are reference works; they are consulted to find answers to questions about the inquirer's life, either directly, or by means of a diviner. The inquiry is often, but not always, about the future; it can concern past events or handling a present situation.

Divination manuals vary greatly in format and style, but all address common concerns of human life. The *Zhouyi* is extremely terse, probably not as a deliberate stylistic choice, but because it was compiled early in the development of written expression in China. For this reason, it consists of only simple images and descriptive phrases; the latter typically provide only limited explanations.

Psychology and the *Book of Changes*

In the West, beginning in the eighteenth century, a variety of cultural movements led to new ways of understanding the workings of the mind. Specialized vocabularies developed to express these new ways and were applied to use to explain many aspects of human culture, notably religion and philosophy, happiness and unhappiness (the latter previously termed melancholia), as well as causes of violence and social power dynamics. By the late nineteenth century depth psychoanalytic explanations of religion became particularly influential. Those of Freud drew upon his own Jewish heritage and, most famously, appropriated figures from Greek mythology, which he then reduced to psychological concepts. Jung famously summarized this as: "The gods have become diseases" (Jung "Commentary" in Wilhelm 1962). Because there was no overt evidence for such concepts as the "Oedipus complex," Freud placed them in the newly invented unconscious, a part of the mind not accessible to normal awareness, but not acknowledging the metaphysical nature of this concept. Jung also drew on the ancient world, particularly India, which he visited only later in life; in contrast to Freud, he was concerned to revalidate religion rather than to refute it. Indeed, it was Jung's seminal Foreword to the Wilhelm-Baynes *I Ching* that made the ancient work accessible to Westerners by explaining it as a way to access the unconscious. A more philosophical approach to spirituality, particularly influential in academic study of religion, was that of William James in *Varieties of Religious Experience*. Many others could be mentioned, including Sir James Frazier, especially in light of Wittgenstein's critique.

I mention these famous figures to alert those beginning to read the reconstructed *Zhouyi* c. 1046 BCE that they will find nothing resembling these modern modes of exegeses. In traditional China nothing analogous to psychological language existed; divination was routinely accepted without need for empirical verification. Beginning with the rise of Ruism in the Warring States, the yin-yang and *wu xing* metaphysics were elaborated and provided the theoretical basis for *Yijing* interpretation. These concepts did not develop until centuries after the *Zhouyi* was composed; the early text never proposes any basis for its efficacy. Not only in China, but in Greece and other ancient civilizations, it was just assumed that divination was a useful and valid way to make decisions. In this sense the *Zhouyi* is entirely descriptive; it states images, prognostications, and prognoses, but these are selected by a random method. It is up to inquirer and diviner to apply these to the inquiry. Later, the profundity of the *Changes* was explained by it being the record of the insights of ancient sages, who understood heaven and earth better than those who came later. It attributes events to the state of the cosmos at a particular moment, not to specific causes.

Origins

It is the beguiling six-line diagrams referred to in English as "hexagrams" that made the *Changes* unique among all the world's divination texts; without them it likely would have long been forgotten.[1] The *Zhouyi* text itself does not refer to the hexagrams; it has been proposed that their original function may have been to find the correct text for a specific divination. They are thought to have evolved from simpler linear marks on pottery, but no intermediate forms have been discovered. Later, as part of the Ruist adaptation of the *Changes*, efforts were made to read the core texts and figures as an integrated whole; this is apparent throughout the *Ten Wings*, particularly the *Tuanzhuan*, *Dazhuan*, and *Shuogua* which refer extensively to line and trigram positions. These basically defined subsequent *Yijing* interpretation. They are clearly based on the core text, though in what form we do not know, and add meanings to the trigrams and lines based on their positions relative to others. The *Zhouyi* makes no mention of this or any other system of interpretation; such must have been in use but we have no source for them.

Even though there is a reasonable consensus about the reconstructed early meanings of the *Zhouyi*, we have little direct evidence as to how the text was actually read and understood, or even the setting in which it was used. The only evidence we have is found only in centuries later sources. We often do not know if those who used the *Zhouyi* memorized parts of it, read it, or had it read to them. There is no record as to whether it was read in solitude, in dyads, or in larger groups; presumably it was used in all such settings. As to whether the interaction was master–student, diviner–inquirer, or free discussion, or most likely, all of these in different circumstances, we do not know. Nor do we know the extent to which it circulated in partial or variant forms. Many excavated texts, including the appendices found with the *I Ching* at Mawangdui, are fragments of a longer work, so it is possible that many users did not know the full work.

Some practitioners resist thinking of the *Changes* as being intended for divination, because they feel that this detracts from its status as a compendium of sagely wisdom. I will take up this issue in more detail later, but here point out that this is based on a fallacious assumption—that use of divination is a sign of ignorance and superstition. Historically, this is entirely incorrect; until modern times divination was practiced by people at all levels of society. In the ancient world, Confucius and Socrates, as well as kings and generals, practiced it. Divination is more usefully conceived as an element of human consciousness—much of our thinking concerns the future. A great variety of theories and techniques have been devised for divining; most recently software for this purpose has proliferated. Knowledge of the mostly unknowable future is still sought by many means because human life has always been filled with anxieties about health, physical security, arbitrary authority, travel, relationships, sexuality, and reproduction, among other uncertainties. This is why despite these broad similarities, ancient life was very different. The *I Ching*, if in a reasonable translation, can tell us much about the details of ancient worries and how they were responded to. Divination manuals tell us much about the form these worries took in their era, as well as measures available to cope with them.[2]

The place of the *Book of Changes* in Chinese culture

The recent arrival of the *I Ching* in the West is only one of many transformations in its long evolution, but resulted in its being read in ways that would have been incomprehensible to traditional Chinese. Hence those who know it only by Wilhelm-Baynes or other translations will have at best a limited understanding of what it means in its culture of origin.

While the *Book of Changes* is not recorded as having been a prominent part of official rituals, so far as I am aware, it was declared canonical in 136 CE by Emperor Wu 武 of the Western Han, thus becoming one of the five so-called Confucian classics (Adler 2022: 17–19; Nylan 2001 passim). This confirms that it had been fully adopted into Ruist 儒 (Confucian) orthodoxy by this time. Ruism designates the ideology of those educated in the classics, in ancient times the six arts of ritual, music, archery, chariot driving, calligraphy, and mathematics. Ruism is a broader and more accurate designation than "Confucianism," which is not used in China and is problematic because much of the ethical and philosophical tradition that has been referred to as "Confucianism" in the West was not in the Master's teachings. For example, the traditional associations of Confucius with the *Book of Changes* are apocryphal, including authorship of the *Ten Wings* and his wanting fifty more years to study it. Thus the conventional designation of the *Changes* as a "Confucian" text is misleading.

Even at times when Daoism or Buddhism were predominant, the *Changes* was studied by virtually all the literati (educated elite). The mythology about its ancient origins placed it at the center of Chinese identity, with the appealing story of the culture hero Fu Xi discovering of the trigrams on the back of a tortoise, or in some accounts, the *Luo Shu* 洛書 magic square (see Figure 1).

In the *Dazhuan*, several of the trigrams are credited with inspiring important aspects of civilization such as plows and markets, thus making the *Changes* part of the mythology of Chinese origins. In the modern world, Chinese as well as many non-Chinese hold it in high esteem, even though most have not read it. (This admiration for unread classics is not unique to China; few in the West have read Plato or Aristotle.)

The *Zhouyi* contains few abstract ethical, psychological or philosophical terms; presumably they had not yet become part of the language. So far as we can judge from the *Zhouyi* texts, its value was providing guidance for handling difficult situations. Presumably many found it helpful, otherwise it would not have survived. Basically a collection of images that could serve as metaphors to

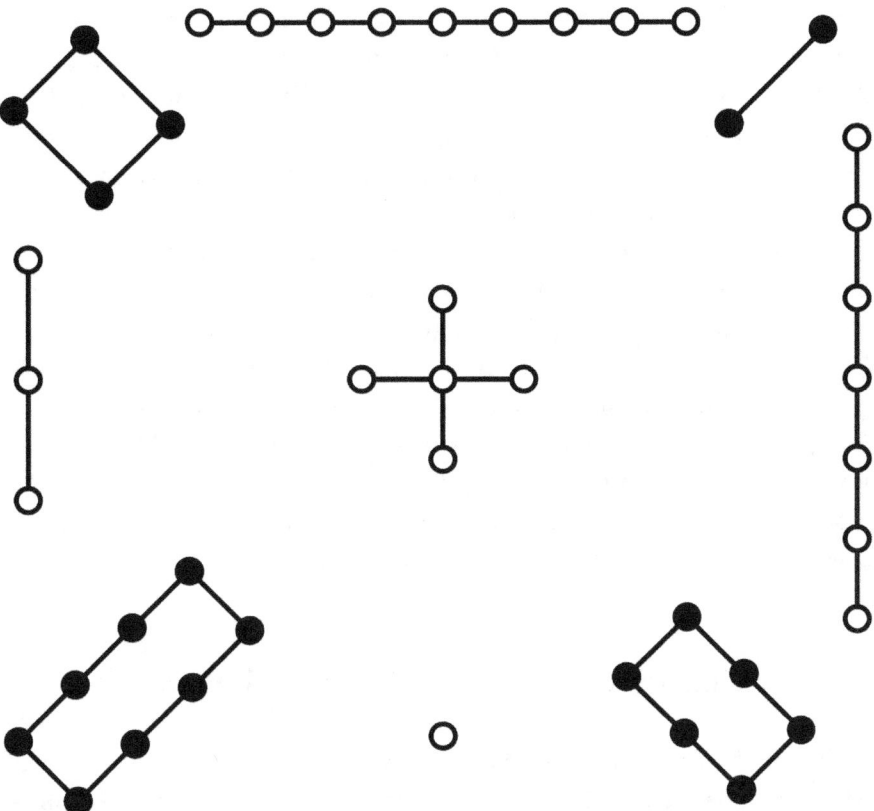

Figure 1. The *Luo Shu* or River Diagram. Public domain via Wikimedia Commons.

represent virtually any life situation, it included a few proverbs and other bits of wisdom material, but almost no abstractions.

It was not until the Warring States that the seminal works of Chinese philosophy began to appear (Redmond 2017: 353). Most of the philosophy associated with the *Yijing* is contained not in the *Zhouyi*, but in the *Dazhuan* 大傳. First attested by Sima Qian 司馬遷 *c.* 100 BCE, this canonical commentary, also referred to as the *Xi Ci* 繫辭, constitutes Wings 5 and 6 of the *Ten Wings* (Rutt: 404).

Selection of texts for divination

For actual divination, specific lines within hexagrams must be selected. These methods are not mentioned at all in the base text, but are referred to, but not explained, in the *Ten Wings*. Yarrow sorting to generate a line number is the earliest known. After the introduction of metal coinage in the Spring and Autumn, the simpler method of tossing of six coins became more popular. There may have been secret methods as well.[3] The ancient procedure for line or text selection by yarrow was lost quite early; in the Song Zhu Xi proposed a reconstruction, but his method is awkward in actual use.

Most of these methods generate a single line, together with its associated text. The process is repeated until all six lines are selected, each of which will be one of the four types—yin, young (8) or old (6), and yang, young (7) or old (9). (Solid lines are yang, while broken ones are yin.) During the Han divination was based mainly on trigram and line positions, often involving intricate numerology (the *Xiangshu* school 象數); with the *Yili* method later attributed to Wang Bi, there was renewed attention to the texts (*Yili* school 義理). (These are discussed in more detail in Chapter 4.) Use of hexagram lines versus the text has been debated over the classic's long history, often acrimoniously.

Spirituality and philosophy in the *Book of Changes*

In my recent translation I attempted to show how the *Zhouyi* seems to contain what might be seeds of ideas that foreshadowed what later became Chinese philosophy (Redmond 2017: 353–80). In the present book I apply methods of literary analysis, including patterns of imagery, rhetoric, and peculiarities of syntax to reveal emergent patterns. In a few cases the patterns seem to hint at nascent philosophical ideas that ultimately were incorporated in the more overtly philosophical texts of the Warring States, Han, and later. While we do not find formal philosophy in the *Zhouyi*, there are a few bits of text that show humanity starting to reflect on its life and place in the cosmos.

A related issue is whether the classic can be considered spiritual; although this is usually assumed, Rutt's argument needs to be considered seriously:

> If the *Yijing* has, in spite of itself, accrued a quasi-spiritual aura and has been used for spiritual purposes, that is because its original meaning was forgotten. (Rutt 51)

Rutt wrote from his background as a Christian missionary for whom spirituality must include monotheism; while this is a limited perspective, but it can motivate us to go beyond the pat belief that it contained the wisdom of high antiquity. Instead, we can set aside preconceptions of what spirituality should be and examine the *Book of Changes* to discover if spirituality is present and, if so, what form it takes. Rutt does acknowledge that, despite the *Zhouyi* not being overall a work of wisdom or philosophy, or spirituality, eventually it did acquire all of these. Despite hints of ethics and philosophy that foreshadow Chinese philosophy, nothing suggests that the *Zhouyi* compilers had an idea of philosophy as a particular way of thought. They simply inserted bits of reflection into the text; it was centuries later that the great philosophical texts began to appear, although in forms unlike those of the West. China had no Socrates or Aristotle, just as Greece had no Confucius or Laozi.

Practitioners and scholars

Those seriously interested in the *Book of Changes* tend to fall into one of two groups—scholars or practitioners. The former have recently focused, as I have, on the reconstructed early meanings, especially in light of the excavated texts, and other recently discovered material related to the Western Zhou. The study of later interpretations of the classic has been revitalized by use of evidence-based methodology, which began to be applied to the ancient classics in the later Qing and became increasingly rigorous from the Republican Period to the present (Elman 2001 passim). Methodology is similar for the study of other ancient texts of China, emphasizing accurate reading of the texts based on advances in historical linguistics (Baxter and Sagart 2014). Scholarly study has concerned itself with the meanings of the texts and hexagrams, but not as much with its divinatory use.

Practitioners, in contrast, find the *Book of Changes* of value for their personal lives, either as an aid for decision making or for psychological insight. A few *Yijing* scholars admit to consulting the book themselves, at least experimentally, while others deny any interest in doing so. I put myself in the first group; it seems peculiar to me to invest great effort in studying a text, yet not experience it as it was actually used. This can be compared to reading about music without actually listening to it. Although it is not always admitted, most feel some anxiety when obtaining a reading, whether by themselves or with a diviner. There is always the possibility of bad news, which can be disturbing, even for those who do not believe in it. Deep in the human mind, primeval fears persist.

Practitioners generally dislike the reconstructed early version and even challenge its validity, in contrast to most Western sinologists who accept the early meanings. An example is Bradford Hatcher, whose self-published works provide a useful, if sometimes hyperbolic, critique of academic sinological approaches:

> I will concur wholeheartedly with the scholars that the *Zhouyi* was not the manual of social engineering that Confucians made of it, nor is it the manual of cosmological mysteries that the religious Daoists saw. But I will not join these modernists and drag it all the way back to the caves of Paleolithic society...I do not consider the Yi to be a work of philosophy in the genre of Warring States teachings. But the idea that the Yi might have been, at least in a small way, an ethical manual does not seem at all incongruous, nor does it seem out of line to see the Yi as a "primitive" book of psychology. (Hatcher 2009: I.15)

I know of no one who considers the *Changes* to be a work of the "Paleolithic," but the reconstructed early meanings do seem "primitive" to those unfamiliar with early texts generally.

Among Chinese there is a wide spectrum of opinion about their most famous ancient classic, although a significant number reject the reconstructed early meanings. Clashes between traditionalists and revisionists are usual with respect to scriptural texts. Those disputing their validity often approach them synchronically rather than as historically conditioned. The Wilhelm-Baynes version lends itself to this approach because it presents the text as timeless, having expurgated most of the many unpleasant images and is seemingly unaware of it having a textual and interpretive history.

Practitioners, who greatly outnumber scholars, are a quite varied group whose only commonality is using the *Book of Changes* in their lives. Online *I Ching* communities exists, but I suspect that most practitioners are solitary, in contrast with astrology and Tarot for which online communities seem more active. Whether one considers these practices religious or not, their followers experience them as spiritual and some at least flirt with supernatural beliefs. This latter aspect is rarely discussed in conferences about Tarot, astrology, or other esoteric practices. The many practitioners I have met seem untroubled about whether or how divination works. *I Ching* readings can be based on the brief texts, whether literally understood or not, or can use elaborate analyses of line positions (*Yili* 義理 and *Xiangshu* 象數 respectively). In actual use, at least since Wang Bi 王弼 (226–249 CE), both methods are used in combination. Chinese usually consider themselves to belong to one of the two schools, while non-Chinese do not.

That the *Book of Changes* is part of a system of practice has been essential to its popularity and longevity. As Pierre Hadot has shown, in the classical world, practice also held an important place in philosophy (Hadot 2004). In the 1960s, many of the young began to feel that their culture was lacking in spirituality and began to search for it outside the mainstream religions. At this time of rebellion and ethical confusion, the Ruist moralism of the Wilhelm-Baynes *I Ching* provided a sort of ethical grounding, more acceptable because of its exoticism. Systems that emphasized practices—doing things—rather than reciting prayers and listening to sermons were more appealing. Asian religions, particularly Buddhism, but also Hinduism and sometimes aspects of indigenous ones, emphasized practices, at least as presented by such emissaries as Episcopal minister turned Zen Buddhist Alan Watts, Maharishi Mahesh Yogi (the Beatles' guru), among others, who preached new systems of belief and emphasized practices. These included meditation, usually with postures novel to Westerners, and sometimes with mala beads, mantra recitation, contemplation of mandalas, and mental gymnastics such as koans. Carl Jung wrote about some of these from a psychological perspective, making them more accessible, although he also warned Westerners not to practice yoga, perhaps having recognized these practices as potential competition with psychotherapy. For many, these practices adapted from Asian traditions were simply fads, but a significant number took them seriously, even to the point of becoming Buddhist monks, or obtaining PhDs in related subjects. Many now established Asian scholars began as practitioners.

The *Changes* is a book, but also something more—the experience of consulting it. If one simply picks it up, starts at the first page and tries to read through to the end, the result is almost always frustration, because it was never intended to be read in linear fashion; like the other early classics, it was not organized thematically. In traditional Chinese use, before the book was opened a simple physical ritual was performed, usually tossing coins or sorting yarrow sticks; these indicated the hexagrams and lines that were the answers to the inquiry. Early editions, at least those which have survived, were on bamboo strips, which form a cluster that is heavy and awkward to sort; manual effort would have been necessary to find the indicated section. Thus the consultation process involved the body as well as the mind.

Contrary to disparagements by a few who saw themselves as defenders of science, the *Changes* tended to be used to suggest possibilities rather than to tell fortunes. Thus it can open up possibilities rather than limit them. Some of the most admired intellects of ancient times, including Confucius and Socrates, believed in divination. In the modern world many report divinatory readings to have been helpful in their lives. In modern vernacular, it facilitates thinking outside the box.

To conclude this introductory chapter, here is an excerpt from a letter I sent in response to an article in the *Skeptical Inquirer* entitled "What's Wrong with the *I Ching*: Ambiguity, Obscurity, and Synchronicity" (Sullivan 2009):

> The article seems to be directed at a hypothetical group who use the *I Ching* in a literal-minded way to make important decisions. Perhaps there are some such, but my experience suggests that for most who are interested in the *Changes* the motivation is to understand ways of thought very different from those of the modern world. Particularly unfortunate is Sullivan's remark that the "words of advice ... appear to be no more illuminating that the words of advice found inside fortune cookies ..."

(My letter received no reply.)

Yes, the language is obscure, hardly surprising since the earliest textual layers are nearly 3,000 years old, in a language quite different from modern Chinese. This sort of condescending dismissal without any actual knowledge of the *Changes* is regrettably common.

I have spent more than twenty-five years studying the *Book of Changes* and before that had a more general interest in divination, mainly Tarot, but also astrology and spiritualism. Despite my long fascination with divination as a mode of consciousness communication, I have no definite conclusion about what happens in the process. Divination may be a religious practice, as in Thailand and other Buddhist countries where some monks perform divination in exchange for donations. Some religions opposite it, at least in theory. The practice of divination does not require any specific belief system or ideology. My approach is to understand it, not prove or refute it.

1

Engaging with the Archaic Text

To understand a text, a reader needs to know what kind of text it is; that is, its genre, and a general idea of what it meant to its writers and readers. This is usually determined so quickly as to be a nearly unconscious process. Yet we cannot read a science article as if it is a poem, nor the reverse. The genre of the *Book of Changes* is the divination manual. Once extremely popular, these are now read mainly by a relatively small group. The *Yijing* does not explain itself, although modern editions, both in Chinese and English, include explanatory material. If we imagine a reader completely naïve to the nature of the text, it appears as a collection of simple images drawn from ordinary life, to which are appended prognoses and fragmentary explanations. The texts are ostensibly organized according to the lines of the diagrams, but why a text was assigned to a specific line is never stated. The primary text does not explain how it is to be used for divination, or even whether that is its function at all. While it has been assumed that it was intended as a collection of answers to divinatory inquiries, the original questions are not included. Many of the texts do not seem to be in the form of answers to questions, so it could originally have been an anthology of text fragments felt to be important enough to be preserved in writing, later made into a divination manual.

My own theoretical preference, based on work with a very ancient text with many uncertainties, is to begin with a traditionally philological approach that strives for accuracy and objectivity, but openly acknowledges when uncertainties cannot be resolved. This requires locating the text both historically as well as linguistically. Once the text has begun to make sense, it can serve as a source for the development of the Chinese written language development and also begin to tell us about the life of its time, the fortunes of its people and their values. One must be clear about what the texts do not tell us.

About the Western Zhou (1046–771 BCE) much remains unknown; surviving texts are limited and tend to be formulaic. In spite of these difficulties, much can be learned by close reading accompanied by archaeological evidence. Given the polysemy of its language, the *Zhouyi* is best approached in an experimental spirit, trying different meanings before settling on what seems most reasonable, keeping in mind that any translation of this archaic work is a hypothesis, not a conclusion.

With very early texts such as the *Zhouyi*, habits of reading that are usual for more recent texts can result in frustration. Even though there is a reasonable consensus about the reconstructed early meanings of the *Zhouyi*, we have little direct evidence as to how the text was actually read and understood, or even the setting in which it was used. We often do not know if those who used the *Zhouyi* memorized parts of it, or had it read to them by others more literate. There is no early record as to whether it was read in solitude, in dyads, or in larger groups; plausibly it was used in all such settings. Interaction may have been hierarchical as master–student, diviner–inquirer, or collegial, between friends. It likely often circulated in partial forms instead of what came to be considered the complete work. Many excavated texts, including the commentaries included in the Mawangdui silk manuscript, are fragmentary, so it is possible that many readers did not know the full work, if there was one

In this chapter I describe a variety of useful ways of approaching early texts and indicate what I believe are some of the insights they can provide. Given that the *Zhouyi* is unique in the world's literature, no one approach is definitive..

Organization

Early Chinese texts were compilations and thus do not have thematic or narrative organization comparable to a modern non-fiction work. Rather than regarding the *Zhouyi* as defective, however, we should recognize the principle of coherence it does manifest—a very precise system for organizing its fragmentary text portions so as to make them quickly accessible by random selection methods. This system is the hexagram array in which each text is associated with a line (except for the judgment texts which are associated only with the specific Hexagram, not with a specific line). This organizational scheme, baffling to most modern readers, enabled it to function efficiently as a reference work in which the selected text could be quickly located.

There are several factors that partially account for the often randomly ordered text portions in the *Zhouyi*. Some may have been based on incomplete or damaged sources and likely some oral material, which by its nature lacks permanent organization. Given the preciousness of manuscripts, the scribes' priority may have been simply to preserve or transmit the words believed to be from sages. Even in modern times, quotations from scripture or iconic authors such as Shakespeare or Proust do not necessarily correspond to their order in the written text. In contrast to some writers of modernist fiction who deliberately vary the order from the chronological, with the *Zhouyi* and other early works, the principle was simply getting the words down on the available medium, bamboo or silk, or for some texts bone, shell, or bronze. When thematic organization is present it extends for a few lines, only sometimes enough to constitute a complete anecdote. Once the reader comes to terms with this, the glimpses provided of early life can be appreciated.

It is natural, although anachronistic, to imagine that the *Book of Changes* was originally more topically organized; some editors and translators have attempted to "restore" the imagined original order. Much as these may appeal to some modern readers, none are supported by any textual evidence. Something like this is found in Field's *Duke of Zhou Changes* "based on the traditional understanding that ... the Duke of Zhou is the author of the line texts of the *Zhouyi*" (2015: xi). This is, however, only one of the traditional attributions for this part of the text. Given that the real duke spent much time waging war, as well as killing or exiling his brothers, it seems improbable that he would have time or interest for literary composition (Nylan 2010a: 94–127). Such attributions to culture heroes were made for all of the Chinese early classics. Field also rewrites and reorganizes the line texts in tabular form. It is interesting to see how he has rearranged the text, but it seems better to at least start with the text as it has actually been transmitted.[1]

Referring to the Laozi, Crispin Williams comments:

> since the Laozi is not a narrative, it does not have a beginning and end; in that sense the sections do not have a correct order. (144)

These remarks apply to the *Book of Changes* as well; although the Hexagrams are numerically ordered in modern editions, this is a later addition. In early use with yarrow, they were built up line by line and hexagrams identified by which lines were changing. With bamboo strip manuscripts, the order would easily change if the leather binding strips wore out, as legend has it happened with Confucius' copy.

Exegesis: The methods of analogy and anomaly

Textual criticism in the classical world developed as early as the third century BCE, with two different schools: that of Alexandria—the method of analogy—and

Pergamum—the method of anomaly (Greetham 299–305). The former held that texts should be regarded as internally consistent and that editing should smooth out what seemed inconsistent. The anomaly method, in contrast, accepted a text's oddities and did not try to resolve them by emendation. Neither method is better for all texts. They also apply to selecting meanings for translation, particularly with the highly polysemous early Chinese language. Applying the analogy method can end up being rewriting—unfortunately all too common with Chinese-to-English translations. With the anomaly method, there is still an effort to try to select the best reading, but without forcing the text into consistency.

The nature of variants in the *Zhouyi* is quite different than those of ancient Greek and Latin texts, which were the initial subjects of Western critical textual scholarship. In contrast with these works, especially the Greek New Testament, for which there are hundreds of extant manuscripts, there are only a few for the *Zhouyi*, only three of which are complete enough to be compared: the received version, that excavated near Ma Wang Dui, and that owned by the Shanghai Museum. The provenance of the received text is unknown. All of the excavated versions were created centuries after even the latest plausible date of the *Zhouyi*. Of the many character variants, only a few are substantive. Most are simply homophone substitutions—replacement of the proper character with another of similar sound. None radically change our readings of the *Zhouyi*, except in one respect—they show that the *Changes* text was remarkably conserved over the centuries. This is extremely important because it establishes that the apparent obscurities are not due to corruption, but are inherent in the text.

The textual problems with the *Zhouyi* are not due to multiple witnesses but to the extreme polysemy of Chinese, compounded by the paucity of phonemes. As a result, many of the characters themselves have multiple meanings, with further ambiguity added by the frequent use of homophone substitutions. Furthermore, even when the word designated by a graph is not ambiguous, its meaning may have changed greatly over the past three millennia. Thus the late Qing meanings that Legge and Wilhelm relied upon for their translations often were substantially different from the reconstructed Zhou meanings.

The usefulness of the analogy–anomaly distinction is to make conscious the need to make ongoing choices between altering a problematic word or phrase and leaving it as it is. As I show throughout, the syntax of the *Zhouyi* has regular patterns, yet more than a few phrases seem distinctly strange. Usually this can be resolved by reasoned selections from the many possible meanings, although there will be more than a few instances when several meanings fit the context. Limitations of the method of analogy is that first, the *Changes* is itself anomalous, being unlike any of the other Chinese classics; second, it is clearly an assemblage from multiple sources so we cannot assume a consistent authorial voice, nor scribal consistency. Finally, altering words from the actual text risks eliminating some of its distinctive features. Nonetheless, the method of anomaly should be tempered with the principle that if the text could be understood 3,000 years ago, it can be understood today, at least most of it. No doubt, as with most texts, ancient or modern, a few inscrutabilities will remain, but these should not excuse introducing obscure meanings without actual evidence, as has been too often the case with this classic.

With the addition of the *Ten Wings,* traditional Chinese interpretation reached the extreme of analogy, the text being in effect rewritten to conform with Confucian ideology. Later, the debunking Doubting Antiquity movement applied the method of anomaly, often to the point of indulging in whimsy. Neither method fully resolves the difficulties of the *Zhouyi*; ultimately instead one must resort to *bricolage,* making use of what fits.

Here are examples of the two methods as applied to a phrase from 4.0; in my translation :

Not I who asks the neophytes; the neophytes ask me.

匪我求童蒙；童蒙求我.

I chose "neophyte" based on the plant component of the second character. Wilhelm-Baynes render 童蒙 as "young fool," (20f), which is similar, if less literal. In contrast, Rutt, following a suggestion of Arthur Waley, renders meng 蒙 as "dodder," a kind of weed (227, 297). Shaughnessy renders it as "shroud" (2014: 73). Choices of Wilhelm-Baynes and myself can be ascribed to the method of analogy, while the latter two are anomalous. Here analogy is appropriate because it yields unproblematic meanings that fit the overall context, which is about treatment of children. The latter two translations have no basis beyond the mystique of Arthur Waley, a great translator, but with a taste for the fanciful.

Modern theories

The Sapir-Whorf hypothesis

This is a hypothesis kept alive by its critics. Few linguists now openly support it. The basic idea, never directly expressed by the two linguists to whom it is attributed, is that language determines what can be thought. This seems to me self-evidently true, if we modify it slightly to state that language is one of the determinants of what can be thought, language and thought being in a constant state of interaction. The necessity of language for thought is most obvious in technical fields such as medicine, mathematics, law, accounting, even linguistics itself. A doctor cannot make a diagnosis without knowledge of the specialized vocabulary, nor can a lawyer construct an argument for a case. The second modification is that the theory cannot contend that language irrevocably limits thought because new vocabulary can be learned or created as needed. The final modification is that language can adapt to expressive needs. The vocabulary of the *Zhouyi* is quite limited, but its range is extended by metaphor and analogy. For example, moral principles are usually expressed as what the cultivated person (君子 *junzi*) would do rather than by abstract terms for virtues and vices.

Despite these work-arounds, the expressive power of the *Zhouyi* language is more limited than we find with the later Chinese classics. Abstract terms are infrequent and we do not find reflections on society, as we do in Confucius, Xunzi, Mencius, Laozi, and Zhuangzi. The later work includes humor and irony, absent from the *Zhouyi* with a few possible exceptions. The expressive power of written language developed gradually over centuries after the invention of writing. In this perspective, the laconic nature can be understood, not as deliberate hiding of esoteric truths, but as having a language only recently being able to be written. Walter Ong argued that the language of non-literates was largely made up of set phrases because more original expressions were soon lost to memory (2002: 33–6).[2]

Context-dependent versus argumentative texts

A distinction proposed by Dirk Meyer (2012: 11 et passim 1) in relation to the Guodian manuscripts *c.* 330 BCE, unearthed 1993; see also S. Cook 2012) can provide a useful perspective on the nature of the *Zhouyi*. The first category he terms argumentative, "which aim to be persuasive by establishing their reasoning on the power of 'good arguments.'" Context-dependent texts, on the other hand, "do not seek to establish argumentative force by virtue of reason. Instead they largely rely on established and identified authorities." Although the *Zhouyi* is more than half a millennium earlier than the Guodian texts, Meyer's insight is useful because much of his description of context-dependent texts applies to the *Zhouyi*. It is only through other sources that we know that it is very ancient, that it is a divination manual, and that it was held in high esteem throughout most of its history. Confucius, although there is no evidence that he actually knew the *Changes*, was invoked as its main external authority. Because of the cultural eminence of the Master, its ethical rectitude and philosophical profundity were placed beyond doubt.

The name of Confucius established the authority of the *Changes*, but not its meanings; the hexagrams in particular had no evident context, while the texts, if not obscure when they were compiled, certainly were by some point in the Eastern Zhou. To the extent that wisdom and metaphysics were present in the *Zhouyi*, it was in seed form (Redmond 2017: 353–80). These first appear in the *Ten Wings*, particularly the *Dazhuan* and *Shuogua*. The most famous concept of Chinese philosophy, yin-yang metaphysics, began to be prominent in the Warring States, and became progressively more in the Han. Thus much of what is usually credited to the *Yijing* actually was not in the core text, but were later additions. This is true of hexagram, trigram, and line position meanings, as well as more abstract conceptions.

Symptomatic of the *Yijing* and *I Ching* being context-dependent is the ample explanatory material included in most editions, even my own with my deliberately terse minimalist glosses. Few readers, including Chinese, can understand the *Book of Changes* without additional material to place it in the context of Western Zhou life and language, as well as the culture of divination.

Unfortunately we do not know anything about how the *Zhouyi* was regarded in the era of its creation. At some point mythology arose that associated it with Fu Xi, one of the legendary founders of Chinese culture, who discovered the trigrams (or the related Luo Shu magic square) on the back of a tortoise. The sages could understand the meanings directly from the trigram patterns, but by the rise of the Western Zhou, there were no sages remaining and so the judgment and line texts were added by King Wen during years of unjust imprisonment, and/or by the Duke of Zhou, with Confucius authoring the *Ten Wings*. This mythology justified the great esteem in which the ancient book was held and is believed by many to this day, although current scholarly consensus holds that Fu Xi was mythical and the supposed roles of Zhou Gong and Confucius apocryphal. These stories are engaging and no doubt contributed to the longevity of the ancient work, combined with the fascination of the texts and hexagrams. Because of the text's ancientness, it would have seemed almost self-evident that it preserved the lost wisdom of sages.

The mythology of its origins enabled it to be adopted by the Ruists to support their ideology, which they superimposed on the primary text. We do not know when the *Changes* began to be read for wisdom. It is tempting to attribute this to the addition of the *Ten Wings*, particularly the *Dazhuan*, and *Shuogua*, but this begs the question of why this highly abstract and philosophical text was appended to it. Importantly, the *Yijing* mythology also served to support the legitimacy of the authoritarian system of government by attributing the authorship of the texts to two of the Zhou founders. Eventually, reverence for the work made it part of China's identity, hence part of the ideology that Yuri Pines (2022) argues was the major reason China was able to maintain unity over the millennia.

While context-dependent texts may seem inherently less informative than argumentative ones, they can be of interest for the ideas that attach to them, as is the case with the *Book of Changes*. Put another way, context-dependent texts inspire us to examine their contexts.

Somewhat akin to context dependence is the method of "patterning" in medieval exegesis, in which "readers were expected to form their own synthesis and to detect meanings hidden in the text" (Olson 162). This could equally well describe how the *Changes* has been and continues to be read, whereby the texts are read with at least as much attention to subjective associations as to literal meanings. At the time of divination, these together with the inquiry and response form a unique set of meanings that, appropriately, change with each consultation of the book. The process would be similar when the book was used as a source of wisdom, because most often wisdom is sought for reassurance or guidance.

Coherence

Although the *Book of Changes* seems incoherent to many moderns, those who compiled it must have had some ideas about what they wanted to accomplish. To infer their principles, we have to attempt to put ourselves in the mindset of those who assembled it and infer how they conceived it would be used. If we hypothesize that what was most important was being able to locate the correct response during divination, the system of organization by hexagrams and lines is quite efficient. An iterative method, such as yarrow sorting or coin tossing, is used to generate six lines, which indicate the applicable Hexagram, then a specific line is used.[3] Presumably, this response would have been read by itself, so that it did not need to be consistent with other lines of the same Hexagram. Essentially the textual structure of the *Book of Changes* is that of a reference book, such as dictionary or encyclopedia.

Later classics, such as the *Lunyu* or Zhuangzi, consist of separate narrative anecdotes often in dialogue form, but not always ordered thematically. So far as I am aware, readers in traditional China were not bothered by this. What then mattered to Chinese readers over the millennia, I would suggest, would have been having the words of a master available to them. Also, with scriptural and other important texts, there are favorite passages that are re-read by themselves, so that their exact position relative to other passages is not important after the first few readings.

The *Zhouyi*, the *Yijing*, and the axial age

The theory of an axial age, originally proposed by the German psychiatrist-turned-philosopher Karl Jaspers (1883–1969), can be a useful heuristic for understanding the *Zhouyi*. Like all grand theories, this has attracted strong dissent from multiple ideological perspectives.[4] In a minimalist form, axiality can be useful—even indispensable—for reading and translating very early texts. Jaspers argued that human thought underwent a fundamental transformation in what he called the axial age, defined as approximately 800–200 BCE, the time of Confucius, Laozi, the historical Buddha, Socrates, Plato, Aristotle, and some philosophers in the Levant and Persia. Jaspers noted that during this time frame self-conscious reflection and philosophy arose separately in geographically disparate locations. In its unelaborated form, the theory was confined to India, Greece, and China. Later critics broadened the concept by pointing out that axial ideas developed at different times later in other locations and that the development of critical reflection or philosophy was not a unitary event but took quite different forms in different cultures.[5]

For analyzing and contextualizing ancient texts the axiality concept is useful in reverse; that is, to avoid projecting post-axial consciousness onto pre-axial texts. By recognizing how archaic thought differs from post-axial thought, we can be better able to avoid inadvertent anachronisms. Early consciousness, it is generally accepted, took the world as it was, rather than having reflective or critical perspectives on the conditions of human life and on the nature of the cosmos.

The term "axialization" generalizes the notion of the axial age beyond China, Greece, and India to refer to similar changes in consciousness when at other times and places humans began to reflect on their lot, often critically. Pre-axially, the supernatural was omnipresent in the form of magic, gods, and spirits, but metaphysical speculation was absent, except on a very simple level, such as the assumed existence of indistinct realms that could be entered by shamans and from which ancestors continued to be able to affect the living. There were implicit behavioral norms, but not abstract ethical theorizing. A familiar Western example is the *Iliad* in which terrible events occur, but without expression of ethical judgments about such behaviors as rape, warfare, and human sacrifice.

An early Chinese example of a pre-axial text is its first historical writing, the *Chunqiu* 春秋 *Spring and Autumn Annals,* a bare record of events in the state of Lu from 722 to 481 BCE. It recorded a few important state matters for each year, such as executions of nobles, but did not explain or comment upon them. We known nothing about its actual composition, particularly how events were selected for inclusion. One theory is that it was composed to inform the spirits of important events among the living. Mencius attributed it to Confucius, leading it to become one of the Five Classics. Based on Mencius' attribution, the *Chunqiu* came to be read as an esoteric text covertly conveying the Master's moral judgments on the events it recounts.

Comparing the *Chunqiu* and the later *Zuozhuan*, in part a commentary on the earlier text, we can see the transition from pre-axial to axial. By itself, the *Chunqiu* is dryly factual but came to be esteemed because of its supposed political moralizing, which was actually a later superimposition of post-axial thought regarding ideal government.[6]

Because pre-axial writings lacked ethical and philosophical abstractions as well as social criticism, historical accuracy must avoid anachronistically inserting these into pre-axial texts. A central trope of post-axial thought is the notion that society and individuals are in a fallen state and in need of transformation. This is quite explicit in the *Lunyu*, the Dao De Jing, and the *Zhuangzi* and even more so in their later commentaries. The present (for the writers) was contrasted with remote antiquity, an era of benevolent rulers and naturally virtuous subjects leading simple, virtuous lives. This was often conceived as cyclical, as in the—perhaps partly mythical—decline of the late Shang, leading to the rise of the Western Zhou. It is harder to find instances of virtuous government in later Chinese history when records were more complete.

Virtue as a concept is only hinted at in the *Zhouyi*, as I have discussed in a previous work (Redmond 2017: 353–80):[7]

> 6.3 Dining with friends of ancient virtue.
>
> ...
>
> Auspicious sometimes to follow the king's affairs for which there is no completion.

六三食舊德. .吉或從王事无成.

When seeking in the *Zhouyi* those elements for which the *Yijing* is most famous—its ethics and its metaphysics of change based on the alternation of yin and yang—one finds only the barest prefigurings. Yin is mentioned but once in the *Zhouyi*, where it refers to a shady riverbank, and yang does not occur at all. Nonetheless yin and yang became fundamental to the *Yijing* and their association with broken and solid lines seems intuitively self-evident. Over time these developed into an increasingly complex system of correlative cosmology (Needham II 1956: 304–64). Similarly, the belief that the hexagrams could represent all possible situations is not mentioned in the *Zhouyi*; they may have originally been only a means for choosing the pertinent text for a divination.

Axialization introduced a radically new view of humanity and the world as fallen, as having lost the true way. Given the unsatisfactoriness of the human plight, hope was offered as the possibility of social and personal transformation, fundamental to the world's most prevalent religions. This is prominent in the *Lunyu* and the *Dao De Jing*, among many other classics. For Confucius the transformation was behaving morally, for Laozi, a change of consciousness, as it was for Buddhism, which came to China much later. The *Yijing* was given a part in this new understanding by being viewed as a means to personal transformation in the form of moral self-improvement.

It was this vision of the book that attracted Wilhelm, Baynes, and Jung:

Wilhelm:
   It is my firm conviction that anyone who really assimilates the essence of the *Book of Changes* will be enriched thereby in experience and in true understanding of life. (lxxi)

Cary F. Baynes:
   If the reader is drawn out of the accustomed framework of his thought to view the world in a new perspective, if his imagination is stimulated and his psychological insight deepened … Wilhelm's *I Ching* has been faithfully reproduced. (xliii)

Carl G. Jung:
   The *I Ching* does not offer itself with proofs and results … It offers neither facts nor power, but for lovers of self-knowledge, of wisdom … it seems to be the right book. (xxxix)

The three creators of this edition of the *I Ching* presented it to a new audience as a guide to personal improvement, even transformation. Subtly they invoked the trope of ancient wisdom as the cure for current malaise. It was this view of the classic that appealed to the spiritual renewal of the 1960s; the philological methodology that utilized new discoveries to reconstruct it followed a separate path. Both can be said to bring the 3,000-year-old text into the modern world, but in different forms. Wilhelm-Baynes is based on the interpretations of late Qing China, but viewed through the lens of twentieth-century Western psychology, while the *Zhouyi* is at once ancient and the product of recent advances in scholarship.

The question remains of how the *Changes* acquired philosophy and eventually became a means for personal development. The answer seems to be that the *Changes* by itself was not the spark that ignited Chinese philosophy, but served as a matrix upon which to organize it. Its ancientness together with the mathematical completeness of the hexagrams would have inspired the idea that they can represent all possible situations. The two types of line, broken and solid, encouraged a dualistic cosmology based on light and dark, fundamental in human life before electric lighting.

Although the *Changes* did take a philosophical turn, it did so on a practical level. The *Yijing* as consisting of sage-like wisdom is emphasized in the *Dazhuan*:

> *Yi*, being aligned with heaven and earth.
> can wholly set forth the *dao* of heaven and earth
> ...
> Being in accord with heaven and earth.
> It does not go contrary to them;
> Its knowledge embraces all things,
> and its dao assists all under heaven.
> Thus it does not err. (Rutt 411)

This implies that the *Yijing* express the dao of heaven and earth, but also includes all things and so guides those under heaven—that is, humanity

Divination and society

Critical theory, particularly as initiated by Michel Foucault, is concerned with discovering covert power interests both in literary materials and in actual history. This has been applied mainly in the study of Western texts, primarily recent ones. In early Chinese the power interests are usually quite obvious, much of Confucianism being an apologetic for the hierarchical structure of society that extended from the highest levels of government to the family. This was justified not as the will of the people, but the will of heaven; that hierarchy was inherent in the nature of the cosmos was rarely questioned. Resistance and rebellion were punished harshly. Those in power were supposed to promote welfare and prosperity, but many did not do so. In extreme cases the mandate of heaven was withdrawn but this was signaled by anomalies, such as eclipses and earthquakes, and often was interpreted as about the rulers' personal behavior, especially excessively frequent sexual intercourse.

The *Yijing* served power interests both as a source of authority for Ruist officials and as a source of hidden knowledge. As I have previously observed, the *Zhouyi* does not question the status quo; indeed, divination was one means of maintaining power (Redmond 2017: 355). This is quite evident in the earliest extant Chinese writings, the oracle bone inscriptions. King Wu Ding divined himself; this was clearly a way that he maintained his power, since he would have the final word on what the oracle meant, even when professional diviners were involved. The diviner is someone who *knows*, no matter how many times wrong, because he or she is in contact with the spiritual forces or beings that determine events on the human plane. Divination confers a transcendent source for authority. In the modern world, divination, like all paranormal claims, invites skepticism, but in the past it held great authority. Just why a specific individual would have this mysterious ability and why he or she would be accepted as having it is difficult to account for. Some reasons are fairly evident—the king would be believed because of his position and power. Some would be hereditary. Certain behaviors, as those of shamans, seem to have archetypal associations with the possession of special knowledge. No doubt some prognosticators were more convincing than others; some were disgraced, particularly if they offended powerful inquirers.

In addition to these political factors, charisma is essential to the credibility of divination. This includes personal psychological factors, but also use of specialized language. With the *Zhouyi* and, to a slightly lesser extent, the *Yijing*, it is the images that carry the authority, often embedded in rhetorical structures. Conversely the language of divination, particularly that of the *Zhouyi*, often seems peculiar unless its specialized use is recognized.

An interesting analysis of early Chinese divination from the perspective of critical theory is that of Rowan K. Flad, based on oracle bone archaeological findings. He notes the polymorphism of the social functions of divination:

> Ritual specialists control a body of knowledge and social status that may be monopolized by elites and employed as a source of authority and legitimacy.

Alternatively, specialist diviners may act outside formal hierarchical structures, representing a distinct realm of information and power that is separate from established social institutions. (2008: 403)

Flad further suggests that state-sponsored divination procedures can develop a high degree of elaboration, as is the case with oracle bone pyromancy, while local methods are necessarily less elaborate. He suggests that divination, by revealing "quarrels and grudges and mediating uncertainty, is therefore a social act that helps ensure that society can continue to function" (ibid.).

These insights are useful in considering divination in terms of its social function, in contrast to the discourse of superstition, which sees it solely as error, or as contact with nefarious entities or forces. I have previously suggested that one reason for attempts to suppress divination is that it can exert considerable influence over individuals and groups that is not entirely under state or elite control.

In contrast to its role in the 1960s counterculture in the West, the *Book of Changes* was orthodox in traditional China, as shown by its receiving canonical status in the latter Han. As I previously proposed, the *Yijing*'s official endorsement was possible because it does not contain criticism of the government, nor other content that might be used as a pretext for sedition. This was particularly important in China as insurrections were generally justified on religious grounds, from the Yellow Turbans of 184–205 CE to the Taiping rebellion of 1850–1864. Accordingly Chinese governments have long been wary of dissident religious movements. The *Yijing* did not lend itself to challenging the social order, although it did include advice on dealing with those of higher social rank. This is apparent in the following recurring phrase, which advises how to best conduct one's self with the bureaucracy, but does not criticize it:

39.6 Beneficial to see the important person.

利見大人

What might seem to be an exception to the argument that the *Changes* does not suggest social transformation is Hexagram 49 革 *Ge*, translated by Wilhelm-Baynes as *Revolution (Molting)* and by Lynn as *Radical Change*. This word eventually came to include change in the sense of revolution, but in the *Zhouyi ge* specifically refers to tanning or curing leather, which would have been familiar to most in the Western Zhou. No other hexagram contains any suggestion of recommending regime change or revolution. The role of the *I Ching* in the 1960s counterculture was less radical than it might seem. Some sought to link the hexagram arrays to the experience of psychedelic drugs, most prominently Terence and Dennis McKenna in *The Invisible Landscape: Mind, Hallucinogens, and the I Ching*, originally published in 1975. No doubt some *I Ching* practitioners used drugs, but to the extent the book was a protest, it was an internal one against the supposed dominance of science and the distrusted "establishment." If the *I Ching* was revolutionary, it was on a spiritual level—a gesture of personal dissent, not itself part of an agenda for social change. One might get the contrary impression from the title of Frances FitzGerald's 1972 best-selling book on the Vietnam war, *Fire in the Lake*, referring to Hexagram 38 睽 *Kui* Opposition, which consists of the trigram for fire over that for lake. While her title and the tag of the hexagram do fit the idea of violent revolution, the judgment and line texts have nothing to do with revolution; disappointingly, the *I Ching* is not further quoted beyond the title page. The book's title is simply another instance of how the *Changes* can be adapted to fit any situation.

Hierarchical relationships are frequently mentioned in the *Changes*:

2.0 The upright person has somewhere to go. At first lost, he obtains a master. Auspicious.

君子有攸往. 先迷後得. 主利.

Junzi, translated here as "upright person," originally meant prince. Wilhelm-Baynes translated this phrase as "superior man"; although the Chinese phrase has no reference to gender; in its traditional use it would nearly always have referred to males. Originally a title of rank, it became a term for a virtuous person. Having "somewhere to go" suggests an errand for a king or high official. A master would have been necessary for having a secure place in society for himself and his family. Lacking a sponsor would mean uncertain status and being vulnerable to others more powerful.

The *Yijing*, by giving advice with the confines of Ruist propriety, helped inquirers function properly within their social role. The philosopher Joshua Ramey in his 2016 *Politics of Divination* expressed this succinctly:

Divination suggests an opportunity to adjust action so as to more deeply participate with (rather than to dominate, through sorcery) these otherwise unaccountable forces. (2016: 148)

2

Divination

Managing Uncertainty

Divination has been practiced at all times and in all cultures, yet is widely stigmatized in the West both in the name of religion and of science. Neither form of disparagement has succeeded in eradicating the practice, but has, until recently, inhibited scholarship on the subject. In many non-Western cultures, including China, divination is widely practiced without embarrassment. The aim of this chapter is not to attack or defend divination, but to replace these prejudicial attitudes with a broader sense of its role in culture and consciousness. The *Book of Changes* is an important creation of early humanity and as such should not be deemed less worthy of study because it is, among other things, a manual for divination.

Divination can be usefully defined as a way for acquiring knowledge not obtainable by normal means. Its scope is much broader than predicting the future; it can be performed to clarify a present situation, choose favorable days for important actions, or even whether to marry a particular person. Divination methods can be as simple as tossing a coin, as laborious as making cracks on a bone with a heated poker, or as elaborate as using a computer to generate horoscopes that include hundreds of aspects (planetary angles). While sometimes dismissed as primitive or ignorant, divination has been and is used by people of all economic and educational levels. Divining, like singing or calculating, is a human capacity, although some have it more than others.[1]

In the twenty-first century, we consider ourselves to be uniquely overwhelmed by information, unaware that our remote forebears also were oppressed in this way. Common events such as bird calls or a fox crossing a river had meanings that one ignored at one's peril, requiring experts to interpret. The *Zhouyi* was, one imagines, a great help; it elucidated circumstances in simple language using set phrases, proverbs, precedents, and historical allusions, usually specifying the prognosis in standard terms. As now with the media, much of the information imparted by diviners was alarming. While climate change had not yet been conceived, weather-related crop failure was an immediate danger. Cosmic events such as eclipses might threaten the rulers' mandate and thus cause social disruption.

Fear is the subtext in all divination; when we know what people fear, we know much about them and their era. The inquirer fears a bad prognostication, yet is disappointed when receiving a neutral instead of a positive one. We can understand ancient divination better when we recognize the analogies with our own hopes and fears. It is the role of a divination manual to warn or reassure, as the situation requires.

Divination is a structured procedure that is carried out in accordance with rules and conventions, although these may be tacit. Both inquirer and diviner assume that the method for obtaining the prognostication is efficacious, with a result that is specific, though not necessarily unambiguous. From a modern disenchanted perspective, divination cannot produce objectively valid information, but in ancient times it was relied upon for all important decisions, even military ones. Now it often serves merely for mild amusement, as with fortune cookies or online horoscopes. Contemporary informal use of divination for entertainment should not blind us to the fact that in the past it was a very serious matter, as it remains in some cultures today. There have always been skeptics, such as Xunzi in China and Cicero in Rome; many more must have had private doubts.

Performing divination is actually complex; the diviner's dilemma has always been to give prognostications that are general enough to fit most possible outcomes, yet seem specific for the inquiry. It was also crucial to avoid displeasing the inquirer, particularly when of high rank. In all times and places some diviners were more esteemed than others; what qualities made a diviner persuasive are not readily ascertained.

The widespread use of divination in the ancient world was in part due lack of knowledge of causation for ordinary life events such as weather, success of crops, and disease; and also the assumption of a network of correlations linking events (Fiskejö 2004: 72–5). Pragmatic knowledge existed, for example in agricultural technology, but underlying knowledge of why particular methods worked was limited. Then, as now, all were anxious about their futures. Given the human need for explanations, in antiquity supernatural ones were better than none at all. Fear was omnipresent because the factors needed to sustain life—weather, availability of game, crop yields, fertility—were largely unpredictable and uncontrollable. Similarly unpredictable were predators, natural disasters, war, acts of the powerful or arbitrary power, illness, and supernatural hazards—particularly terrifying because invisible were curses and vindictive spirits of the dead. The need to placate gods and spirits created needless worry and immense waste of resources.

In traditional China both men and women from a wide range of social levels made their living from supposed psychic abilities. Although the Ruists disapproved of women diviners, many availed themselves of their services nonetheless. The effort to shun women diviners seems to have been greater among the literati than lower demographic groups. Divination could stir up social discontent, and as a livelihood could be hazardous, risking retaliation for wrong or unwelcome prognostications, or even accusations of witchcraft.[2]

Shamans provided divination despite Ruist disapproval, as did Buddhist and Daoist monks, many of whom supported themselves by divining, as well as selling charms, curses, talismans, cures, and the like, despite these being contrary to monastic regulations. The status of divination is ambiguous, being associated with outsider status, yet sought even by the most respectable.

Over the centuries, with increasing interest by the literati as well as professionalization, divinatory theory and practice overlapped with metaphysical speculation and became progressively more convoluted, presumably in part to impress inquirers, but also in the (vain) hope of greater accuracy. If the method was assumed to be valid, it would follow that refinement of it would produce greater accuracy. Competition between diviners must have been intense, as no objective credentials were required, although like many occupations in the premodern world, it was often passed on from father to son. Regrettably, we know little about women diviners because under Ruism they tended to be excluded from the historical record. Mentions of women in the *Zhouyi* are discussed in Chapter 11.

From the Warring States and Han with the development of yin-yang metaphysics, and numerological interpretation of the hexagram lines, the *Yijing* became a vehicle for philosophizing. All these accretions further reinforced the repute of the *Yijing* as a repository of ancient wisdom that was revealed during the process of divination.

The *Zhouyi* texts are diverse and many do not obviously lend themselves to divination; this may be the reason that appended to most line texts are prognostic terms consisting or one or two characters that were selected from a fixed set, as analyzed in Chapter 5. These terms can be reduced to being favorable or unfavorable, but have some nuance as to just how good or bad the situation was and whether a particular action was favored or not. Often the prognostic terms are attached to omens, such as bird calls, that are not self-evidently favorable or unfavorable. In other cases, prognostic terms simply add emphasis. In the *Zhouyi*, it is often unclear to which phrase the prognostic term applied, and some prognoses even seem to contradict the sense of the rest of the text. Although not interesting by themselves, these terms would have had intense emotional impact in fraught circumstances.

It is the images that make the texts interesting and would have stimulated the imagination of the diviner, who could fit them to the inquiry. The inquirer is also active in this process—modern studies show that recipients of divination tend to remember the correct parts and ignore the rest. The setting of divination, together with the inquirer's expectations, can give the give the response considerable psychological impact. Quite apart from the question of superstition, divination could cause real world harm both by issuing of frightening prognoses or by auspicious prognoses that might cause real problems to be overlooked.

A balanced view of divination

The effects of divination can be positive, negative, or neutral. It can be used to defraud or extort, but this properly belongs to the study of criminal psychology. Some offering fortune telling use it as gimmick to make easy money, but do not charge significant amounts; I suspect a large portion of internet psychics are in this category. The contemporary diviners I have met do readings because they find the process inherently interesting, are a way to socialize, to can help others by providing what amounts to cheap (and mercifully brief) psychotherapy. Although the diviner, and probably the inquirer, presumably enter an altered state, this is not the extreme change of consciousness induced by psychotropic drugs. (Shamanism and the Oracle of Delphi are exceptions.) In my experience observing readings, the appearance is of a normal conversation without a conspicuously "woo woo" atmosphere. Yet one senses that one is witnessing a special kind of interaction, although the actual state of consciousness is, of course, unobservable. That some diviners are much better than others becomes apparent if one observes multiple readings. Psychotherapists also vary greatly in skill. Both talent and skill are involved, although these seem to elude rationalistic description.

The modern Western revival of *I Ching*, Tarot, astrology, and less popular methods such as runes began in the 1960s, although drawing much from the occult renaissance of the turn of the century. Books describing the various methods as well as coins and sticks for *I Ching*, Tarot decks, and ephemerides and other paraphernalia became easily available. To fully understand the theories underlying these methods, especially the *I Ching* and astrology requires considerable study and practice. In actual use, however, prognostications can be produced with only very basic knowledge; these would not convince the experts, but most inquirers want the reading, not the theory. The very elaborate metaphysics described in Chinese commentaries, notably those of *Shao Yong* 邵雍 (1011–1077) of the Song, were not understood even by most literati in its day.[3]

Divination, prophecy, and science

Most scholarship on divination tends to be historical, yet we have similar examples in our own world. A very interesting book by Lynda Walsh (2013) discusses how the role of prophet is now often occupied by a few scientists, as well as economists and other experts, who speak to the public about critical issues. Walsh mentions as fitting into this category Richard Dawkins, Carl Sagan, Stephen Jay Gould, and Stephen Hawking. All have published best-selling books; all have appeared in the media in educational programs to explain science to lay people. Pronouncements are made on issues such as evolution, cosmology, and climate change. (To these could now be added sexuality and gender.) Walsh is not so much interested in taking sides on these issues as showing how the style of their communication is rhetorical, describing the similarity between scientists and prophets: "In both cases we have self-sacrificing individuals who use technical means to divine transcendent visions of truth" (2013: 10).

Whether prophets and diviners (not quite the same as prophets) are self-sacrificing is doubtful. While prophecy is about society, since Biblical times often diatribes on moral deterioration, divination is on a personal level intended to advise individuals; it may or may not include moral guidance. The *I Ching* in its Confucian interpretation was moralistic; the *Zhouyi* was not explicitly so.

Walsh enumerates five attributes shared by prophets and public scientists; these apply equally to diviners: motivation to establish certainty in a crisis; confirmation of privileged access to knowledge; descrying messages from beyond the political ken; framing the crisis in terms of shared values (2013: 9–10).

Stated directly, prophets and diviners have access to truths not available to others. I am not suggesting that science is merely divination, but rather that, given the abundance of difficulties in human life, expert advice is always sought. The advice given, whatever its basis, has always employed similar patterns of language and expression. Technology has changed how people access the advice, and the rise of science has provided a new source of authority. In the ancient world systematic knowledge was quite limited; now science has taken up much of the mental space once occupied by divination, such as weather forecasting and diagnosis of disease. Many life issues, however, are not resolvable by science so advice is sought, and often offered unsought, by figures such as family, teachers, psychotherapists, financial advisors, religious and spiritual teachers including gurus, and government officials. All, like divination, use specialized forms of rhetoric intended to convince, although these are not always successful.[4]

I am not arguing that the *I Ching*'s advice is as valuable as that of one's mother or therapist, rather that the rhetorical form of the advice is almost the same. Authoritative advice from sources like these have mostly, although not completely, supplanted divination, but are not invariably more apt. Experts frequently disagree, making their advice in a sense random. This is evident in stock market recommendations, often wrong, yet many still pay for this sort of advice. however uncertain. Indeed few sorts of advice are absolutely reliable. I offer these observations not as a criticism of science, or authority in general, but to point out that confusion about vital issues continues to cause much anxiety. With this perspective, we can look back at divination, not as mere credulity, but as an inevitable response to the enduring human need for certainty in the face of incomplete knowledge, a need still not satisfied by advances in science and social support.

We all wish for certainty, despite its impossibility. As Walsh observes, "It is true that scientists have never been prophets; it is also true that their audiences keep saying they are, and keep working with them toward certainty" (2013, 8). The same can be said of diviners, except that they do claim to be prophets.

Divination and economics

Not only has divination been compared to media punditry, it has also been connected to "neo-liberal" economics; that is, the market-oriented economic philosophy of Friedrich Hayek and Milton Friedman. As proposed by Joshua Ramey, "Neo-liberal authoritarianism dominates the space of divination in modern culture" (2016: 6).

In a literal sense, not only the *Book of Changes* but other methods of divination of which I am aware have nothing to say about economic theory, although there are occasional claims that they can predict the stock market. Ramey's theory, summarized in the following quotations, is intriguing:

> Neo-liberalism attempted to conflate "expert knowledge of the markets" with *knowledge of the unknown*. (2016: 4; italics in original)

> Market expertise ... has come to occupy an ancient and perennial place in human cultures ... the site where human cultures have, from time immemorial, practiced many forms of divination procedures by which human beings attempt to access knowledge of the unknown. Divination is systematic solicitation, generally on the basis of chance, of more-than-human wisdom. (2016: 5)

This notion can be expanded from economics to political and social control generally; I propose the term "oligarchy of the unknown" to refer to control by a few of knowledge that is essential for human thriving. What the experts control is not the future, but hopes and fears about the future. Like prophecy, divination has authority that is intrinsic; because not based on evidence it is difficult to refute, as is also true of much expert opinion. In traditional China divination served to validate official authority but sometimes to undermine it. Both divination and prophecy can be tools for exerting power or justifying rebellion; in traditional China, anomalies, such as earthquakes and eclipses, were often interpreted as heaven's condemnation of the ruler's conduct. Contemporary divination, as part of New Age culture, is generally not applied to politics or power interests; rather, it is practiced to circumvent perceived limitations of conventional ways of knowing. It also provides a personal spirituality not subject to regulation by establishment institutions such as religion or psychology.

Learning from contemporary divination

As part of my study of divination, I have attended conferences for practitioners of Tarot and astrology, and also more general New Age thought. I have also presented papers and organized panels at academic societies including the Association for Asian Studies, the American Academy of Religion, and the Association for the Study of Esotericism. Academic and practitioner conferences differ in their atmosphere and the viewpoints expressed, but together they provide etic and emic perspectives.

My experience meeting and speaking with practitioners of these arts has dispelled the notion that divination is mainly used by the ignorant and uneducated. Many I have met are articulate and intelligent, even critically so; quite a few have advanced degrees. (On the other hand, a few are noticeably eccentric.) Some retain a degree of skepticism, yet still find value in divinatory consultation. That some diviners have advanced degrees does not prove divination works, but confirms the breadth of is appeal, establishing that it is worthy of study as part of the history of thought.

Some interested in Tarot and astrology, and to a lesser extent *I Ching*, form communities; they hold local and national conferences and have substantial presence on the internet. Although my experience with these communities suggests most who are involved are sincere, some who advertise on the internet hype their abilities and charge excessively. On the other hand, there are also many free sites, including some that select a hexagram by computer.[5]

Coming of age in the 1960s, a time of increased interest and tolerance for what James Webb termed "rejected knowledge" (1974;1976), including divination and occultism generally, I have felt both curiosity and cautious sympathy regarding these modes of thought, which persist despite all efforts to debunk them.[6]

Fortune telling is a common expedient for fraud. Those who use it to swindle typically have no actual knowledge of the method; a few set prognostications suffice for them to mislead the credulous. Claims of psychic powers, or use of Tarot and other occult exotica, are merely props. Their actual expertise is in exploiting the vulnerabilities of those seeking their advice. A common ruse is a request for large sums of money to remove curses, or dark clouds, or to open one's third eye, as I was recently offered. Another necessary precaution is awareness that extreme heterodox ideas can be a sign of mental disturbance.[7] Being open-minded about divination and esotericism does not mean abandoning common sense.

Experiencing divination

While I have long been fascinated by divination as an aspect of human communication and consciousness, I am not really a believer. In studying these phenomena, however, I do my best to be open-minded, at least when the beliefs and practices are harmless, as most of them are. I recommend that scholars and others seriously interested in the *Book of Changes* try doing readings so as to have actually experienced the process. A question is asked, which may be general or specific, the *I Ching* is consulted, and the selected texts pondered to intuit how they might apply to the question. The question should be sensible, but not about serious life issues, such as careers or relationships. A useful perspective is that expressed by Greg Whincup, author of one of the better *I Ching* translations: "My own experience suggests that it does work—how I am not sure ... But rather than allow the *Changes* to make my decisions for me, it seemed better to make them myself" (1985: 223).

In traditional China, *Yijing* consultation was taken very seriously and often concerned grave matters. In modern use, particularly in the West, it flourishes liberated from this rather grim atmosphere and is usually not taken entirely seriously. It is commonly justified as a way of "thinking outside the box"; that is, freeing the mind to consider multiple possibilities. It can also facilitate fantasizing, as a sort of assisted daydreaming. If so inclined, one can imagine being in the lineage of Fu Xi, Wen Wang, Zhou Gong, Cheng Yi, Zhu Xi, and perhaps even Confucius, including his supposed wish for fifty more years to study the *Changes*. More formally, Carl Jung explained *I Ching* consultation as a way to explore the psyche, based on his famous concept of synchronicity (Jung 1960). Like fiction, it can liberate the mind from quotidian preoccupations so as to open it to fresh perspectives. Later one can apply rationality and common sense to decide if this mental meandering contains a useful message for the conscious mind. That divination is unscientific is besides the point when it is an aid to intuition. There is, of course, no obligation to follow what seems to be the *I Ching*'s advice.

Modern scholarly understanding of the *I Ching* differs from that of most practitioners as just described. It advances by being evidence-based, historically contextualized, and ideally, accurately translated.

Finally, it must be admitted that despite the fascination it evokes, the *Book of Changes* is not a page-turner, but something even more gripping—the world's longest obsession, a 3,000-year one.

3

Is the *Book of Changes* Esoteric?

As with any seemingly obscure text, with the *Book of Changes* the question arises as to whether it is esoteric; that is, whether its most important meanings are hidden. To anticipate my more detailed discussion, the answer is: it depends on the reader's preconceptions. Over its long history it has been read in many ways and its meanings cannot be reduced to one correct reading. When a text or image is esoteric, recognition as such is essential to a complete appreciation. At the same time, esoteric meanings can easily be projected onto a text, resulting in neglect of its surface meanings. Because the term "esoteric" is itself polysemous, its use in reference to the *Changes* requires some clarification. Here we can benefit from the explorations of Arthur N. Melzer in his 2014 monograph, *Philosophy Between the Lines: The Lost History of Esoteric Writing*. Although Melzer's monograph is about classical and European texts, his erudite discussion of the issues can illuminate texts of other cultures. Crediting Leo Strauss as reintroducing discussion of esotericism into modern criticism of Western philosophical thought, Melzer provides a concise initial definition as "something difficult to understand because hidden or secret" and "as a secretive activity—as well as an alien, deceptive and elitist one . . . it has a particularly hard time getting the fair and sympathetic hearing that it particularly requires" (2014: 1).

Melzer's interest is in philosophical and political esotericism, which he distinguishes from the mystical varieties. This distinction is less useful with early Chinese works, which often combine the mystical with the philosophical and political. Divination in Chinese history has often been political, with potential to be disruptive because it can be very persuasive, yet beyond government control. On a personal level it can be disturbing because hearing about one's fate is scary, whether credible or not, as is the notion that a magical procedure can reveal it.

Melzer draws attention to the fundamental problem posed by esoteric writing, referring to Western philosophy, but also applicable, I suggest, to that of China:

If they wrote esoterically and we do not read them esoterically, we will necessarily misunderstand them. We will systematically cut ourselves off from their thought precisely in its most unorthodox, original, and liberating part. (2014: xii)

With the Chinese classics we often face the opposite dilemma in which esoteric meanings are emphasized at the expense of the explicit ones. This was the rule, not the exception, in the early classics, not only the *Zhouyi*, but also the *Classic of Songs* and the *Spring and Autumn Annals*. All three were compiled much earlier than Confucius' lifetime; the Ruist readings were superimposed on them much later. These readings can be considered esoteric in that they were not apparent in the earliest forms, so far as they have been reconstructed. The traditional explanation is that the ancient sages did have these meanings in mind but expressed them through the hexagrams. According to this mythology, the meanings of the hexagrams were self-evident to the sages, who apparently did not anticipate the gradual decline in wisdom over ensuing generations. This account is not plausible as objective history, but in Chinese culture, certainly by the Spring and Autumn, the Ruist meanings *were* the *Yijing*.

Esoteric interpretation can also result from philological challenges such as language change, plentiful variants, and textual corruption; readers and editors are frequently tempted to fill in lacunae, or to amend phrases whose sense is not clear. There is also the strangeness—and cruelty—of ancient life, which later Chinese and Western interpreters often glossed over.

Another source of pseudo-esotericism is created by translations that are really paraphrases based on the translator's belief of what the text really wanted to say. This is particularly true of Wilhelm-Baynes, although James Legge, also a missionary, also deviates from the Chinese, particularly by rendering its simple syntax into awkward complex sentences with frequent interpolations, as here from the first of the *Ten Wings* gloss on Hexagram 61 中孚 *Zhong Fu* Captives Within:

> LXI. I 'Pigs and fishes (are moved) and there will be good fortune :' – and sincerity reaches to (and affects even) pigs and fishes. (Legge 1899: 263)

This introduces unnecessary confusion; for example, sincerity somehow affecting pigs and fishes. Without the parenthetical additions the passage is quite clear, with the pigs and fishes being a sign of future abundance, or simply a feast about to happen:

> 61.0 Suckling pigs and fishes, auspicious.
> Beneficial to ford the great river. Beneficial to divine.
>
> 豚魚, 吉.

This image with its interpolations is the sort that invites allegorical or other esoteric interpretations. While Legge merits esteem as the first to create reasonably accurate translations of the early classics, his convoluted syntax, I suspect, helped perpetuate the stereotype of Oriental wisdom being beyond the comprehension of Westerners.

Both exoteric and esoteric

Hidden meanings can be discovered, or imagined, without necessarily having been intended. With scriptural texts, new meanings sometimes arise that eventually become standard, often attributed to culture heroes or other eminent historical figures. With *Book of Changes* these include Fu Xi, King Wen, the Duke of Zhou, and Confucius. These figures were central to Chinese civilization's sense of itself so that doubts about this mythology were rarely expressed, and often met with resentment when they were.

Textual fundamentalism—the dogma that a text is to be understood literally, often as the words of a deity or sage –does not effectively resolve debates about its meaning. The *Book of Changes* has been read both exoterically and esoterically and often anhistorically. Melzer rightly points out that failing to discern hidden meanings can result in overlooking an ancient text's most important ideas. Yet, awareness of this risk can create a sort of, what I term exegetical anxiety, a form of "fear of missing out," leading to ascribing meanings on shaky evidence. Even more common is creation of meanings to support a pre-existing ideology. This is frequent with scriptural texts and common with literary ones as well.

In China, doubt about attributions of ancient texts appeared sporadically in the Song, but had limited influence until the rise of the evidentiary scholarship movement during the Qing, as described by Elman (1984). Textual skepticism reached its extreme in the early twentieth century with the Doubting Antiquity movement, which took an agonistic, frequently openly hostile, stance toward the Confucian meanings of the classics. Some of its revisionist work, such as disputing Sima Qian's account of Shang dynastic succession, has been refuted and it is still resented by many Chinese scholars. While the doubters overreached, they did initiate reconstruction of the early meanings of the *Zhouyi* and as such advanced the dialectic of *Changes* studies. Their exegetical approach can be considered esoteric as its intent was to sought to reconstruct meanings that had been disguised by later Ruist readings. Their approach was adversarial rather than critical; often their suggested emendations meanings were obscure, merely pretexts for display of erudition.

The reconstructed and received meanings need not be considered contradictory because each can be considered correct for its stage of Chinese intellectual history. This approach is not, however, consistent with the mythology of the *Changes* origins, nor with its wisdom being timeless, and so it is not acceptable to some practitioners.

The revival of esotericism

Esotericism usually involves the assumption that certain truths must be hidden. Most obviously, dissenting opinions are often hidden to avoid retaliation from those they might offend. This has not usually been a concern with the *Book of Changes* in that it does not encourage social criticism. A different, although sometimes overlapping, reason for concealment is to withhold powerful truths from the unworthy. Often the secret material was in the form of mantras, words of power, and talismans that are kept secret, lest they be misused by the unscrupulous. In the West this second form of esotericism is the most common, particularly with the revival of interest in hermeticism, the occult, divination and "rejected knowledge" that began in the late nineteenth century with the Hermetic Order of the Golden Dawn, and other secret societies.

There is no indication that any of these forms of esotericism were present in the *Yijing* although there were cults that appropriated its metaphysic. Divination, however, involves what might be termed ad hoc esotericism since the selected text (or hexagram line pattern) needs to be interpreted to serve as an answer to the inquiry. This is created, depending on the beliefs of those involved, by intuition or a special power.

The two schools: *Xiangshu* and *Yili*

Divination systems tend to grow in complexity, partly in the hope that a more elaborate system will be more accurate and probably also because intricacy would impress clients and thus provide competitive advantage. For practitioners, the complexity of a system was part of its fascination. Many would-be savants devoted themselves to finding the true order of the hexagrams, and thus the deep truths hidden in them by the ancient sages. By the Western Han, two distinct schools of interpretation had developed: Images and Numbers *Xiangshu*i 象數 and Meanings and Principles *Yili* 義理. The *Xiangshu* school focused on the hexagrams, sometimes to the point of ignoring the texts. The *Yili* school is traditionally held to have begun with Wang Bi, who advocated more attention to the texts in order to return to use of the *Changes* for moral edification. Line positions continued to be used, however, and even Wang Bi frequently referred to line positions in his commentary. In this sense the *Yili* school is more balanced, tempering the quasi-mathematical extravagances of *Xiangshu* with the concreteness of the texts.

The *Xiangshu* school is inherently esoteric as the abstract line patterns have no intrinsic meanings, and therefore could be quite freely interpreted. In practice, however, the interpretations were based on line positions and yin-yang metaphysics. The lines of the hexagrams were numbered, from 1 to 6, with 1 being the lowest; thus they were able to represent levels and sequences. At least three interpretive systems made use of this. Most obvious was to regard the lines as positions, as with the dragons in Hexagram 1 *Qian*. In the first line, the dragon is hidden, then occupies progressively higher positions until soaring in heaven in line 5 and finally over-reaching in line 6. This scheme fits well with the first Hexagram, *Qian*; higher lines are associated with the dragons occupying progressively higher positions. For most Hexagrams, however, only free exercise of imagination can relate the text to the line position.

The second mode of interpreting the line positions is based on social hierarchy, always of great importance in Chinese culture, though often invisible to outsiders. In this system line 5 represents the most powerful person; 4 could be beneficial, but also dangerous as being close to power.

The third system designates lines as correct or incorrect. Positions 1, 3, and 5 are yang because odd numbers, leaving 2, 4, and 6 to yin. (Line 4 was not inherently unlucky; this was a later innovation in Southern China.) A line position is incorrect if a broken line in a yang position, or a solid one in a yin position. Considerable ingenuity was applied to connect this rather abstract notion to the problem divined about.

Two of the most celebrated of the Song commentators, Zhu Xi 朱熹 (1130–1200) and Cheng Yi 程頤 (1033–1107), also combined texts with line positions. Although Zhu Xi was more associated with the *Yili* school, he included line positions in his reading. Here is an example which I have chosen to show the level of complexity characteristic of *Yijing* interpretation.

In my translation, based on early meanings:

 *Lin* Wailing

19.0 Begin with an offering, beneficial to divine.
Until the eighth month will be ominous.

元亨，利貞．至于八月有凶．

Adler in his work on Zhu X translates as follows, with the first phrase rendered in accord with Ruist understanding: .

> 19.0 Supreme and penetrating, appropriate and correct. Reaching the eighth month there will be bad fortune.

Here is an excerpt from Adler's translation of Zhu Xi's commentary, which I have condensed somewhat:

> Lin means to advance to confront and in on something. The two yang line gradually rise to close in on the yin: hence "approaching" ... Also, as for the trigrams, below is the pleasure of *Dui* and above is the compliance of *Kun*. The 9 in the second, as a firm line occupying the center corresponds with 6 in the fifth; therefore the diviner will greatly succeed and will benefit from being correct. (Adler 126f)

For those literati who devoted themselves to serious study of the *Yijing* and knew much of it by heart, this would not be excessively difficult to follow. Although Zhu Xi clearly considers himself to be explaining what is present in the classic, it is not self-evident to those not familiar with the *Xiangshu* interpretive system. Accordingly, it is an esoteric system of reading, one that imposes meanings, rather than discovers what was deliberately hidden. Zhu Xi wrote two millennia after the traditional date for the *Zhouyi*'s compilation; in that time, the classic had evolved into to a degree that would have made it unrecognizable to its Western Zhou compilers.

Cheng Yi's *Yi River Commentary on the Book of Changes*, recently translated by L. Michael Harrington, composed earlier than that of Zhu Xi, is also metaphysical and even more abstract than Zhu Xi's. Here is a portion of the translation of Cheng's commentary on 19.0 to give a sense of his mode of thought:

> In the Watch [*lin*] hexagram, two *yang* lines are born. It is the moment when *yang* starts to be more abundant step by step. This is why the sage gives a warning, saying that although *yang* is starting to grow, nonetheless, "when the eighth month is reached, it will disappear and "there will be misfortune" ... *Yang* begins

and is born in the Turn hexagram in the Flee hexagram ... Concerning the *yin* and *yang qi*, one may remark that their disappearance and growth are like tracing a circle than cannot be changed. (Harrington 2019: 161f)

This reading is equally metaphysical, but stylistically more dynamic in its references to yin and yang. As with Zhu Xi's commentary, its interpretive framework is esoteric in being based on concepts not in the core text.

My expectation is that the literal meanings of the texts of the *Book of Changes* will withstand the passage of time, while the elaborate interpretations using line positions seem to me only a curiosity of intellectual history. Few other than specialist scholars will want to expend the time and effort to learn the complex traditional systems of line positions. The yin-yang duality, however, has become part of world culture, mostly as stand-ins for feminine and masculine, although among sinophones its more subtle correlations, such as cool-warm and hidden-visible, are still in use. Some practitioners make use of line positions in a simplified way, but they are no longer part of the wider culture of the *Book of Changes*.

Western esoteric readings of Chinese texts

Some of the early Jesuit missionaries in China held to a doctrine called "figurism," which was based on the belief that as the universal religion, Christianity, must be present in some form in the early Chinese classics, including the *Yijing*. Figurism was an esoteric method of exegesis that served as justification for study of these works by some of the early Jesuit missionaries, notably Fr Joachim Bouvet, S. J. 白晋 or 白進 (1656–1730), who devoted much of his time in China under the Kangxi emperor to seeking Christianity in the *Yijing*. While his interpretations now seem fanciful, they are of interest as an example of an intelligent, highly educated scholar attempting to understand totally unfamiliar ideas. His fellow Jesuit, Matteo Ricci 利瑪竇 (1552–1610) worked particularly hard to find common ground between Chinese culture and Christianity. (Mungello 1985). Figurism soon came under vehement attack by European Catholic clerics, particularly the Dominicans. At stake was whether Chinese religion merited study as a debased version of Christianity, or should be suppressed as a form of "paganism," the pejorative term applied by missionaries to the local religions with which they had to compete.

The *Book of Changes* continues to be a fertile source of speculative theories ranging from imaginative to decidedly eccentric, from profoundly philosophical to bizarre. Somewhere in this spectrum exist the several books by Carol Anthony and Hanna Moog, who claim that the real message of the *I Ching* is psychological—that we need to overcome the "ego." Perhaps more extreme are the mathematical elaborations of José Argüelles (1984) and Richard Sterling Cook (2004–6). While these are more about their author's imagination than the *Book of Changes*, they are nonetheless part of its continuing fruitfulness.

Ultimately, it is the reader's choice whether to construe the *Book of Changes* as esoteric or exoteric. The texts are capable of esoteric reading, while line positions require knowledge of a separate system. When I have lectured in China I am always asked if I belong to the *Xiangshu* or *Yili* school. Since I am never asked this by Americans or Europeans, I had considered myself to be neutral in this regard. On reflection I realized that I fit with *Yili* because it is the texts that interest me, both grammatically and for their content. Line interpretation is akin to numerology and appeals to those who like mathematical games. There is no evident explanation for the hexagrams and the texts being together in a single literary creation, but it is to a great degree this improbable combination and the tension it creates that has maintained the dynamism of the *Book of Changes* over three millennia.

Part Two

Grammar and Structure

4

Divinatory Prognostic Terms

The underlying anxiety of anyone seeking divination is whether the result will be favorable or unfavorable, hence the need for explicit prognoses. In the *Zhouyi* a fixed set of terms, which recur throughout the text, serve to indicate the outlook. At least that seems to be their function, but it is often unclear why a particular prognosis fits the rest of the adjacent text, or even which phrase it applies to. In translation the confusion tends to be even greater because the terms are often translated imprecisely; this is unfortunate, because correctly understanding these terms tells us much about the mind of the Western Zhou. For this reason, I discuss the prognostic terms in considerable detail. For those who need a quick reference as they are reading the *Zhouyi*, I have provided a Table of Prognostic Terms, which lists them in Chinese and pinyin, together with the closest English equivalents.

By themselves the prognostic terms are empty; their significance arises from their proximity to specific images and supplemental phrases. By labeling actions and events as favorable or not, they reveal some aspects of the values of early China, which not infrequently are contrary to the values of the modern West, such as beating children being beneficial 利 *li* (4.1), or sacrificing captives being honorable 光 *guang* (5.0).

Although the prognostic terms are clear by themselves, their positions within the texts often creates uncertainty as to which phrase the prognosis applies; some prognoses seem contradictory to their adjacent phrases, or even unrelated at all to the phrases in the judgment or line text. While this can be puzzling to the modern scholar or practitioner, it would not have been to a diviner, who would pick only those parts of the texts that seemed pertinent to the inquiry. Here is a prognosis that seems unrelated to the image:

35. 4 Advancing like a squirrel
Divination harsh.

九四晉如鼫鼠. 貞厲

We can easily explain this as warning that advancing timorously, as does a squirrel, will make a bad impression, or even invite attacks from predators. It is also possible that the prognosis might refer to now forgotten mythical attributes of squirrels. We cannot tell which, if any, of these putative meanings were intended, but any could serve for a divination response.

A common structure is what I term a split prognoses, which pairs favorable and unfavorable prognoses:

28.3 The ridgepole sags, ominous.

九三棟橈, 凶.

28.4 The ridgepole bends upward, auspicious.

九四棟隆, 吉.

These prognoses, like many others in the *Changes*, seem arbitrary; it is not apparent why the direction of bending would be auspicious or ominous, since there is no indication that this has anything to do with the structural integrity of the building. It is simply an omen.

The same act may be beneficial or not, depending on which line is selected:

5.0 Beneficial to cross the wide river.

利涉大川.

6.0 Not beneficial to cross the wide river.

不利涉大川.

As here, the *Zhouyi* usually does not specify an exact time; it is assumed to apply to circumstances at the moment when the divination is performed. Since choice of a line is based on a random method, the prognosis will usually be different each time selection is performed.

Favorable prognoses

One of the most common prognostic terms in the *Zhouyi* is 利 *li* beneficial or favorable, appearing 99 times and sometimes negotiated as 不利 *bu li*, not beneficial. In context, it usually indicates whether or not a particular situation or action will be advantageous for the inquirer. By implication, the prognosis is specific for the time the divination is performed:

13.0 Assembling in the wilderness, making offering.
Beneficial to cross the great river.
Beneficial for the upright person to divine.

同人于野, 亨. 利涉大川. 利君子貞.

"Beneficial to cross the great water" is a set phrase metaphorically indicating that a major undertaking will be advantageous. Three of the four characters of the standard invocation appear in this judgment text: 亨 *heng* offering, followed later by the remaining two characters 利貞 *li zhen* of the invocational formula, with 君子 *junzi*, upright person, inserted. The later suggests the idea, later emphasized in Ruist ideology, that only the virtuous will receive correct answers from the *Yijing*.

Double negation is frequently employed as a literary flourish to emphasize that everything will be beneficial:

14.6 Nothing not beneficial.

无不利.

Here a split prognosis contrasts alternative actions in terms of benefit:

4.6 Not beneficial to attack bandits; beneficial to resist bandits

不利為寇, 利禦寇

This form also makes the advice more precise: *Bu li* warns not to attack the bandits; *li* by itself indicates the better response would be simply to resist them. This trope of split prognosis is relatively sophisticated for such an early text as the *Zhouyi*, and continues to be common in later Chinese texts.

It seems unlikely that with attack by bandits imminent, soldiers or officers would take a few minutes to consult the oracle. Even if one did, odds would be against receiving this specific line. The line best makes sense as a record of a previous divination that was preserved to use metaphorically in new circumstances—recycled, in effect. It could be a general warning that when encountering hostility, one should resist rather than attacking back. This is the sort of divination response that is certain to come true, as everyone encounters hostility from time to time.

In the following, the set invocation is followed by a time frame specification:

19.0 Begin with an offering, beneficial to divine.
Until the eighth month will be ominous.

元亨, 利貞. 至于八月有凶.

We are not told what will be ominous, but presumably that would have been apparent from the inquiry. The eight-month duration is not quite hemerology because it does not indicate an exact date.

While 利 *li* indicates a direct benefit resulting from an action, in effect, "You should do this," 吉 *ji* means overall auspiciousness or good fortune. In modern Chinese it tends to mean "lucky," but in the *Zhouyi* it usually has a more serious sense, "auspicious" or "fortunate," because luck implies a random event, not one caused by correct or skillful behavior.

Often a favorable prognosis follows practical advice:

6.1 Do not persist for the long term with the matter.
With a few words it can end fortunately.

初六不永所事．小有言終吉

This line text does not state an image directly, but one gets a clear sense of a conversation.

In Hexagram 6 訟 *Song* Dispute, *ji* appears in the judgment and five of the line texts, for example:

6.3 Fortunate sometimes to follow the king's affairs for which there is no completion.

吉或從王事无成．

In context, 利 *li* as beneficial might have been as appropriate as 吉 *ji*; choices between similar prognostic terms are sometimes a stylistic preference on the part of a compiler or editor.

Li 利 beneficial appears directly and negated within a split prognosis in the judgment text of this Hexagram:

6.0 Beneficial to see the important person.
Not beneficial to cross the great river.

利見大人．不利涉大川．

Here repetition creates anti-parallelism for rhetorical effect. The assumption behind such tropes seems to be that the same line selection has different implications for different sorts of action—in effect, "Don't do this; do that." It is usually not clear why the particular actions were selected for this contrast.

Ji can also recommend behavior for the long term:

6.3 Fortunate sometimes to follow the king's affairs for which there is no completion.

吉或從王事无成.

15.3 By laboring humbly, the high-born person has an auspicious outcome.

九三勞謙，君子有終吉.

In the following, two prognoses are provided—placing troops in the center is not only favorable, it will also avoid blame. This seems similar to what is now termed "plausible deniability"—when dealing with the powerful, avoiding blame is of paramount importance:

7.2 To situate troops in the center is auspicious and averts blame.

九二在師中吉无咎.

"No blame" has other implications to be discussed below.

Chinese historians tended to conceive history as cycles alternating between virtuous and corrupt government. Here is the good phase of a cycle:

11.0 The petty depart; the great arrive. Auspicious, make offering.

小往；大來. 吉亨.

In this phase, virtue is rewarded:

12.5 Refusing the bad, for the important person, auspicious.

休否大人吉

Unfortunately, the opposite state of affairs is all too common:

12.2 For petty people, auspicious; for great people, not.
Make offering.

六二包承. 小人吉；大人否. 亨

Auspiciousness can come in quite unexpected situations:

10.4 Treading on a tiger's tail, terrified, terrified—but ends favorably.

九四履虎尾，愬愬—終吉.

This suggests being careless in the presence of extreme danger, yet somehow escaping the consequences.

Sometimes *ji* rather than recommending an action, endorses one already in progress:

11.5 King Di Yi bestows his younger sister (and/or) cousin in marriage.
For happiness, an auspicious beginning.

六五帝乙歸妹. 以祉元吉.

The final phrase was likely a standard expression of hope for a happy marriage.
Sometimes the prognosis seems unconnected to the rest of the line text:

15.1 The humble and the high-born alike must wade to cross a wide river.
Auspicious.

初六謙謙君子用涉大川. 吉

This is a proverb vividly conveying the truth that the powerful cannot escape all of life's difficulties. It is not clear why this is auspicious, unless for the envious. Presumably an editor saw this phrase and felt a prognosis needed to be included.

Less frequent is the prognostic term 光 *guang,* meaning honorable or glorious. It appears only three times (5.0, 20.4, 64.5) and would seem to be a favorable term:

64.5 The upright person is honored.
Holding captives, auspicious.

六五貞吉; 无悔. 君子之光. 有孚吉.

However, as *guang* is again associated with sacrifice in 5.0, its usage does not fit any modern notion of what is honorable.

Unfavorable and negated prognoses

A common form of prognosis in the *Zhouyi* consists of negation of an adverse outcome; that is, reassurance that something will *not* happen. Particularly common are no blame 无咎 *wu jiu* and no regret 无悔 *wuhui*. There are several possible reasons for this preference for negations. Stylistically negative statements are more elegant and emotionally they are more engaging than simple positive ones. Fears are more likely to be alleviated by a specific negation than by a general statement that everything will be auspicious. The ancients had much to be fearful about, not only personal and political dangers, but the omnipresence of supernatural ones as well.

Fears are present in any divinatory interaction. As noted by Marshall McLuhan, "Terror is the normal state of any oral society, for in it everything affects everything all the time" (1962: 27).[1]

Given this pervasive fearfulness, it is not surprising that adverse prognostic terms appear quite frequently, although sometimes negated. The most unfavorable prognosis is ominous 凶 *xiong*, which appears 57 times; the other unfavorable prognostic terms are regret 悔 *hui*, blame 咎 *jiu*, and *lin* 吝 shame or remorse. These terms have slightly different connotations, although these are not distinguished in most translations. Because precise understanding of the subtle differences between these terms helps clarify some obscurities in the text, I discuss them here in some detail.

In contrast to the other unfavorable prognoses, *xiong*, ominous, is never negated, although it is "set aside" in 23.1 and 23.2, apparently because of sacrifice of a ewe. In a few cases it is qualified, as in 28.6, "ominous but not blameworthy," and 42.3 "Advantageously used for an ominous affair." In a few cases 凶 *xiong* follows *zheng*, to form 征凶, meaning an ominous portent:

> 9.6 Moon nearly full; for the cultivated person a long journey is an ominous portent.

> 月幾望；君子征凶.

In the *Zhouyi*, prognoses are only occasionally provided with timeframes:

> 19.0 Begin with an offering, beneficial to divine.
> Until the eighth month will be ominous.

> 元亨, 利貞. 至于八月有凶.

In this line and in 43.3 is it paired as 有凶 *you xiong*; one wonders if this was a preference of a specific compiler, although with an ancient text, this is merely conjecture. Here, rather than being a divination response, it might be part of a cynical proverb:

> 32.5 Divination for a married woman is auspicious; for a husband, ominous.

> 貞婦人吉；夫子, 凶.

By far the most frequent of the adverse prognostic terms is *jiu* 咎 blame, with 99 occurrences; the majority, 74, of these are negated as 无咎 *wu jiu* no blame. This negation suggests evading blame for an action that might get one in trouble, but the usage of this phrase is more complex—sometimes the action does not seem blameworthy at all, but in other instances the action definitely seems deserving of blame. The reasons for what seem to be peculiar uses of this word are discussed below.

Also sometimes negated is 悔 *hui* regret, appearing 34 times, six of which are preceded by 无 *wu* 无悔 to mean "without regret." The least frequent negative prognostic term is 吝 *lin* "shame" or "remorse" with 20 occurrences.

There is ample evidence for 悔 *hui*: meaning regret

16.3 Open eyes to prepare. Regret—tardiness will bring regret.

六三盱豫. 悔—遲有悔.

This text is a self-evident warning that for an important occasion one must prepare and not be late.

Here is an odd instance of this word:

1.6 Overbearing dragon will have remorse.

上九亢龍有悔.

One does not imagine that dragons have much conscience, but the phrase can be understood metaphorically as stating that even the powerful can go too far and suffer consequences.

In the *Zhouyi*, *hui* usually denotes the sort of regret that is felt when one's action creates difficulty for oneself. It is not so much a moral self-judgment as an indication of unpleasant consequences. In vernacular English, it is closer to "I would be better off if I had not done it," or " What I did was a mistake," rather than "I feel bad that I did it." There may have been mental pain or sorrow but such are at best only hinted at by the actual text. (Regret is considered from another perspective in the section on human sacrifice.)

The exact consequences that produce regret are not always stated:

34.4 Divination auspicious—regrets will go away.

九四貞吉—悔亡.

This could be translated less literally, "Don't worry, you won't make any mistakes that will get you in trouble." It could also be a charm to avert regrets. Since *hui* occurs 32 times in the *Zhouyi*, making mistakes was a major source of anxiety in this often unforgiving society.

Rutt provides a useful graphic summary of the meaning changes of the prognostic terms, although by compressing millennia of language change into a few lines, it creates as many questions as it answers (1996: 206). Regarding *hui*, he proposed the following (I have replicated his typography):

HUI: TROUBLE >> regret >REMORSE

In Rutt's formulation, bringing trouble or misfortune upon oneself gradually transforms from regret to a more Christian-like emotion of remorse.[2]

A third unfavorable prognostic is 吝 *lin*. In modern use this usually means humiliation; in my translation I have usually rendered it as "shame" in the sense of disgrace or suffering unpleasant consequences for one's actions.

Sometimes a double negative is used as a literary flourish:

> 40.6 Using an arrow, the duke shoots a falcon high above the city wall, bagging it. Nothing not beneficial.

> 上六公用射隼于高墉之上獲之．无不利．

Prognostic terms can occur in combination:

> 44.6 They meet with horns.
> Shame, not blame.

> 上九姤其角．吝，无咎．

This is one of those passages that resists efforts to make sense of it. Presumably the first phrase refers to an encounter between bulls or goats, although as I previously suggested, it might be a euphemism for sexual intercourse. To have two prognoses in which one qualifies the other is unusual in the *Zhouyi*. Perhaps shame is a less negative prognosis than blame and thus moderates it. Also possible is that shame is public embarrassment, while there is no blame from supernatural entities, such as ancestors.

Why "no blame"?

The word 咎 *jiu* occurs 99 times in the *Changes*, usually translated as "blame," but can also mean calamity or misfortune. Significantly it is negated by 无 (or 無) *wu* in 74 of its appearances so as to form the phrase 无咎, usually translated as "no blame." There are a few variants of the phrase, such as in 9.1, where the preceding phrase is, as below, "what blame?"

> 9.1 Returning along the road, what blame? Auspicious.

> 初九復自道，何其咎．吉．

The only other uses of this form 何咎 are in 17.4, and 38.5.

The following shows the sort of uncertainties one faces in trying to fix the meanings of this text:

14.1 Cannot cross, catastrophe.
Bandits are blamed for this difficulty.
Thus nothing blameworthy.

初九无交，害．匪咎艰．则无咎．

However, in the Mawangdui version, in which this Hexagram is # 50, this phrase appears as 非咎 meaning "no blame," rather than 匪咎 *fei jiu* meaning "bandits blamed" (or punished) (Shaughnessy 1996: 136 f). Most likely the MWD character is correct as it is consistent with the usual phrase containing *jiu*. On the other hand, 非 is easier to write, so might be a scribal substitution for 匪.

Blame: Natural and supernatural

When first reading the *Book of Changes* in Chinese or almost any translation, one is struck by the frequency of the phrase commonly translated as "no blame."[3]

Averting blame was clearly important to those who composed and used the *Zhouyi*, but who would do the blaming and the exact consequences are not usually stated. There is evidence, though to my knowledge not previously applied to the *Zhouyi*, that the blame feared was that of offended ancestors or spirits, who could inflict revenge upon the living. In ancient times these entities were aware of the behavior of the living, especially their relatives, and could affect their well-being. These entities and the nature and place of their existence are not described in the *Zhouyi*, perhaps because this seemed a matter of common sense.

Fear of being blamed by spirits had also been pervasive in the Shang, as indicated by frequent use of the same phrase in the form 無咎 *wu jiu*. Constance Cook has shown clearly that these terms referred to blame on the part of ancestral and other spirits. The fear pervaded all aspects of life because it was impossible to know what daily life activities might offend them. In some situations there were prescribed propitiatory rituals, but otherwise the spirits' demands could only be learned by divination. This is why the phrase, or charm, "no blame" appears so frequently in the *Zhouyi*, although there must have been other apotropaic methods for this purpose. Since it could never be ruled out that present and future misfortunes were due to invisible entities, elaborate rituals and costly sacrifices were regularly carried out to propitiate them (C. Cook 2006:

80). One such ritual is described in a passage from the *Baoshan*, an Eastern Zhou text in part derivative of the *Zhouyi*:

> Hexagram Sun moves to Hexagram Lin. (Wu) performed an exorcism to get at its source. (He) performed the proposition prayer to Grand Occluded Unity with a whole gelded pig. (He) performed proposition prayer to the Earth Alter (spirit) with a whole pig's worth of dried meat. (C. Cook 2006: 171 f)

The passage goes on to mention further sacrifice of a white dog, as well as a fattened piglet, wine and food. As a result, he was told by the diviner that he would be without blame by spirits for the subsequent three years. As Cook suggests, during the Warring States, supernatural blame was still deemed a cause of sickness and death, but violation of Confucian morality was now a possible etiological factor. Divination by either tortoise shell or stalks was necessary to determine the state of blame and its outcome. Blame 咎 *jiu* could now be incurred for failure to maintain proper behavior.

It is not always possible in the *Zhouyi* to distinguish supernatural blame from that on the part of humans. The following, because it mentions no specific act that might be blamed, seems to be a general purpose apotropaic ritual:

> 17.0 Begin with an offering, beneficial to divine.
> There will be no blame.
>
> 元亨利貞. 无咎.

This passage consists of the full four-character invocation, which states that an offering is to be made, followed by the phrase, "there will be no blame." This set phrase could be a charm to avert supernatural blame, or reassurance that it will be avoided, or, most likely, both. The early users of the *Zhouyi* may not have made such fine distinctions.

In Hexagram 19 臨 *lin* wailing, in which the title character appears in all the lines, seems to refer to lamenting the dead, as suggested in the final two lines:

> 19.5 Controlled wailing—proper for the great master. Auspicious.
>
> 六五知臨—大君之宜. 吉.

> 19.6 Loyally lamenting. Auspicious. There will be no blame.
>
> 上六敦臨. 吉. 无咎.

In Chinese culture from very early, proper mourning behavior, especially display of grief, was considered imperative lest the aggrieved deceased retaliate upon the living relatives. Here in context "no blame" expresses the hope that the wailing and lamenting was adequate to appease the recently deceased.

In the following passage, plans for an enjoyable occasion are described; "no blame" seems to be a routine spell to prevent anything from spoiling it.

> 24.0 Coming and going there will be no infirmity.
> Friends arrive.
> There will be no blame.
> They turn back on their way and in seven days return.
> Beneficial if having to go somewhere.
>
> 亨． 出入无疾． 朋來． 无咎；反復其道七日來復． 利有攸往．

Since concern about supernatural blame is so frequent in the *Zhouyi*, it is curious that spirits are never referred to directly. This could be because the *Changes* was conceived as a source of guidance for practical, earthly matters. Perhaps more likely would have been an unspoken taboo against mentioning spirits or ancestors, although there is no such taboo apparent in the Wu Ding oracle bone inscriptions (OBI). Rather than an absolute taboo, it could have been a matter of decorum, which could also explain why Confucius famously never spoke of spirits (*Lunyu* 7.20). Perhaps having their names mentioned would offend some spirits, or, nearly as bad, attract their attention.

The shame/blame controversy

A recurrent controversy in Western scholarship about Chinese ethical thought that needs brief mention here is whether China had a shame culture but not a guilt culture. (To the best of my knowledge this issue has not been raised in China.) The notion that China is a shame rather than a guilt culture was proposed by Herbert Fingarette (1988) and Jane Geaney (2004), among others. As used in this debate, the English word "shame" refers to the distress felt when one's faults or misdeeds become known to others; "guilt," in contrast, involves conscience, the inner sense of having thought or done something wrong. According to this conception, people in a shame culture feel remorse only if publicly shamed. In guilt cultures there may be shame, but because of conscience there is also an uncomfortable inner state of self-blame.

While not always explicit in these arguments, the Western notion of guilt culture stems from Christian doctrine, which teaches that all are born with original sin and unavoidably continue to sin throughout life. To be released from the consequences of sin requires awareness that one has sinned—that is, guilt, and consequent contrition and atonement. Ultimately divine forgiveness is possible only through the intermediation of Christ with the God the Father, who knows all acts and thoughts. The Christian narrative of sin, guilt, and redemption, still prevalent in the West, is often erroneously assumed to be universal, but guilt is understood differently in other cultures.

Before the arrival of Christianity, Chinese were not aware of this narrative; it does not have an analogue in Confucianism. They were therefore "unreached people," for whom conversion would be necessary to save their souls. The notion of China as a shame culture seems to have arisen because from Christian doctrine. It should not be assumed Chinese never felt guilt or remorse; rather, it was expressed in different terms. Given these differences, care must be taken not to equate the early Chinese words referring to blame, regret, and shame with these in Christian usage.

It is not self-evident whether or not people of the remote, pre-axial past felt guilt in addition to shame; yet all civilizations have ideas of what actions are right or wrong. In early China, the transcendent beings who judged were ancestors, not an omniscient deity. Whether the early Chinese, or any other non-Christian peoples, felt guilt involves a semantic issue. Traditional Chinese had great fear that misbehavior, particularly neglect of ritual obligations, would adversely affect their lives. As with Christianity, there was fear of supernatural retribution for misbehavior, but otherwise there are many differences. With the rise of Ruism, there was great anxiety to observe propriety in social interactions. Indeed, the *Lunyu* largely consists of Confucius expounding proper ethical decision making. The Song dynasty philosopher Zhu Xi 朱熹 (1130–1200 CE), generally regarded as second in importance to Confucius, advocated intense self-examination for ethical self-improvement, based in part on frequent consultation of the *Yijing*. The idea of moral self-improvement implies conscience and thus guilt, but in Ruism this was based on lessons embedded in the ancient classics, not on the drama of sin and divine forgiveness.

Chinese no doubt feel shame at times, as do members of all cultures, but this does not establish inability to feel guilt. In the interest of brevity, I will confine myself to only one of Geaney's claims: her analysis of the character 恥 *chi*, which she translates as "shame." While this character does not appear in the *Zhouyi*, shame has an obvious relationship with regret and blame, which do appear in the Western Zhou text. Geaney notes that the first component of the character for *chi* means ear, which she takes as indicating that the word refers only to social disapproval, but ignores the second component, which is usually translated as "heart-mind" and therefore implies an inner mental state. Inferring meanings from character components is a dubious undertaking, but if applied here would be as consistent with guilt as with shame.

We need to be careful about making overly subtle distinctions about mental states based on very early Chinese sources, because they had not yet developed an extensive vocabulary for this purpose. Most *Zhouyi* prognoses, as with divination systems generally, are about the personal consequences of wrong or imprudent actions, not the inner feelings of the inquirer.

Divination as word magic

Divinations are generally undertaken to better understand a present situation or to foresee the future, but as with no blame they may also be intended to bring about the desired outcome. As I have suggested, in practice these intentions probably often overlapped. The phrasing of many *Zhouyi* texts can be read with equal plausibility as predictions or appeals:

24.0 Make offering.
Coming and going there will be no infirmity.

亨．出入无疾

30.0 Beneficial to divine; make offering. For breeding cows, auspicious.

利貞'　亨．畜牝牛，吉．

38.1 Regret goes away
Losing one's horse, do not pursue it. Naturally, it will return.

悔亡．喪馬勿逐．自，復

Magical or supernatural elements in the *Book of Changes* became less apparent as metaphysical theories emerged, as in this passage from the *Dazhuan*:

Hexagram statements refer to figures,
　line statements refer to alternations.
Auspicious and Disastrous mean failure and success;
Trouble and Distress refer to minor mistakes
No misfortune means mistakes can be mended. (Rutt 410)[4]

In these lines supernatural causality has been supplanted by the concept of good and bad fortune as cyclical, prefiguring the yin-yang metaphysics that later became fundamental to *Changes* interpretation.

Determination of prognosis using line positions

We do not know whether the *Zhouyi* utilized lines as well as texts from its earliest beginnings, but they are present in all known related versions, those of the Shanghai Museum, Guicong, Fuyang, and MWD manuscripts. There is no mention of their use until the *Dazhuan* (Wings 5, 6 and 8) and *Shuogua* (Wing 9), both usually considered to be of late Warring States or early Han origin.

Here is the explanation of the significance of the *Yijing* figures from the *Dazhuan* (*Ci Xi*), attributed to the *Tuan* (Wings 1 and 2):

> The *Tuan* [彖] speak of the emblematic figures (of the complete diagrams). The *Yao* [爻] speak of the *Changes* (taking place in the several lines). The expressions about good fortune or bad are used with reference to (the figures and lines, as) being right or wrong (according to the conditions of time and place) ... those about repentance or regret refer to small faults (in the satisfying those conditions); when it is said "there will be no error," or "no blame," there is reference to (the subject) repairing an error by what is good. (Legge 1899)

象者，言乎象者也。爻者，言乎變者也。吉凶者，言乎其失得也。悔吝者，言乎其小疵也。无咎者，善補過也

The notion of trigrams or lines being correct or incorrect is based on the yin-yang metaphysics, in which odd-numbered line positions (1,3,5) are yang, while even-numbered positions (2,4,6} are yin. Thus a yin line at position 1,3, or 5 would be incorrect, as would a yang line at 2,4, or 6. (See Adler 2022: 35–8, 75–86; Redmond and Hon 2014: 161–9, among many others.)

Legge's translation, although rather awkward, has the advantage of separating the interpolations of the translator, which are enclosed in parentheses, from the text itself. In less convoluted form it states that the hexagrams describe the overall situation, while the lines describe what will change. Whether lines are right or wrong refers to whether yang lines are in odd-numbered positions and yin in even-numbered ones. In this excerpt, both texts and line positions contribute to the prognostication.

This combined use of the text and line systems does not appear in the *Zhouyi*, but was already well-developed in several of the *Ten Wings*, and predominated in the *Yijing*'s subsequent history. While acknowledging the ingenuity and importance of *Xiangshu* interpretation, from my perspective it is a major reason for the classic's seeming difficulty. Trying to connect line and text meanings creates a kind of forced marriage between incompatible partners, which scholars have sought to harmonize ever since. My view is not likely to be well received by practitioners; all I ask is recognition of the heuristic value of interpreting the figures and texts separately. Considering the texts and the *Xiangshu* methods separately has great heuristic value because the texts make sense when not forced to be paraphrasing what the line positions mean. This is not to deny the fascination of the diagrams, which are unique among all divinatory texts. The Wilhelm-Baynes translation only adds to the confusion because the primary text is combined with interpretive material of uncertain sources. I am not suggesting that the core texts are the "real" *Book of Changes*, rather that it combines two quite different systems.

5

The Grammar of the *Zhouyi*

Much of the seeming peculiarity of the *Book of Changes* for modern readers stems from two inherent attributes, one historical and the other grammatical. In its depiction of the life of 3,000 years ago, hierarchy was strict, servants could be killed for spilling a duke's stew, and blood sacrifice was routine. What is being described is clear, but the sensibility that sanctions such acts is not. Unrelated, but also difficult to resolve, is the extreme polysemy of the early Chinese language, combined with its "isolating" syntax. Here, isolating languages are those that offer relatively few clues as to the grammatical relationships of adjacent or nearby words. Subjects are often omitted, making it often difficult to determine if a noun is the object of a phrase or the subject of a succeeding one. Modern Chinese has many characters that indicate grammatical relationships (often mischaracterized as "empty words"); all but a few are lacking in the *Zhouyi*. Furthermore, between the early Western Zhou and the Spring and Autumn many words changed their meanings.

One must remind oneself when reading the *Book of Changes* in modern format that the text was composed very early in the development of literacy. Words and clauses lack connectives—words and phrases such as "but," "because," "as a result of," and other forms of subordination. Because the Chinese writing system does not allow for inflections, the part of speech to which a word belongs must be inferred from context. Other sources of difficulty include unrelated phrases placed adjacent to each other, and events of narrative being out of order.

As a result of these characteristics the *Zhouyi* texts often seem like "word salad," evading attempts at grammatical categorization. Comprehensibility is, however, from the perspective of users of the language and so our working assumption must be that the *Zhouyi*'s syntax made sense to Western Zhou users. As I hope to establish, the apparent jumble of words can be resolved with recognition of the underlying patterns of the language.

Parataxis

The modern term for the predominant syntactic structure of the *Zhouyi* is *parataxis*, in which clauses are placed together without connectives, thus leaving it to the reader to determine their relationship. Parataxis can be a deliberate, even affected, stylistic device, but for the *Zhouyi* compilers it was simply the way they wrote. Its antonym is *hypotaxis*, in which clauses are coordinated or subordinated to one another within sentences. Other terms have been used to describe this distinction, such as "agglomerative versus subordinative"; even contemporary Chinese tends toward the agglomerative end of the spectrum, although the addition of grammatical markers has provided greater clarity. Walter Ong refers to this mode of composition as "additive," providing as an example the Douay version of Genesis 1:1-5 in which the only connective is "and." Modern versions of ancient texts nearly always have punctuation added, usually without noting that it did not exist in the original language version. Christoph Harbsmeier, one of the leading anglophone authorities on Chinese language and logic, describes the situation as follows:

> In the oldest inscriptions we have from the oracle bones, punctuation, even in the forms of gaps indicating pauses, is so erratic that no systematic pattern arises ... the various symbols we find on many bamboo strips do not coherently relate to the notion of a sentence in which we are interested.
>
> ...
>
> What we have of punctuation, as opposed to grammar, would not give us any set of reliable clues at all to sentence boundaries and clause boundaries in Classical Chinese. (Harbsmeier 1968: 177)

To modern English language readers paratactic texts seem disordered, hypotaxis being the default assumption in reading. While parataxis may seem a defect in written, expository prose, it is usual in ordinary conversation because tone of voice, gesture, emphasis, and other mannerisms add clarity in ways not possible in written language. It is also usual in situations in which the writer minimizes effort: notes from lectures, minutes of meetings, and other transcriptions of spoken language. Text messages are often paratactic, but understandable to the intended reader.

Young children's speech is often paratactic:

> They speak their ideas as they come to them, one after the other, without logically connecting the ideas together.[2] Parataxis may use commas, semi-colons, and periods to force juxtaposition, but it can also replace these punctuation marks

with "and" to seamlessly string the speech or written pieces together and present the words as each being equally important. Works utilizing parataxis as a style may emit a staccato rhythm. This can result in phrases with words that don't seem to go together at all. (Hale 2013)

Parataxis in Modernism

In early texts, parataxis was simply the way people wrote because most of the grammatical means for indicating relationships between words had not yet been invented. Parataxis in modern works is something quite different, a deliberate choice or even affectation, particularly in avant-garde or countercultural works. Examples range from the bitter rants of the French novelist Louis-Ferdinand Céline (aka Destouches) to the hypomanic rush of words in Jack Kerouac's *On the Road*. Parataxis can go only so far without creating gibberish, as William Burroughs demonstrated in the cut-and-paste sections of *Naked Lunch*, of no interest except that it was done.[1]

The parataxis of the *Changes* is different from that of postmodernist works in that grammar is present, but must be exposed by the reader or translator.

Punctuating archaic texts

Few modern readers consciously identify the grammatical functions of words as they read, but this is necessary in reading or translating the *Zhouyi*. As the syntax is being worked out, addition of modern punctuation can serve to distinguish separate phrases and indicate word relationships. This improves readability with only minimal modification of the text being translated. Tedious as this process is, it can set free the meanings of the *Zhouyi*. Knowledge of the history of the era is also important because it narrows the choice of possible meanings.

Over years of puzzling over the peculiarities of the *Book of Changes* I have come to feel that most of the texts make sense once they are divided into clauses, which are then identified by punctuation. By recognizing parataxis, one avoids trying to force unrelated phrases into a coherent whole. The classic then presents itself to us as an agglomeration of mostly banal phrases, but it would not have appeared this way to its early readers, who were familiar with the genre of divination manual. For this genre, a collection of distinct phrases works quite well, because in use it would not have been read straight through from beginning to end; rather, one or a few phrases were selected by a random method to serve as the response to the inquiry.

At some point, the *Changes* was adapted to indicate how events would unfold over time by means of line positions, or by using changing lines to generate another hexagram. This method was the basis of the *Xiangshu* school which became active in the Han, emphasizing the diagrams with little attention to the texts. Wang Bi is usually credited with restoring use of texts in the *Yili* school, but he also made use of diagrams. In the *Zhouyi*, the hexagrams are thought to have served to organize the texts so as to permit access. There may have been divinatory use as well, but we have no record of such.

While the hexagrams are the distinctive feature of the *Book of Changes*, it is important to understand how they actually function within the work, beyond adding visual interest. On the most basic level they constitute a template upon which the text is organized, saving it from being a jumble of fragments lacking any evident pattern. Most important, they lent themselves to selection of the proper text as the divination response. Yarrow stalks (milfoil) seem to be the first method for selection, with tossing of three coins eventually becoming more popular because of its ease of use. Thus the usual way of reading the *Changes* was not from beginning to end, but as a few lines selected by a random method.

Punctuating without rewriting

The greatest value of translations of ancient texts is, for me at least, the opportunity to glimpse how our remote forebears thought and lived. With paratactic texts this means maintaining the style of the original, to the extent possible, by minimizing addition of connecting words and paraphrases. Other approaches are possible, as illustrated by Wilhelm-Baynes' translation of 19.3:

> Nothing that would further.
> If one is induced to grieve over it,
> One becomes free of blame

However, it is possible to have the passage make sense while preserving the paratactic style:

> 19.3 Willingly wailing.
> Nowhere beneficial.
> Now sorrowful; There will be no blame.

> 六三甘臨. 无攸利. 既憂之；无咎

As often occurs, the two translations read like different texts. Wilhelm-Baynes' version seems to make more sense, but only because it adds meaning not present in the original. My version preserves the parataxis and is intended to convey the mood of sadness. In contrast Wilhelm-Baynes ends on a positive note but achieves this with a subtle anachronism, the modern psychotherapeutic commonplace that expressing one's emotions is beneficial. Presumably this was introduced by the translator of Wilhelm's German into English, Cary F. Baynes, an American woman in the circle of the psychiatrist Carl Jung.

These translations had different goals; Wilhelm-Baynes was to adapt it to readable English while emphasizing (or perhaps adding) spiritual content. My intent, on the other hand, was to capture the literal meaning while preserving the archaic syntax and mood. If the Wilhelm-Baynes version seems easier to understand, it is because it adds familiar psychological ideas not in the source.

As is usual in the *Zhouyi*, this passage does not specify dates or durations, in contrast to works on hemerology, which provide methods for selection of favorable dates. These techniques attained a high degree of elaboration, but were not based on the *Yijing* (Harper and Kalinowski 2017).

Parsing the *Zhouyi* texts

The key to making the *Zhouyi* comprehensible is parsing and punctuating the texts so that the function of each word becomes apparent. Forming words into phrases has particular difficulties in the Chinese of the *Zhouyi*. While all verbal constructions permit of syntactical analysis, early Chinese as an isolating language is particularly difficult to characterize in formal terms because of its loose syntax, polysemy, paucity of grammatical markers, and frequent omission of the subject. However, that the text now seems obscure does not mean that it was obscure at the time of its composition in the Western Zhou.

Cultural context often resolves seeming obscurity. The following phrase, seemingly obscure, would have been clear to it contemporaries:

31.3 Sensation in one's thigh. Grasping it while following. Going, regretted.

九三咸其股. 執其隨. 往吝. (191 ff)

As I have divided the phrases, the literal meanings are clear, but their significance is not—until the sensation in the thigh is recognized as an omen, which is interpreted to mean that going somewhere (unspecified) will lead to regret.

Omens are spontaneous natural events that were believed to foretell important happenings; they could be significant on a personal level, as a bird call, or the state level, as with eclipses. (Bodily movements and sensations as omens are discussed in Chapter 11.) As discussed in the previous chapter, in the *Zhouyi* the term 吝 *lin* regret usually means not the emotion, but consequences causing regret: accident, punishment, etc. Alternatively, it might be that the painful thigh would be made worse by extended walking. The passage is straightforward once recognized as stating an omen and explaining its significance.

Parsing by function

Richard Rutt proposed a system, based on that of the Chinese scholar Li Jinchi 李鏡池 (1902–75), for parsing the texts into five types of expression; this is summarized in the addendum to this chapter. Because his categories are somewhat indistinct, I have developed a different system that emphasizes recognizing the *function* of each syntactical element. I offer this simply as an aid for making sense of the *Zhouyi* texts. While this proposed system is intended to elucidate the grammar, and hence the meanings, of the ancient text, it does so using modern critical methods. It is heuristic in that it does not claim to replicate what was in the minds of the compilers as they created the classic. Previously I have termed this approach as "translating backward and forward," that is, using modern knowledge to reconstruct older meanings, while being careful to avoid anachronism.

My proposed system works by identifying the functional role of each word, thus indicating how they can be combined into meaningful phrases. I postulate six kinds of functional role for words and phrases in the *Zhouyi*, although most lines do not have all six. Within the texts the ordering of these elements varies.

The elements of the judgment and line texts are: an **invocation**; an **image**; a **descriptive or supplementary statement**; a **prognostication**, which may be a **conditional**; and a **prognosis**. The image and descriptive statements are substantive in that they contain specific information. The prognostication is usually, and the prognosis is always, a standard term or set phrase.

The judgment (hexagram) texts

The first line of text associated with each Hexagram is unnumbered. In English these have usually been referred to as the "Hexagram text," or "Judgment text," based on the traditional Ruist reading which considered them to summarize the meanings of the entire Hexagram chapter (figure, tag, judgment text, and the six- or seven-line texts). Literally translated, however, these are not summaries, but are usually invocations to initiate the divination. I have referred to these lines as judgment texts to avoid the implication that they function as summaries. The full invocation is found in the first line of both the received and MWD versions:

> 1.0 Begin with an offering; beneficial to divine
>
> 元亨利貞 (*Yuan, Heng, Li, Zhen*)

Since divination is nearly always ritualized, use of an invocation to begin the procedure is unsurprising.

Wilhelm-Baynes translate quite differently, presumably based on the late Qing views of his informant:

> THE CREATIVE works sublime success,
> Furthering through perseverance. (4)

Lynn's translation, based on the commentary of Wang Bi, is similar in being a list of virtues:

> *Qian* consists of fundamentality [*yuan*], prevalence [*heng*], fitness [*li*], and constancy [*zhen*]. (Lynn 129)

In these translations, the judgment text is no longer an invocation, but an enumeration of virtues. Possibly the invocation did not fit with Ruist practice, or a different way of beginning the divination came into use.[2]

In the *Zhouyi*, the word offering 亨 *heng* refers to a ritual offering, usually to begin a divination. In 31.1 the divination is "for choosing a woman." We are told what the offering is in 坤 *Kun* 2.1, in which it is sacrifice of a mare:

> 2.0 Begin the offering, beneficial if a female horse, for the divination
>
> 元亨，利牝馬之

Wilhelm-Baynes seem not to have been aware that blood sacrifice was usual in early China; luckily for the mare, in their version she is no longer a victim, but instead exemplifies the virtue of perseverance:

> The RECEPTIVE brings about sublime success,
> Furthering through the perseverance of a mare. P11

It seems unlikely that something as valuable as a horse was sacrificed every time a *Zhouyi* divination was performed, suggesting that this line might be a record of another divination for a particularly important purpose. Early sources that mention divination by yarrow never, except for 2.0, refer to blood sacrifice. By the Song the usual offering was lighting of incense.

In many judgment texts, only part of the invocation appears, most commonly, 貞 *zhen* or *li zhen* 利貞, but sometimes only "to make offering" 亨 *heng* as in 4.0:

> 4.0 Make offering. 亨

In such cases, *heng* is probably an abbreviation for the full oral invocation.[3]

Possibly the reason the invocation was so often abbreviated is that it was routinely used in oral rituals to begin divination, thus familiar to all early users of the *Zhouyi*. This is characteristic of many sorts of verbal formulas, such as mantras.

Some judgment texts lack any element of the invocation and thus read more like line texts, as in this example:

> 43.0 Displayed in the king's courtyard, the captives wail at this harshness.
> Get out the word in one's own county that it is not beneficial to go to battle.
> Beneficial if having to go somewhere.

> 揚于王庭，孚號有厲．告自邑不利即戎．利有攸往．

Plausibly these were misplaced line texts; the compilers were not entirely systematic in arranging the texts.

The line texts and images

The line texts form most of the *Zhouyi* content and because of their varied content are often more interesting than the judgments. The images, although simple, are usually the most vivid element of each text and thus what engages the imagination. Grammatically, the image may be a solitary noun, or a noun with an adjective or verb. It is usually a living creature, human or animal; when an event or action, it is always one related to human life. The image makes possible the divinatory response. The *Zhouyi* never explains why a randomly selected image, such as a bird calling or a muddy well, can foretell human events; such explanations seem not to have been thought necessary.

Most divination makes use of visual images such as cracks on bone or shell, numerals or letters, planetary positions, the shape of a sheep's liver, or pictures on a Tarot card, although some, such as bird calls, are auditory. With the *Changes*, the hexagrams are visual and the texts create mental pictures. The relation of image to prognostication is ultimately intuitive, even though there may be guidelines for interpretation. Dream interpretation also is based on images, although dream images are often indistinct.[4]

The images in *Zhouyi* line texts can be single or multiple; some extend across several line texts, notably the dragons in *Qian*, Hexagram 1. Often there is also a supplementary statement and/or prognostication that expands the image. Usually, however, images within adjacent texts seem unrelated.

The image is the substantive component of the response because from the perspective of correlative cosmology, the omen or other image is a message from the cosmos intended for the inquirer, but requiring decipherment. Thus creating a divination response using the *Zhouyi* begins with contemplation of the image, in light of explanatory or prognostic statements, if present. The one- or two-word prognosis is usually at the end of the phrase and seems to be a conclusion. The syntax of most lines is in the form "Gray sky, rain, ominous," or in more usual English style, "The sky is gray; therefore it will rain, ominous." Sometimes, the prognosis does not seem consistent with the rest of the associated text, or to be in the wrong place.

A few line texts do not follow this pattern, such as the following in which the prognosis is self-evident:

16.5 Divination: Sickness long-lasting, but not fatal.

六五貞：疾恆，不死.

The value of images for divination

Images engage the interest of inquirer and diviner and help hold the divination in memory. Prognostications tersely explain the significance of the images and sometimes add to the interest. They also provide further raw material for the diviner to develop into a coherent narrative. The more closely the diviner can connect the images to the inquirer's concerns, the more the inquirer will be persuaded. The process moves in both directions; however, the reactions of the inquirer—agreement, argument, relief, anger, distress, or even boredom—provide feedback to the diviner, who can adjust the reading accordingly.

Images can be quite simple, yet reassuring:

24.0 Make offering.
Coming and going there will be no infirmity

Here an offering is suggested to ensure that in the ordinary activities of the day, nothing harmful will befall. This is directed toward the universal slight anxiety felt when leaving one's home to face the world, an anxiety that must have been much greater in the ancient world. This simple apotropaic phrase, that coming and going will be without difficulty, remains in common use in Chinese communities 3,000 years later, demonstrating the efficiency of oral transmission. Bright red posters bearing this phrase in gold characters are universally available in China and Chinatowns and, in fact, one has adorned our front door for many years—a prudent precaution in New York City, where we live.

Prognostication and prognosis

As pointed out above, most lines also provide a **prognosis**, a one- or two-word direct statement of whether the outcome will be favorable or not. The prognostic terms are explained in detail in Chapter 4 and summarized in Part IV. The connection between image and prognosis often seem tenuous; greater specificity is often provided by a **prognostication**, that is, a description of what might happen. These different components do not always seem clearly related to each other. Often, prognostications are conditional: the outcome depends upon the gender, character, or other traits of the inquirer. Or, it specifies that one kind of action will be beneficial, while another will be harmful. Rutt suggests that some elements in the line texts may be later additions intended for clarification and that prognoses were particularly unstable through the Han; this conclusion is supported by the variability of these terms in the Mawangdui silk manuscript (Rutt 134f). Nonetheless, deciding what is a later addition is ultimately a matter of guesswork. Time and geography may have been factors as well.

Do the prognoses imply fixed fate?

When divination is considered, the question of free will versus determinism arises. I have no insights to offer about this as a philosophical problem, but will consider the viewpoint of the *Book of Changes* 易經. The very title suggests that fate is not fixed; but we do not know if this was the original title, although it has long persisted. Since 易 *Yi* also means "easy," some have suggested that the title may originally have meant Easy Classic. Many prognostications and associated prognoses in the *Changes* are conditional; that is, whether the outcome is favorable or not depends on the inquirer. This suggests that the *Changes* was not based on an assumption that fate is fixed, but rather is somewhat dependent on choices and character:

> 33.4 A good piglet, for the upright person, auspicious.
> For the petty person, not.
>
> 九四好遯, 君子, 吉. 小人, 否.

The piglet might be an omen, or it might be a meal. Either way, it is the upright person who benefits.
   Sometimes the prognosis is different sorts of inquirer:

> 32.5 Divination for a married woman is auspicious; for a husband, ominous.
>
> 貞婦人吉; 夫子, 凶.

Similarly, when divining about travel, the prognosis may depend upon the direction.

> 39.0 Beneficial in the west and south.
> Not beneficial in the east and north.
> Beneficial to see the important person.
> Divination auspicious.

Sometimes bad people come out ahead:

> 20.1 For the petty people there will be no blame.
> The upright people will have regret.

The *Zhouyi* does not discuss fate versus free will as a philosophical issue, but it is addressed indirectly in the *Dazhuan* (*Great Commentary*), Wings 5 and 6 of the *Ten Wings*:

> Thus when a superior man prepares to act or move,
>   he puts his question in words
>   and receives instruction like an echo.
> Nothing is too far or near, hidden or obscure;
>   he is able to know what will happen.
> If Yi did not reach the innermost core

of everything under heaven,
what else could do so? (Rutt 416)

The term 君子 *junzi*, often translated as "superior man," is difficult to convey in English without it seeming snobbish. The cultivation or superiority it refers to is moral—being able to choose the proper course, especially with the aid of the *Yijing*.

Many judgment and line texts include a **supplementary phrase** or general statement, such as a set phrase or proverb. These may clarify other components of the phrase, although some give seemingly unrelated information, such as a reference to an historical event.

Contemporary Western divination tends to avoid negative prognostications consistent with the New Age movement's emphasis on positive thinking. In earlier times, however, inquirers seemed to want the unvarnished truth, although the process must have often been emotionally wrenching. Still, another hexagram can always be selected in the hope of a more positive message, so there seems to be a place for at least some control over one's fate.

It is sometimes suggested that the *Book of Changes* expresses a philosophy of change, or time. However, the *Zhouyi* itself contains no analytic or metaphysical statements about the nature of time. (Philosophy of time did became a central concern of Chinese philosophy in the Warring States, notably in the *Dao De Jing* and *Zhuangzi*.) It is possible, however, that the title character *Yi* 易, translated as "change," referred not to an abstract or metaphysical theory of time, but to hexagrams transforming into other hexagrams by means of changing lines.[5] Whether viewed metaphysically, or just as a given of life, change is still central to the classic because divinations can be repeated to keep track of changing circumstances.

The *Dazhuan* commentary expresses the traditional Chinese admiration for the *Yijing*:

> Thus: a superior man
>   has a place in life
>   resting content
>   in the succession of *Changes*;
>   finds his satisfaction
>   taking delight
>   in the words of the statements.
> ...
>   when he acts

> observes the alternations
> and takes delight in the omens. (Rutt 410)

The *Changes* in the hexagrams are derived from natural processes:

> All in heaven and earth alternates and transforms:
> sages followed suit.
> Heaven gave celestial figures
> to declare what is *Auspicious* and *Disastrous*;
> sages made hexagrams from them
> ...
> Sages took them as norms. (Rutt 419)

Here the *Yijing* is celebrated for its wisdom in the sense of explaining the cosmos in terms of alternation. The "superior man" is delighted because the *Yijing* makes sense of the cosmos, both philosophically and by making it possible to anticipate auspiciousness and disastrousness. While there is no shortage of unfavorable prognostications in the *Changes*, its overall concept of change *Yijing* is optimistic; with its guidance it is possible to have some control over one's life.[6]

Addendum

Other Approaches to Parsing the *Zhouyi* Text

I will briefly summarize two alternative systems for parsing the *Changes* text; there may well be many more that I have not encountered. Ultimately they cannot differ very much as they are all about the same text.

Richard Rutt

Richard Rutt (131–6) paid close attention to the syntactical structure of the *Zhouyi*; his book has not received the scholarly attention it deserves (Redmond 2017: xxiii f). I have found it indispensable; although I often arrived at different conclusions, these were often stimulated by his carefully reasoned views. My parsing scheme method described above derives from his, but I feel is more precise. Given that no one system can encompass every possible meaning of the *Changes*, I have provided a brief description of two others here.[7]

Rutt's first category is *Shici* 示辭 The "oracle," that is, the theme (Rutt 118–44). Rutt further describes this as "the heart of the line statement, a phrase or sentence that encapsulates the divinatory value of each line." He notes that some are proverbs. Although Rutt argues against terming these elements "topics" or "images," for me, the latter term would be clearer than "oracle," which can refer to multiple aspects of the divinatory process.

Gaoci 告辭 The "indication," that is, the type of problem divined about. Since the *Zhouyi* texts are responses rather than questions, determining the type of problem is often a matter of inference.

Rutt's term for the "prognostic" is *Duanci*斷辭, of which five are listed by Rutt: *ji* or auspicious; *li* or dangerous; *jiu* or misfortune; *xiong* or disastrous. The Chinese term Rutt uses here is somewhat confusing as it usually has negative meanings such as unhappiness or calamity, yet some of the prognoses are favorable. (In my discussion I identify more prognostic terms; these are discussed in detail in Chapter 4 and the table in Part IV.)

Yanci, an observation, usually modifies a negative prognosis. In my proposed categories this is part of the prognosis. An example is *wu jiu*; two morphemes but functioning as a unit to form a specific kind of prognosis.

Although our categories differ, Rutt's and my systems are not contradictory.

Myth-based parsing of the *Zhouyi*

Stephen Field, author of an important work on Chinese divination (Field 2008), considers the *Changes* from unusual perspectives, both in his account of its history and in his way of presenting the texts. His account of the text's origins is engaging, but an eccentric mix of the traditional mythology with the actual history based on recent scholarship. Almost nowhere does the work indicate what its author must have been well aware of: that Fu Xi could not have been based on an historical figure; and that the other mythical individuals mentioned in the *Dazhuan* could not have invented the basic elements of culture, such as marriage or laws (32f). Nor did the Duke of Zhou compose the *Shijing* or *Shangshu* (Books of Songs and Documents, which were traditionally, also apocryphally, attributed to Confucius instead) (16f). These myths are worth retelling, but their nature should be acknowledged.

It is Field's mode of parsing the text that is of interest here. He divides the texts of each Hexagram into three columns, designated as omen, counsel, and fortune. So far as I am aware, the *Changes* texts never appeared in this format in

China at any stage of its history. It has been reorganized in other ways, including the translations of Legge and Wilhelm-Baynes. Although these are meant to make the text clearer, they deprive the reader of experiencing the book as it has come down to us, limiting possible interpretations. To those who know the *Changes*, however, it offers a new way to read it, as devised by a knowledgeable scholar.

Field's division into omen, counsel, and fortune is a reasonable approximation of the functional elements of the *Zhouyi* texts; they do provide an image (often, but not always, an omen), an explanation, which is not always advice, and a conclusion that Field calls "fortune," and I have labeled "prognosis." There are several limitations, however. "omen" and "fortune" are less fully descriptive terms than "image" and "prognosis," although casual readers may not be much bothered by this. Particularly problematic is his statement that "there is no structural difference between *guaci* or hexagram [judgment] statement and the *yaoci* or line texts" (48). These texts are thought to have separate origins, and many include a distinctive element, the formulaic four-character invocation 元亨利貞, "Begin with an offering; favorable to divine." This is the first line in both the received and Mawangdui versions; in the former it appears in complete or partial form in eighteen Hexagrams, but only two of the line texts.[8]

The important phrase 无咎 *wu jiu,* almost universally translated as "no blame," becomes, for example, "no harm will come."

10.1 He walks in plain silk shoes
On a journey no harm will come. (89)

This misses the meaning of this phrase, which almost always refers to averting supernatural blame, rather than a general reassurance of safety. Perhaps because of Ruist influence, interpretation of the *Book of Changes* has generally ignored or concealed such elements of early consciousness as fear of vengeful ancestors or spirits, and the consequent belief in the necessity of offerings, usually blood sacrifices, to propitiate them.

Field's version is not without some strong points; the mythical origins are described in a lively and detailed manner, although misleading in not being labeled as such. The parings are presented visually, in an easy-to-understand system. While I would not recommend it as a place to start study of the *Zhouyi*, it does present interesting perspectives for those already familiar with it.

6

Rhetoric and Forms of Expression

Despite the voluminous writings that analyze the *Book of Changes*, seemingly from every possible angle, little has been said about it as a work of literature; that is, its rhetoric and style of expression. This is not surprising given its indistinct syntax and the disjointed texts. Yet virtually any written work uses words to convince and has a distinctive style, even if not consciously chosen. Although at first encounter the *Zhouyi* text may seem muddled, we should heed Harbsmeier's pronouncement that "In order to fill in the right sort of linguistic forms the ancient Chinese must have had an operative notion of a statement versus other strings" (1998: 177–81). They did not help the reader by punctuating, but cannot be blamed, as this aid to quicker comprehension had not yet been invented. Even Classical Chinese, a later elite form of the written language, was not punctuated. Harbsmeier suggests:

> To a seasoned scholar, an unpunctuated text has something virginal about it … so there is a sublime quiet joy in punctuating a Classical Chinese edition as one reads it for the first time. After all, Classical Chinese was never meant for the impatient modern reader. (Harbsmeier 1988: 181.)

Although the language of the Western Zhou differed considerably from the later Classical language, similar challenges confront the reader/translator, as both lacked punctuation.

Amidst the hard life of the Western Zhou, when writing was brushed on bamboo and scribes may not have fully understood the meanings of the characters they were writing, conditions were not yet suitable for refinements such as punctuation. Even the Shanghai Museum bamboo manuscript (*c.* 300 BCE) lacks punctuation, although the start of each chapter is indicated by its hexagram and space is left at end. Despite lacking grammatical indications, the Chinese language managed to communicate complex ideas for many centuries before Western-style punctuation became nearly universal in the modern era. Before this, punctuation-like marks (句讀 *Judou*) could be added by readers.

The consequence for the *Zhouyi* is that division into clauses must be inferred by the reader, who also must determine to what part of speech many of the words belong. Given the polysemy of the language, many text portions can be read in more than one nominally correct way. Because of this, translation unavoidably adds a fixity that did not exist in the original. An unfortunate result is that many translations are actually paraphrases that take liberties with the Chinese text.

Greek and Latin are highly inflected languages, which facilitates precise structuring of rhetorical figures. Many of these were oral in origin, as is apparent in the Homeric epics; later systems of rhetoric reached a high degree of elaboration, which were described in manuals and which influenced literary style in the West from classical times through the Renaissance. In early Chinese texts rhetorical structures are present, but usually less elaborate than those in Greek and Latin classical texts.

The term "rhetoric" originally referred to what is now termed "public speaking." More specifically, the term refers to artifices in spoken or written language that are intended to convince. Any divinatory method needs to establish credibility, both of the method and of the person doing the reading. The *Zhouyi* uses simple diction and practical solutions; in contrast, Ruist adaptation of the classic gave it a preachy quality entirely absent from the early meanings. This enhanced credibility with the literati as it affirmed their ideology by employing the language of propriety and virtue. Knowledge of these constituted the expertise that was the basis for their qualification for public office. This knowledge was supposedly learned from study of the ancient classics. So as to fit this purpose, those ancient classics whose composition had long preceded the rise of Ruism—not only the *Yijing*, but also the *Shijing*, and *Spring and Autumn Annals*—had this ideology superimposed on them. While this might seem philologically problematic, it was effective in maintaining Chinese culture and civilization for the ensuing more than two millennia.

Confucian simplicity and the *Zhouyi*

What is most characteristic of the rhetoric of the *Zhouyi* is its terseness. This is not apparent in the convoluted James Legge translation, nor the prolix Wilhelm-Baynes version. The *Ten Wings*, as well as the arcane philosophizing of the

Warring States and early Han, obscure the plain language and conceptual simplicity of the core text. Once freed from its 2,500 years of encrustations, the *Zhouyi* is a collection of simple images whose meanings are usually on the surface. In this it is early an early exemplar of a strand of Chinese thought that favors the laconic and down-to-earth over the strange and metaphysical. We find this articulated much later by Confucius:

> People in old times were sparing in their words ... (*Lunyu* 4.22; Watson 2007: 34)

Confucius clearly admired terseness:

> This man doesn't say much, but when he does speak, he's sure to hit the mark. (*Lunyu* 11.14; Watson 2007: 74)

This is a recommendation for simplicity in thought.

This preference for laconic expression is evident in the *Zhouyi*, which also does not delve into strange doctrines; these became plentiful beginning in the Warring States. Its imagery is drawn from ordinary life and explanations, to the extent they are provided, they are not fanciful. The style, if we can use such a term for an archaic work, is minimalist. There is no reason to regard this as a deliberate choice; this was the way written works were composed in its time. Also worthy of remark is the rarity of magical and supernatural elements in the *Zhouyi*, perhaps due to a taboo against mentioning them in certain settings:

> Subjects the Master did not discuss: strange occurrences [anomalies], feats of strength, rebellion, the gods. (*Lunyu* 7.20; Watson 2007: 50)

Given that Confucius in the *Lunyu* held forth on many subjects, his refusal to discuss these specific topics is significant. It might be that he wanted to avoid matters that were doubtful or titillating, or that might have magical significance, or that might be taken as portents, which could be a pretext for rebellion, and thus destabilizing. Events such as eclipses or earthquakes could be interpreted as signs that heaven had withdrawn its mandate from king or emperor. Recurrently in Chinese history such events were used to inflame the populace and justify rebellion; possibly this was the reason Confucius would not speak of anomalous happenings. The *Zhouyi* contains no mentions of these subjects that Confucius avoided, although it has references to kings and nobles,. Thus, it can be speculated that this was a long-standing taboo that preceded the Master by several centuries. In a sense, what is not said constitutes a from of rhetoric. As the Master summed it up:

> To delve into strange doctrines can bring only harm. (*Lunyu* 2.16; Watson 2007: 22)

While the *Changes* may seem to a modern reader to contain strange doctrines, they would not have seemed so to the early Chinese.

Some clarification is necessary regarding Hexagram 49 革 *Ge* Tanning Leather, sometimes interpreted as "Revolution" presumably because tanning symbolized a radical change. There is no textual or other evidence for this meaning in the *Zhouyi*.

Confucius also avoided the supernatural, advising:

> Respect the gods and spirits but keep them at a distance—this can be called wisdom. (*Lunyu* 6.22; Watson 2007: 45)

The almost complete avoidance of anything supernatural must have been deliberate on the part of the compilers or editors of the *Zhouyi* project. I do not suggest that they were somehow Confucian *avant la lettre*, rather they were likely observing a taboo or a principle of decorum. Other classics do mention some of the topics excluded from the *Zhouyi*; two examples are the *Zhuangzi* and the *Classic of Mountains and Seas* 山海經 *Shan Hai Jing*, which is filled with fabulous creatures and events.

Zhouyi rhetoric is unaffected and pragmatic

Records of speeches composed with formal rhetorical devices are prominent in the ancient classics of China as well as the West. Most esteemed among the former was the *Shangshu* 尚書 *Book of Documents*, a collection of speeches by notable ancient figures that was considered one of the five Confucian Classics (Nylan 2001: 120–67). I mention the *Shangshu* to show that early Chinese used rhetoric in a way similar to the Greeks, and to contrast this formal style with the plain style of the *Zhouyi*. The stylistic difference is apparent throughout the *Shangshu*, as in this extract from its first line:

> Examining into antiquity ... the Di Yao was styled Fang-xun. He was reverential, intelligent, accomplished, and thoughtful ... The bright (influence of these qualities) was felt through the four quarters (of the land), and reached to (heaven) above and (earth) beneath.[1]

This brief passage includes formal expressions resembling the rhetoric of the Greek and Roman classics, possibly in part because of its Scottish translator, James Legge. "Examining into antiquity" is a *topos* or topic intended to invoke the wisdom of the ancients; the long clause about the four quarters is similarly a *topos*, a standard way to praise an important person. Rhetorical figures of this sort were likely to be familiar to the audience, thus likely to engage attention and agreement.²

The *Zhouyi* also uses recurrent topics and phrases that serve the same purposes of familiarity and engagement, but they are down-to-earth and unadorned rather than elegant. Easily recognized images and familiar prognostic terms would facilitate understanding between inquirer and diviner; the former would feel on familiar ground and the latter would be better able to weave the text into an acceptable response.

Characteristics of early literacy in the *Zhouyi* texts

Rhetoric must have long preceded literacy; as early as humans assembled in groups, there would often be occasions when some would use eloquence in efforts to convince others. The invention of writing allowed rhetoric to be more elaborate by releasing it from the limits of memory. The change was more gradual than moderns can easily imagine, occurring over centuries. Many of the verbal devices were simple. Repetition was frequent to aid retention in memory, so that content and form would be familiar to intended audiences. In addition to repetitions of important words, set phrases, and proverbs, illustrious historical events such as military actions and royal marriages were often mentioned. These very devices that make many early texts, including the *Zhouyi*, seem stilted and tedious to modem readers helped early readers and also non-literates, who would have had texts read or recited to them.

Walter Ong's insightful explanation for the formulaic nature of oral material can help us appreciate its stylistic nature:

> In an oral culture, to think through something in non-formulaic, non-patterned, non-mnemonic terms, even if it were possible, would be a waste of time, for such thought, once worked through, could never be recovered with any effectiveness, as it could be with the aid of writing. (2002: 35)

Much of the *Zhouyi* consists of fragments of evident oral origin; it would have been the images that were memorable, as well as the occasional proverb. For prognoses a small set vocabulary was employed, which would have been familiar to those receiving the divination.

Ong further characterizes the style of orality in a way suggestive of the style of the *Zhouyi*:

> In the absence of elaborate analytic categories that depend on writing to structure knowledge at a distance from lived experience, oral cultures must conceptualize and verbalize all their knowledge with more or less close reference to the human lifeworld, assimilating the alien, objective world to the more immediate, familiar interaction of human beings. (2002: 42)

This description clearly fits the *Zhouyi*, as a compilation of fragments, many of which were originally orally transmitted. Virtually all its phrases concern human interactions, many with animals, ubiquitous in agricultural societies. Ong's formulation is similar to the concept of pre-axiality, in which early humans lived close to nature and had very limited concepts of transcendence. Centuries later, for example with Zhuangzi's Peng bird and carp that enjoy swimming, Chinese thought could move far beyond actual experience; such fantasy elements are absent from the *Zhouyi*. Confucian writings, with a much fuller conception of individuals as existing within society than the *Zhouyi*, still stayed within the lifeworld.

Convincing the inquirer

That the *Zhouyi* is derivative of oral fragments, or at least the style of orality, is why it now reads as stylistically inelegant and repetitive. For its contemporaries, its concise advice, though needing to be interpreted, would have seemed direct and to the point. The very ordinariness of its subject matter corresponded to the life of its time and so, we can presume, did not seem strange at all to its contemporaries 3,000 years ago. Often overlooked is how this bland diction embodies the hopes and fears of the early Chinese.

Given that rhetoric is use of language to convince, we need to consider how the language of the *Zhouyi* accomplished this purpose. (I think we can assume it did, since it is still in use 3,000 years later.) Such an inquiry is unavoidably speculative because we have no early external sources for use of the *Zhouyi*. First, the encounter of inquirer with the book, with or without the aid of a diviner, sets expectations. Anxiety about the future is universal, so inquirers were likely to pay close attention during the divination process and would be aware of the status of the *Changes* as the creation of the ancient sages, who could recognize incipience sooner than ordinary mortals. This was not necessarily a psychic power, but a special ability to observe what most overlook. The aura of numinosity engendered by the hexagrams also contributes to credibility; indeed, it is unlikely the *Changes* would have its reputation for profundity without them.

Ong makes the interesting claim that non-literate cultures often use language in a way he terms "agonistic," by which he means contestational, as in debates, athletics, or war. Ong's work was based on genres, which, although diverse, were quite different from those of early China. Among these were the Bible, the Homeric epics, and African and European oral story-telling. Given this observation, it is of interest to consider whether the rhetoric of the *Zhouyi* can be described as agonistic. (Anyone seeking modern instances of agonistic discourse need only spend a few minutes browsing the internet.)

I suggest that the style of *Zhouyi* might be agonistic in certain settings, but only by implication, as it does not record discussion between inquirer and diviner. It would not have been unusual for an inquirer to be dissatisfied with the response, resulting in argument with the diviner. That there could be outright argument is demonstrated by one of the *Yijing* anecdotes in the *Zuozhuan*, in which Lady Mu Jiang is under house arrest and asks if she will get out:

> The diviner tells her she will get out soon; she replies, itemizing the four characters *yuan, heng, li, zhen* as a list of virtues, none of which she possess and concludes, "I have chosen evil . . . I shall not get out." (Rutt 187; Redmond 2017: 368–71)

In my many observations of contemporary divinations, there is much interchange between inquirer and diviner, but mostly to reconcile the divination with the inquirer's actual life details. Hence divination is usually dialogic, sometimes argumentative, but less often agonistic.

Who used the *Book of Changes*?

Much of what we know about the *Changes* has been learned from excavated manuscripts. Although these were found in tombs of the affluent and therefore were clearly luxury goods for the rich, this does not establish that its practical use was confined to the elite. Much of its content could have been transmitted orally among users who were not fully literate; this fits with the simplicity of its language and images. The 士 *shi* or educated professional class, whose employment depended on literacy, had not yet emerged. I have no basis for challenging the usual assumption that literacy was confined to a few, yet parts of what we known as written texts may have been accessible to the non-literate in at least two ways. The affluent non-literate may have had followers who would read to them, especially a practical text such as the *Changes*. For the less well-off there were almost certainly itinerant diviners; some may have owned the book, or fragments of it, or knew parts from memory. They need not have memorized the entire book to have used it for divination; even a few phrases and images with standard prognostic terms would have sufficed to impress inquirers. Divergence from what become the received text would have passed unnoticed, especially as the content may have circulated in variant forms. Granted that the foregoing is speculative, it seems plausible that the *Zhouyi*, or bits of it, was in use at all levels of society.

I am frequently told by Chinese, and occasionally by Americans, that they regard the *Yijing* as profound, yet cannot claim to understand it. This is actually common with scriptural and canonical texts of many cultures; the plain fact of their existence provides spiritual benefits. Only a few of the devout have read the entire New Testament word for word; the great classics of the West from Plato and Aristotle and even Shakespeare are rarely read, except by specialists. Even Confucius is respected far more often than he is read. Millions of Mahayana Buddhists chant the Heart Sutra while admitting to not understanding it.

The *Changes* is a guide for making correct life decisions, but also is something more: reassurance that life can make sense. Regrettably, there are no more sages, but providentially those of high antiquity understood all possible situations and preserved their insights in the classic. That the *Book of Changes* was never lost preserves the hope that one day the truths of the ancients might be recovered. This hope is a reason why scriptural texts endure; their existence supports a sense of faith that there is meaning. The difficulty of the ancient Chinese book is an essential part of this, because mystery is at the heart of all spirituality.

Part Three

Imagery

7

The Nature of Omens

Fortuitously, the second edition of the Wilhelm-Baynes version of the *I Ching* was published in 1961, just in time to benefit from the emerging fascination with non-Western philosophy and spirituality that was part of the so-called countercultural movement of the 1960s. The seeming exoticism of the *Book of Changes* allowed its Confucian, socially conservative ideology to pass nearly unnoticed by a youth culture eager to throw off restraints. Works on Western occultism also become widely popular, and at first the *I Ching*, too, seemed to belong to the genre of metaphysical, occult, or esoteric literature. It was used for divination and developed a reputation for wisdom, but awareness of its role in Chinese intellectual history was limited. Given their expectations, young readers in the West were often attracted to the Chinese classic because it bore little resemblance to the metaphysical and visionary works of Western esoteric traditions. Instead, it consisted mainly of simple images drawn from daily life that somehow constituted a divination manual. Many of these images were omens, part of a way of experiencing the world that had mostly, if not entirely, vanished from Western consciousness. In the ancient world, however, almost everything perceptible could hold prognostic significance:

27.0 Divination auspicious according to observation of the jaw.

貞吉觀頤

Here the position of the jaw is significant only because it serves as an omen—a chance event carrying prognostic significance. Omens are typically minor happenings without self-evident significance:

15.2 The humble bird calls, auspicious.

鳴謙．吉

As in this instance, most omens are only arbitrarily related to their prognosis. While we might imagine that the bird call was auspicious because pleasant to the ear, just as often they carry an ominous prognosis:

16.1 A bird calls. Prepare—ominous.

初六鳴. 豫凶

In the process of divination, omens are usually interpreted metaphorically, but most are not symbols; rather, they are messages from the cosmos signaling whether particular circumstances or actions are favorable or hazardous. The *Zhouyi* simply attaches prognoses to omens; reasons as to why an omen had its assigned prognosis were rarely provided, perhaps because there were none. It assumed what later developed into systematic as correlative cosmology, the idea that each level of the cosmos is congruent with every other level.

The body was a common locus for omens: facial features, spontaneous sensations, involuntary movements such as twitches, and sightings of people with deformities or injuries could all serve as omens, the latter being usually inauspicious. Animal movements and vocalizations also could be omens. While most prognoses do not seem intuitively related to the omen, some are derived from its emotional impact, such as sightings of people inflicted with injuries or other misfortunes:

21.6 Carrying on his shoulders a cangue, the ears disappear. Ominous.

上九何校滅耳. 凶

Omens in the *Zhouyi* are usually not miraculous, but normal events interpreted as having special significance. In a few instances, however, they are symbolic rather than realistic, as in these powerful images of sterility:

54.6 The woman offers a basket; there is no fruit
The official cuts a sheep, there is no blood.
There is nothing beneficial.

上六女承筐无實. 士刲羊, 无血. 无攸利

It is useful to distinguish omens from other sorts of prognostic events. Omens, or rather their interpretations, could be socially disruptive; in traditional China, natural calamities such as floods or earthquakes could be interpreted as signs of heaven's displeasure with the emperor and thus justify uprisings. Omens on this higher level can be referred to as "signs." When all of society is involved, the signs, often supernatural, are the basis of prophecy, which typically exposes widespread moral decadence. Only a few lines in the *Zhouyi* are prophetic, most notably 11.0, "The petty depart; the great arrive," and 12.0, "the great depart; the petty arrive." The first phrase announces that the morally good will replace the corrupt; the second, that the dissolute will come to predominate.

Omens are objective events that are apparent to everyone present, although their interpretation is entirely subjective. Mental phenomena that should be distinguished from omens include visions and hallucinations; these are private experiences, but are often communicated to others. Visions usually occur only a few times in a devout person's life; their images are drawn from the person's spiritual or religious belief system. Although experienced as different from normal perception, visions do not necessarily suspend consciousness. Hallucinations are abnormal brain events, whether spontaneous or drug-induced. The distinction between visions and hallucinations is not absolute; historically the former have been interpreted religiously, but in recent decades spiritual claims have also been made about hallucinogens. Neither sort of mental event is referred to in the *Changes*, despite its enthusiastic adaptation into the 1960s counterculture, which sometimes associated the hexagrams with psychedelic experiences.

Divination of all sorts, including interpretation of signs, visions, and omens, inherently assumes a metaphysics in which all levels of the cosmos are interrelated, so that random events can reveal information about the human plane. That a bird call indicates a prognosis cannot be understood from a scientific perspective, but some light is shed by "terror management theory," developed by several evolutionary psychologists.[1] Although the details are complex, the basic conception is that belief systems, often religious, but not always, are protective against the terror of death. In this perspective, belief in divination serves to avert fear by seeming to identify hazards and proposing ways to respond to them.[2]

While omens are spontaneous, most divination uses a system or device to generate a prognostication. Such methods are quite diverse, ranging in scale and complexity from a coin toss to calculating positions of planets. Physical devices used to asses prognoses vary greatly, from coins, to reflective surfaces, to manuals such as the *Book of Changes*, and even the livers of sacrificed sheep (haruspicy). All of these employ apparent randomness, which sets it apart from science. (In practice, divination may not be random, as the diviner may know enough about the circumstances to provide an accurate answer, or may employ cold reading.) Much human ingenuity has been expended in creating ways of divining, ranging from the refined, such as using books, charts, or pictures, to the cruel and repellent, such as haruspicy. It is not that much of a stretch to believe that planets' position at birth or the words and diagrams of the sages could provide useful knowledge, but much harder to understand why the civilization that produced Plato and Aristotle believed that sheep livers could foretell the future.

Recycled divinations

The omens in the *Zhouyi* are not actual omens—the bird calls are read about, not heard; instead they are textual records of omens. How they made their way into the book is uncertain. Perhaps they were actual omens that proved accurate and were therefore thought to possess special potency. Selection of a line with an omen might indicate that the present situation resembles the original one:

> 15.2 The humble bird calls.
> Divination auspicious.

六二鳴謙. 吉

The interpretation might be, in effect, "Your situation is similar to a previous one when a bird called and it was auspicious." Thus it is a recycled divination. The tacit notion of causality that underlies divination is quite different than that of science, being based on affinity or congruence. In this way of thinking, because the omen was correct before, it could also be correct whenever this phrase was selected. Put more directly, "This divination was correct before, so it will probably be right again." This does not make sense in terms of causality, but makes a sort of intuitive sense.

Divination responses can easily morph from predictions to being charms or spells to bring about an outcome such as rain, a pregnancy, safe travel and the like. Oracle bones evolved in this way from being predictions to related word magic. This can be uncharitably described as wishful thinking, but put in a more nuanced way, it was an effort to control life circumstances in an era in which few resources were available, even for the affluent. Thus divination responses cannot be reduced to predictions; they may comment on the uncertainties of life, or be apotropaic formulas, or hope for manifestation of intents. They overlap with charms, prayers, and mantras.

Viewed psychologically, the belief that the mind can control the external world is primitive, yet it persists. In New Age culture, bringing about what is desired by concentration or rituals is referred to as "manifestation."[3]

Most omens are open-ended; that is, their meaning is not intrinsic or self-evident, but requires decipherment be applied it to the inquiry. Many of the texts do not seem to be suitable for divinatory responses, yet there must have been principles that the compilers followed, although these are unclear to us now. Indeed, the greatest mystery of the *Book of Changes* is the source of the prognostications—we are never told from whom or where the prognoses originated. Omens are messages, but there is no mention of humans, nor ancestors, nor spirits as their source. This problem does not exist with interpretation of the hexagram line positions as these can have any meanings imposed upon them.

8

Divining About Numbers and Durations

Time and work

Divinations usually provide a time frame for when a predicted event will occur. Methods that provide exact calculations of favorable dates are referred to as hemerology, which has been, and still is, necessary for selecting auspicious dates for a planned activity, particularly important events such as weddings. The *Book of Changes* rarely provides exact times or dates, in contrast to the OBI. Its advice seems to be directed to immediate or short-term situations.

Hemerology, selection of favorable dates, reached a high degree of complexity in China, indicating that it was widely practiced. Early Chinese hemerology became known to the modern world only in 1975, with the excavation of a tomb in Hubei dated to 217 BCE. The earliest texts in these manuscripts are of Warring States origin; we have no sources from the Western Zhou, but it seems almost certain that some sort of hemerology existed in that early era. (The definitive work on early hemerology is Harper and Kalinowski 2017.) Daybooks were generally quite different in character from the *Changes*, using the systems of ten stems 天干 *tiangan* and twelve branches 地支 *dizhi*, often combined with the five phases 五行 *wu xing*. While some of characters of the stems and branches appear in the *Zhouyi*, in context they have other meanings. It is possible that some of these are coded messages about dates, but this degree of esotericism seems inconsistent with the plain style of the early work, although other scholars more adept at hemerology might find some instances that I have missed.

Given the later proliferation of daybooks, it is curious is that the *Zhouyi* provides no advice on selection of dates or times. Its usual advice is whether an action is beneficial or auspicious, but not *when* it should be done. There are, however, some statements of time intervals, usually three or seven days. If this was part of a larger system of numerological divination, there are no other remnants of it. A plausible explanation is that the *Zhouyi* was intended for advice on immediate situations, and could be consulted repeatedly as circumstances evolved.

Duration statements often accompany instances of tireless work:

36.1 The upright person walks for three days without eating.
Has someplace to go—his master has spoken.

君子于行三日不食. 有攸往—主人有言.

Extreme exertion to fulfill one's duties is exemplary in traditional Chinese texts. It is possible that the first phrase is a proverb to the effect that "An upright person will even go without eating to promptly fulfill his responsibilities." The model for this is Yu the Great, legendary creator of flood control who, during the many years he labored over flood control, passed his house three times, but never entered.

Three and seven as duration

The *Zhouyi* often indicates intervals before or after which specific events will occur. In most cases these are based on three, as in 36.1, quoted above. The reason for preference for this number is not stated in the *Zhouyi*, nor the *Ten Wings*. It may simply mean "a few days," just as 10,000 stands in for "very many," even in modern Chinese. Numerology is found in many cultures, but they vary as to which numbers are lucky and which unlucky. As to why there was a preference for three and seven in the early Western Zhou, I have been unable to discover.

In several instances, these numbers refer to arduous activity:

7.1 Buttocks obstructed by stumps and trees while entering into a deep and secluded valley.
Then three years no face-to-face meeting.

初六臀困于株木, 入于幽谷. 三歲不覿.

This seems almost humorous—seeing the buttocks but not the face, although it probably refers to forest growth that is high enough that walking through it is grueling. The difficulty in traveling may be why there is no face-to-face meeting. Three years is a set phrase, as below, in a line text consisting entirely of set phrases.

18.0 Begin with an offering.
Beneficial to cross the great river.

Before starting (jia 甲), three days.
After starting, three days.

元亨．利涉大川。先甲三日。後甲三日。

This can be read as a narrative: an offering is needed to be able to cross the great river, but one will need to prepare for three days before starting and also, for unclear reasons, after starting. (The rest of the *Ge* Hexagram, except for 18.6, is about disease from parental sexual activity and is discussed elsewhere.)

29.6 Tie using braided cords.
Lay them crowded together in a bramble bush.
For three years cannot find, ominous.

上六係用徽纆．寘于叢棘．三歲不得，凶．

Binding or other restraint most often refers to captives, but this would not make sense here, and 徽 *hui* to tie does not appear elsewhere in the *Zhouyi*. This line text seems to mean that something was hidden under a bush and then could not be found. This is the sort of *Zhouyi* text that might make sense if more details were included; we are not told what was put under the bush, nor even why someone would leave something under a bush. Presumably with such texts the source was considered important enough that mere fragments from it had divinatory power.

Phrases that include the number three can have auspicious or inauspicious outcomes, so the number itself does not seem to have divinatory significance:

53.5 Wife after three years not pregnant. In the end nothing successful or auspicious.

婦三歲不孕．終莫之勝吉．

55.6 All quiet—there is no one.
For three years, no one is seen, ominous.

上六豐其屋蔀．其家闃其戶．闚其无人．三歲不覿，凶．

One example does imply a specific day:

57.5 Nothing begins but has an end.
From three days before a *geng* day to three days after *geng*, auspicious

无初有終．先庚三日；後庚三日吉

In two examples, the three years duration refers to years:

63.3 The high ancestor (king Wu Ding) defeated Guizong, the demon land, in the course of three years.

高宗伐鬼方，三年克之

64.4 Divination auspicious, regret passes away.
Zhen used a military expedition against Guifang, the devil land.
In three years got his reward from the great country.

震用伐鬼方．三年有賞于大國．

The following indicates three years astronomically; such references are rare in the *Zhouyi*:

13.3 The forces ambush from the thicket.
They climb the high hill, but for three passings of Jupiter, not achieved.

九三伏戎于莽．升其高陵，三歲不興

The interval meant here by "three passings of Jupiter" is unclear; for Jupiter to reappear at the same point in the Zodiac takes slightly more than eleven years.

Number three in other contexts

6.2 Not successful in the dispute.
Returns, but from his town three hundred families had fled.
There was no mistake.

歸，而逋其邑人三百戶．

6.6 It happened that given a big leather belt, on the same day three times it was taken away.

上九或錫之鞶帶，終朝三褫之

7.2 The king three times confers rank.

王三錫命．

35.0 Bestowed upon Marquis Kang were numerous horses.
They became abundant, mated three times a day.

康侯用錫馬蕃．庶，晝日三接．

40.2 In the field catch three foxes and find a bronze arrow, divination auspicious.

九二田獲三狐得黃矢，貞：吉.

The next example is a proverb:

41.3 If three people walk, then lose one person.
If one person walks, then obtains a companion.

六三人行，則損一人. 一人行，則得其友.

This is similar in meaning to the English proverb, "Two is company; three's a crowd."

49.3 Binding with leather, speak three times while approaching the captives.

革言三就有孚.

57.4 In the field get three kinds of game.

田獲三品.

Other numbers

While most numerical references are to three, a few lines refer to other quantities:

24.0 They turn back on their way and in seven days return.

亨. 出入无疾. 朋來. 无咎；反復其道七日來復.

51.2 Thunder comes, harshly.
Many thousands of cowry shells for the funeral.
Ascend nine times to the burial mound.
Do not pursue, in seven days will be obtained.

六二震來，厲. 億喪貝，躋于九陵. 勿逐，七日得.

While there are many references to numbers and durations, we do not find explicit numerology or hemerology in the *Zhouyi*. It is possible, although not attested in any other source of which I am aware, that there were other manuals for forms of specialized divination absent from the *Zhouyi*. The two famous military manuals, the *Thirty-Six Stratagems* and the *Art of War*, particularly the former, list possible actions and thus could have incorporated material from earlier military works specifically intended for divination.

9

Joys and Hazards of Daily Life

Daily life is a broad category, hence this section contains a rather miscellaneous assortment of images; many other aspects of daily life are placed within more specific categories. As throughout the *Zhouyi*, many of the events referred to seem quite banal, yet are of great interest as accounts of the actual life of the Western Zhou, which are not available in more formalistic writings such as bronze inscriptions.

I explicate most of the images except when the meaning is self-evident in context. Some images could be placed in more than one category and other systems of classification could be devised, but that used here should provide easy access to a reader's areas of interest.

I have usually quoted only the phrases of the judgment or line text that contain the image and omitted the rest of the text, so as to focus on what is being analyzed. On the other hand, I have kept more of the text when the context was needed to understand the image.

Well-being

To begin on a happy note, here is one of the most quoted lines from the *Book of Changes*:

> 61.2 Cranes calling from the shady riverbank; their young answer.
> I have a good wine goblet; I will give to you generously.
>
> 九二鳴鶴在陰；其子和之．我有好爵；吾與爾靡之．

The first phrase evokes love between parents and offspring; the second, friendship and generosity.

Rather gratingly, it is followed by:

61.3 Take the enemy! Sometimes beating drums, sometimes stopping, sometimes sobbing, sometimes singing.

六三得敵！或鼓，或罷，或泣，或歌.

This is toned down in Wilhelm-Baynes by removal of the military context, which leaves the sobbing unexplained:

61.3 He finds a comrade.
New he beats the drum, now he stops.
Now sobs, now he sings.

There are many such incongruous juxtaposition of topics in the *Zhouyi*, presumably because the scribes often put phrases where a slot was available. This accounts for the paratactic structure of the *Zhouyi* and frees the reader from struggling to find connections between thematically unrelated text portions. Since each line text usually served as a separate divination, there is no reason to seek a connection between the cranes or goblets of 61.2 with the military images of 61.3. Given that the *Zhouyi* was a very early effort at composing a prolonged written text, the compilers deserve credit for their accomplishment.

20.3 Observing our lives going forward and retreating.

六三觀我生，進退

This is a somewhat philosophical reference to the ups and downs of life. It is also an easy one for diviners, as both favorable and unfavorable events can be included in the response, making it likely to be correct.

Some lines are mere common sense:

24.2 Resting before returning is auspicious.

六二休復吉.

Home

In premodern China, all but the poorest had servants, necessitated by the magnitude of work required for maintaining households with no conveniences available to ease such continual tasks as making repairs, preparing food, sewing clothes, and child care. Servants received subsistence, but for poor families providing for them was a major cost:

41.6 Obtain a servant without a family.

得臣无家

This was almost certainly a cost-saving matter, although a servant family with older children could provide more labor for a large household. The divinatory meaning could be interpreted metaphorically to advise keeping expenditures down.

Several line texts evoke the precariousness of village life in the ancient world. Proximity to bandits or other dangers could cause residents to abandon their homes:

6.2 Not successful in the dispute.
Returns, but from his town three hundred families had fled.
There was no mistake.

九二不克訟. 歸, 而逋其邑人三百戶. 无眚.

The next example is somewhat obscure, perhaps meaning that the neighbors are stealing or somehow damaging the reputations of others in the neighborhood:

11.4 Fluttering, fluttering.
Not wealthy because of their neighbors
Not on guard with the captives.

六四翩翩. 不富以其鄰. 不戒以孚.

Cities in early China were vulnerable to being attacked without warning, hence the need for city walls:

11.6 The city wall collapses into the moat.
Do not use the army; one's own city declares the order.
Divination—regret.

上六城復于隍. 勿用師；自邑告命. 貞一吝.

The second phrase is not entirely clear, but possibly means to use the city's own resources rather than risk being conquered by an outside army.

28.0 The ridgepole sags.
Beneficial if having somewhere to go. Make offering.

棟撓. 利有攸往. 亨.

The ridgepole is the beam under the center of the roof upon which the structural integrity of the house depends. Changes in the ridgepole may have been interpreted in magical terms (Redmond 2017: 180).

"Having somewhere to go" is probably a set phrase that means that it is good to live with purpose, or to have employment.

The following seems to be ancient interior decorating advice:

28.1 For mats use white grass.
Nothing blameworthy.

初六藉用茅. 无咎.

This seems to resemble the use of rushes in Renaissance England, which were thrown away only when thoroughly soiled. Neither is particularly hygienic.

Health

Considering the devastations of malnutrition and infectious disease in the premodern world, it is surprising that there are few references to health and disease in the *Zhouyi*.[1]

When illness occurs, particularly when there are no effective treatments, prognosis is the main concern:

16.5 Divination: Sickness long-lasting, but not fatal.

六五貞: 疾恆, 不死.

Here the prognostication is that the disease will persist, it will not cause death. While practitioners of traditional medicine may have possessed an intuitive sense of disease outcomes, accuracy would have been limited. For example, distinguishing a cough due to a harmless URI from potentially fatal pneumonia would have been problematic; only as the disease advanced would its severity become clear. Hopeful prognoses would always be welcome:

41.4 To those diminished by illness, quickly send some joy.
There will be no blame.

六四損其疾, 使遄有喜. 无咎.

Divination was also used to select remedies, but these are not mentioned in the *Zhouyi*. It is possible there were separate divination methods, and probably different practitioners, for medical matters. The *Baoshan* and *Wangshan* divination texts translated from the tomb of an official buried in 316 BCE contain references to Hexagrams used in diagnosis and treatment (C. Cook 2006: 171, 195, et passim). The similarity of these works, although more detailed, to the OBI sacrifice recommendations is striking, given that they were in existence nearly a millennium after the King Wu-Ding inscriptions. Divination methods were thus highly conserved over long periods of time. Etiology in these works is generally ascribed to deceased ancestors, demons or curses; suggested offerings include jade objects, pigs, cap strings, and white dogs (ibid. 179). Causation in these works is always supernatural; there is no reference to the metaphysical physiology found in the work most famous in the West, the *Huangdi Neijing Su Wen* 黃帝內經素問 (*Yellow Emperor's Classic of Medicine*).² Likely different practitioners used different theories to explain disease.

Accidents

Accidents have been, and still are, a major cause of death in developing countries. The belief that accidents are due to bad luck rather than carelessness discourages prudence:

> 28.6 Mistakenly drowns while wading.
> Ominous, but not blameworthy.
>
> 上六過涉滅頂. 凶, 无咎.

On the other hand, common sense was not altogether lacking:

> 29.3 Coming to pit after pit.
> Risky now to rest one's head.
> Do not enter into a pit or cave.
>
> 六三來之坎坎. 險且枕. 入于坎窞勿用.

Food and drink

As a narrative, the following two lines describe a household waiting for a meal, only to be joined unexpectedly by important guests who cannot be refused:

> 5.5 Waiting for food and wine.
> Divination auspicious.
>
> 九五需于酒. 貞吉.

> 5.6 Go out from the pit.
> Uninvited, several guests arrive.
> Respecting them ends auspiciously.
>
> 上六入于穴,. 不速之, 客三人來. 敬之終吉.

Meals must almost always have been communal, given the labor needed for food preparation:

> 6.3 Dining with friends of ancient virtue.
>
> 食舊德.

This is one of only four occurrences in the *Zhouyi* of the word 德 *de*, part of the title of the *Dao De Jing*,. There is some variation in meaning in different contexts, but in the above phrase the usual later translation as virtue seems correct.

The following might mean drinking wine to allay worries, but more likely is a libation to appease a troublesome spirit:

> 41.1 Finish the matter, will not be blamed.
> Pouring wine diminishes it.
>
> 初九已事遄往, 无咎. 酌損之.

This seems to be practical advice, although it may be a ritual detail:

> 29.4 Wine in a *zun* bronze vessel and a two handled *gui*.
> Use a narrow-necked earthenware jar so one can receive at the window.
> Ends without blame.
>
> 六四樽酒簋貳. 用缶納約, 自牖. 終无咎.

The importance of the well

After oxygen, water is the most essential substance to maintain life; in premodern times, failure of a well would have been a potentially devastating event. Anxiety about the function and safety of wells is apparent in Hexagram 井 *Jing*, which contains several vivid images of barrenness:

> 48.0 The well is almost dried up; when they arrive; it does not have a well-rope and its jar is worn out. Ominous.
>
> 井汔至亦未繘. 羸其瓶. 凶.

48.1 The well is muddy, not drinkable.
By the old well there are no birds and beasts.

初六井泥，不食．舊井无禽

48.3 The well has been drained. It cannot serve for drinking; our hearts are saddened.

井渫不食。為我心惻

Along with markets, wells were the social center of early village life so that their failure would be a communal disaster.

One line, in contrast, expresses the pleasure of good water:

48.5 The well is cold, a frigid spring for drinking.

九五井冽，寒泉食．

Weather

As might be expected, mode of dress depended on the season:

63.4 Multicolored silk padded jacket to be prepared for winter days.

六四繻有衣袽冬日戒

The silk jacket seems to be a display of status; archaeological finds suggest that luxury goods were as desired in the ancient world as they are today.[3]

Agrarian societies live and die by rainfall, which was unpredictable, thus one of the most common subjects for divination:

9.6 Now rains, now stops.

既雨既

38.5 When going, if caught in the rain, then auspicious.

往遇雨則，吉

Walking in the rain seems to be a sign of virtuous determination:

43.3 The upright person very determinedly walks alone, though caught in the rain. If drenched, irritated but nothing blameworthy

君子夬夬獨行，遇雨．若濡,有慍无咎．

On the other hand, lack of rain is worrisome:

> 62.5 Dense clouds but no rain from our western outskirts.
>
> 亨．密雲不雨自我西郊．

This might be a simple weather forecast, but seems also to be an image of sterility akin to those quoted previously. Drought would result in crop failure and starvation. Rain would have been awaited anxiously:

> 50.3 In the area the rain is diminished—regretted, but ends auspiciously.
>
> 方雨虧—悔，終吉．

Extreme weather could evoke fear:

> 51.1 Thunder comes—terrifying, terrifying.
> Afterwards, laughing, tittering, ha, ha, ha. Auspicious.
>
> 初九震來—虩，虩．後笑言啞啞．吉．

Since cities could be attacked without warning, thunder could be particularly frightening. This is indicated by the combination of fear and laughing, which is described in a way similar to the behavior of captives awaiting sacrifice:

> 45.1 Wailing when grabbed by a hand, then tittering
>
> 若號一握為笑．勿恤

In both lines, the word I have translated as "tittering" is 笑 *xiao*, approximating "nervous laughter" in English. That extreme fear would be expressed by laughter seems strange, but the vocabulary available to express emotional nuance was limited. The various translations of this line differ considerably: Rutt's, which I have basically followed, translates as "They cry, then laugh" (268), while Shaughnessy renders it as "A scream once grasped becomes laughter" (20004: 117). Wilhelm-Baynes' version begins by referring to sincerity, but the rest of the text does not quite fit: "If you call out . . . Then after one grasp of the hand you can laugh again" (175).

10

Women's Lives

In dynastic China, women's freedom and well-being were restricted, although to varying extents. Ruists were generally misogynistic, rarely referred to women in their writings, and advocated confining them to the household; yet many women were able to evade these restrictions to some degree (Yip 2014). In early China, women seemed able to play more active roles in society; this is suggested by high-born women participating in oracle bone divination. Given the paucity of such references, the *Zhouyi* texts that mention women are of particular interest to supplement the findings of archaeology.

Traditionally, rulership was limited to males, although a few women managed to become *de facto* rulers.[1] Misogyny was not only textual, it was built into ritual regulations; the preference for male children was reinforced by the restriction that only males could perform the all-important rituals for the ancestors.[2]

The OBI contain many references to women, both alive and deceased. They were of high social level, as this elaborate and laborious divination method was mainly for the king and his close relatives. The OBI are of interest here because they often included details lacking in the *Zhouyi*, such as the names of diviners and the outcome of the events divined upon. The use of shell and bone as writing media was an early, but probably not the earliest, form of writing in China, since its language is well-developed. Keightley (1978: 139) suggests that the Wu Ding OBI are stylistically sophisticated, raising the possibility that pyromancy had been in use earlier. The earliest Chinese writings were almost certainly on perishable materials and so have not survived. The OBI of interest here are the earliest known, those from the reign of King Wu Ding 武丁 (r. 1250–1192 BCE), some of which include references to Fu Hao 婦好 (died *c.* 1200 BCE), his second wife (of a total of 64). Fu Hao was one of the most interesting figures of the Yin 殷代 (late phase of the Shang 商朝) dynasty, having served as a victorious general, thus exercising a degree of agency that contrasts with later restrictions on women appearing outside the home. Since the literal meaning of Fu Hao— her name as passed down—is "good woman," she perhaps was regarded as a model for women generally, although our knowledge of her life is regrettably limited.

An inscription about Fu Hao's child birthing is on display in the Museum of the Institute of History and Philology at the Academia Sinica in Taipei. Probably because of its shock value, it is perhaps the most frequently quoted OBI in recent times:

> If it be a *ding*-(day) that she give birth, it will be good; if (it be) a *geng*-day (that she give birth), there will be prolonged luck, if it be on *renxu* (day 59) (that she give birth), it will not be lucky. (Keightley 2000: 24)

The outcome of her pregnancy was recorded in a later inscription:

> On the thirty-first day (after the day of divination), *jiayin* (day 51) she gave birth. It was not good, it was a girl. (Keightley 2000: 38)

There is the intriguing possibility that the latter inscription might indicate a belief that the sex of the child is not fixed at conception, but determined by the date on which birth occurs. In any case, this inscription demonstrates that despite the prejudice revealed by the inscription, Fu Hao was able to attain power and influence

Fu Hao was sometimes the subject of a divination:

> Lady Hao's dream was not due to Father Yi (Xiao Yi, K20). (Keightley 2000: 101)

Presumably Father Yi was an ancestor and the dream had prognostic significance.

There are other inscriptions that suggests women could have ritual competence:

> Lady Yang ritually prepared the ten scapulas. (Signed by the diviner) Zhang. (Keightley 2000:104)

There is also a category referred to as "Ladies' OBI" (Takashima and Serruys 2019: 6). Unfortunately, I have not been able to find more information about this group of inscriptions.

Among other early texts the *Shijing* 詩經, *the Songs of Chu* 楚辭, and the *Zuozhuan* 左傳 mention women more often than the *Zhouyi*. Although those mentions in the latter text are frequently unfavorable, those in the *Zhouyi* are mostly neutral description, with a supposed exception to be discussed below. Ritual participation by women is not mentioned. The activities most often divined about in the *Zhouyi*, such as travel, warfare, and human sacrifice, seem to have been mainly carried out by males, but caution is necessary when speculating about what is not in a text, particularly one that is 3,000 years old. The most common character I have translated as wife is 婦 *fu*, which indicates a married woman, although in very early use it suggested high-born status.[3]

Those lines referring to women's concerns use the same set phrases as others in the *Zhouyi*:

> 63.2 The wife loses her hair ornament.
> Do not look for it—in seven days will be found.
>
> 六二婦喪其勿逐一七日得.

Finding lost people, farm animals, and objects is a common trope in the *Zhouyi* but, as I have previously pointed out, the interval before return or finding an object is always seven days, perhaps indicating "a few days," rather than an actual duration. The seven days, or, less often, three-day interval can apply to any gender or species.

Marriage and choice of wives

Until modernization beginning early in the twentieth century, polygamy was practiced in China, and sometimes still is, although without legal recognition. Supporting multiple concubines was a sign of wealth. In traditional China the first wife had authority over the later ones; although often referred to in English as "concubines," they are better described as "secondary wives," because they had legal status sanctified with a ceremony. Polygamy was banned with the establishment of the PRC in 1949, but in Hong Kong was not made illegal until 1971, although it continues unofficially.[4] In the past, affluent men in Europe could openly support mistresses and sometimes a contract was involved, although the woman did not have status as a wife. In later Chinese folklore and fiction, relations between the household women were often fraught, although there were exceptions. In the *Zhouyi*, there is only one mention of conflict between women within a polygamous family, that in Hexagram 54 歸妹 *Gui* Marrying Maiden. Because one of a few "gossipy" passages in the ancient work, it is one of the best-known:

> 54.5 Di Yi gave his daughter in marriage.
> The lady's sleeves were inferior to those of her younger sister.
>
> 六五帝乙歸妹. 其君之袂. 不如其娣之袂良

This suggests that a bridesmaid upstaging the bride has been a form of malicious behavior since the beginnings of civilization. The marriage referred to here was probably sororal, with the younger sister probably having transgressed sumptuary rules for women based on hierarchy within families. We are not told whether this was a serious breach of decorum, but it was important enough to be included in the text.

While the *Zhouyi* does not refer to the relations between wives within a household, there are two other references to sororal marriage, probably that of Di Yi 帝乙, the penultimate Shang king:

54.1 Marrying the maiden with her younger sisters

初九歸妹以娣.

54.3 Marrying a maiden with concubines. Turns back, marries with her younger sister.

歸妹以如嬬[須]. 反歸以娣.

Nothing in these texts suggests there was anything unusual about these polygamous weddings. Choice of a wife was thus fundamentally different from that in monogamous societies, because the rich and powerful could have as many as they could afford to maintain. Given the short life expectancy of the time, only to the mid-twenties for women, with approximately 5 percent dying in childbirth, choosing women for the household was likely frequently necessary. Omens could be important in selecting a suitable woman and an auspicious date for the ceremony. Although we have no detailed record, there must have been special divinatory methods for selection of wives and other additions to a household. Omens could not be ignored for such special events:

4.3 Do not use to obtain a woman, upon seeing a conscripted metal worker. Not having bowed, nothing will go towards benefit.

六三勿用取女. 見金夫, 不有躬, 无攸利

The conscript has no direct relationship to the woman, or the person choosing her, he is an omen that it would be bad luck to choose at this time. Another reference to choosing a wife or other woman for the household has frequently been misinterpreted:

44.0 Though the woman is robust, do not choose this woman.

女壯, 勿用取女

As I have previously explained (Redmond 2017: 248), this has been mistranslated into English to imply that the woman should not be chosen *because* she is robust (or strong). Nothing in the Chinese text suggests this; the misogynistic implication was included by Wang Bi in his commentary to Kun 2.0 and Gou 44.0, although it might have originated earlier (Lynn 142f; 410f).

Given the hardships of life in the ancient world together with the inability to alleviate chronic, debilitating diseases, robustness would be highly desirable in a wife. In this context, the line actually means something like, "Even though the woman is robust, she should not be chosen [for a wife or servant]."

Here is another example of an omen regarding choice of a woman, in this case a concubine; as has been customary in traditional Asia, the mother chooses for her son:

50.1 The cauldron topples over—beneficial for releasing the bad.
To obtain a concubine for her son. Not blameworthy.

初六鼎顛趾―利出否. 得妾以其子. 无咎.

The toppling cauldron might seem a bad omen but is here cleverly interpreted as beneficial. This line reminds us that in traditional cultures, the choice of wife or consort was not necessarily made by the man and definitely not by the woman herself. This is not to say people did not fall in love in early China, but family considerations usually predominated. Arranged marriages are still usual in some parts of the world. In China since the passage of the he 1980 Marriage Law, choice of spouse is entirely up to the man and woman involved. (Gay marriage is not recognized in China at the time of this writing.) However, parental pressure can still play a decisive role, with the prospective husband's financial status being of particular concern to the woman's family, as in many cultures. The one-child rule has resulted in there being a shortage of women, who therefore have the stronger negotiating position.

As now, in ancient China marriages were not only between the young:

28.2 From a withered poplar come forth sprouts.
An old man gets his daughter married.
Nothing that is not favorable.

枯楊生稊. 老夫得其女妻. 无不利.

A slight variation on this suggests that sometimes the partners could choose for themselves:

28.5 A withered poplar brings forth blossoms.
An old woman gets herself a gentry husband
Not blameworthy; not praiseworthy.

九五枯楊生華. 老婦得其士夫. 无咎; 无譽.

The first phrases of both are proverbs, meaning that sometimes the elderly can renew themselves, or perhaps can have children. It would have been obvious even then that while age sets a limit for women, many elderly men are fertile. The second phrase suggests that the woman took the initiative, or was at least willing, and that she was fortunate in that her husband had some social status.

As now, not all matches were good for both partners:

32.5 Long-lasting is their effectiveness,
Divination for a married woman is auspicious; for a husband, ominous.

六五恒其德. 貞婦人吉; 夫子, 凶.

This is an instance of the recurrent rhetorical formula of split prognoses—divinations that are favorable for one category of person, unfavorable for the other. Other instances provide contrasting prognoses based on differences in character (11.0, 12.0, and 12.5) or directions of travel (2.0).

Women's activities and the household

Hexagram 37 家人 *Jiaren* Family Members includes several lines that give a sense of life within the household:

37.0 Beneficial for a woman to divine.

利女貞

This is one of only four mentions of women in the judgment text invocations. This phrase is clearly an invocation because it contains the final two characters (利 *li* and 貞 *zhen*) of the formulaic phrase. This might suggest that a woman could herself perform divination, but could instead mean that a particular divination was favorable for a woman.

Another line is enigmatic:

53.0 The women return home. Auspicious. Beneficial divination.

女歸, 吉. 利貞.

The reason the women left is unstated, but as their return is auspicious, it seems that the household was relieved to have them back. This could be simply that they were safely home from errands, or perhaps they had fled because of harsh treatment. The latter is suggested by the Fuyang excavated text specifying that the women referred to in this line were servants or concubines (Redmond 2017: 281f).

The tag for this Hexagram 漸 Gradual Approach is taken from the second character of each of the line texts and also fits with the women returning. Whether the historical Confucius intended confining women to the home is uncertain, but not improbable. The *Lunyu* only mentions women briefly; Wang Bi's centuries later commentaries on the *Yijing* were overtly misogynistic, as in this passage from the *Commentary on the Judgments* (*Tuanzhuan* 彖傳; Wings 1 and 2) for Hexagram 家人 *Jiaren* Family Members, in the translation of Richard John Lynn:

> As far as the Family is concerned, the woman's proper place is inside it. (This refers to Second Yin and the man's proper place is outside it. This refers to Fifth Yang ... and this is why the text mentions the woman first.) Male and female should keep to their proper place; this is the fundamental concept expressed by Heaven and Earth. (1994: 263)

This metaphysical pretext for the confinement of women is rationalized based on the concept of yin and yang, but is not supported by anything in the core text. However, the *Zhouyi* does hint at women's place being in the home:

> 37.2 Nothing goes forward.
> Inside for women's work, divination auspicious.
>
> 六二无攸遂. 在中饋, 吉。

It is likely that restriction to housework was mainly true for affluent families, as a subsequent line suggests:

> 37.4 For wealthy families, greatly auspicious.
>
> 六四富家, 大.

Poor farm families must have needed the women and children to work outside the home at times, as is still true in much of the world.

Line 37.6 does not seem to fit here; human sacrifice, as far I can tell, would not have occurred within a home, but rather outside in public. This does not mean that killings did not occur indoors, as in line 50.4. The *Spring and Autumn Annals* and *Zuozhuan* mention many executions and murders among the high-born, but we know little about violence in lower demographics.

Household security was a source of worry, as it is today:

37.1 The household is gated.
Regret is gone.

初九閑有家. 悔亡.

Overall the ancient world was not good for women, but not much better for most men.

Fertility

Anxiety about fertility is universal, because pregnancy is never certain until it happens; even then it may end in miscarriage or stillbirth. In the present era, in both Asia and the West, childbearing has become a lifestyle choice, but in traditional China children were essential for labor, to continue the family line, and to care for parents when they were too old to work. The requirement for filial piety extended beyond the deaths of parents; proper mourning was obligatory. Particularly important was provision of offerings for the deceased, who might bring misfortune if not propitiated.

Sterility is described with somber images:

53.3 The wife, pregnant, does not give birth, calamitous.

婦孕不育

54.6 The woman offers a basket; there is no fruit
The official cuts a sheep, there is no blood.
There is nothing beneficial.

上六女承筐无實. 士刲羊, 无血. 无攸利.

Children

In traditional China, children were expected to be completely obedient to parents and other elders in authority, such as teachers. Since children frequently misbehave, the *Zhouyi* provides advice for adults on how to respond in Hexagram

4 蒙 *Meng* Neophytes. In context, it is clear that *Meng* refers to the young, although age is not specified. Given the presence of the bamboo/vegetation component as the top line of the character, "neophyte" seems a reasonable equivalent. (For the controversy about the meaning of *Meng* see Redmond 2017: 83f.)

At least as presented in this Hexagram, expectations for children's obedience were rigid and physical punishment usual. There is no indication that the child's feelings and needs were considered. Yet, as today, adults must have varied in their strictness. We get some sense of child rearing in this hexagram, although nothing about who taught the children and what was taught. Deference to parents and teachers was expected:

4.0 Make offering. Not I who asks the neophytes; the neophytes ask me.
The initial yarrow divination informs, but to repeat it several times shows disrespect.
When disrespected, then it does not inform.

亨. 匪我求童蒙; 童蒙求我.

初筮告, 再三瀆. 瀆則不告.

The first phrase refers to children asking repeated questions of an elder or teacher to the point of irritation. This interpretation is supported by 4.1, 4.4, and 4.6, which advocate physical punishment, although 4.1 seems to suggest scolding as an alternative.

The second phrase also states that repeated questioning is improper, but here it seems to be the *Book of Changes* that is being queried repeatedly. The Book was personified as a sage and entitled to the same degree of deference as an exemplary teacher. A traditional principle of *Yijing* consultation was that it would not give helpful answers to repeated or frivolous inquiries. This, of course, could conveniently excuse it giving contradictory answers to the same question.

Harsh physical punishment has been thought appropriate for discipline of children in many cultures and in some, unfortunately, still is. This was clearly the case in ancient China:

4.1 In teaching neophytes, it is beneficial to use physical punishment.
Use scolding to restrain, in order to lead to remorse, before.

初六發蒙, 利用刑人. 用說桎梏. 以往吝.

The following, as I have translated it, suggests some awareness that harshness should not be excessive:

37.3 In the household, regretting harsh scolding is auspicious.
Wives and sons giggling—ends in regret.

九三家人，嗃悔厲吉

婦子嘻嘻—終吝

As I point out elsewhere, in the *Zhouyi* giggling is an expression of anxiety or fear, not pleasure. This line suggests that not only children but women also could be subject to severe rebukes, although it could equally be taken to mean that it is the recipients of the scolding who feel regret. While this text suggests that early Chinese domestic life was harsh, it must be kept in mind that a few fragments from a very ancient text do not give us a complete picture. Divination texts are, after all, inherently about life difficulties. Despite the many cruelties mentioned in the *Zhouyi*, we should not assume that sympathy and compassion did not exist in early China.

A more positive side of domestic life is expressed in another line text:

4.2 To bundle up neophytes is auspicious.
To receive a wife is auspicious.
The son is capable of managing the household

九二包蒙吉. 納婦吉. 子克家.

The first phrase seems to mean that children should be kept warm; bundling or swaddling infants has been a widespread practice to the present day. That the son can manage the household suggests that it is well ordered and will continue to be, even as the father ages.

I suggest, without absolute proof, that the regret in the following is light-hearted, unlike most of the *Zhouyi*:

4.4 Beset upon by neophytes. Regret.

六四困蒙. 吝.

4.5 A young neophyte. Auspicious.

六五童蒙. 吉.

This could mean children crowding around adults, probably many children at once in a polygamous household. The person beset upon might be annoyed, but also happy for there being children in abundance.

While there is no indication that women had any role in compiling the *Zhouyi*, a few passages do suggest female agency: women could divine and could sometimes choose their husband. Still they were subject to scolding within the household, although the *Zhouyi* warns that it should not be excessively severe. Sometimes women went out and returned; this might indicate freedom, or fleeing ill treatment, only to realize that they had no place to go.

On the positive side, phrases in the *Zhouyi* that mention women are no more likely than others to have a bad prognosis. Taboos about female bodies, such as menstruation, are not mentioned, although such almost certainly existed. Although there are many unfavorable prognoses in the *Zhouyi*, none seem to have been directly caused by women; even the awkwardness about sleeves in 54.5 concludes auspiciously.

11

Emotions and the Body

References to the body in the *Zhouyi* mainly describe it as a location of omens. The elaborate treatises that conceived physiology in terms of yin-yang metaphysics date from the Han. We should not assume that there were no conceptions of the inner workings of the body in the Western Zhou, but we have no record of such. Disease was attributed to supernatural factors. The complex disease theories based on the virtual physiology of meridians and energy transformations as in the *Huang Di Nei Jing Su Wen* (*Yellow Emperor's Inner Classic of Essential Questions*) were a much later development but never completely supplanted earlier notions of etiology such as poison, curses, witchcraft, and inimical spirits (Unschuld 1985; 2003).

Expression of emotion

The body is the center of every person's world, yet much of what happens with the body is not consciously initiated by the mind, making it the locus of many events that seem random. In ancient times these were commonly interpreted as omens, given the very limited understanding of anatomy and physiology. With rare exceptions, interpretation of bodily omens had no relationship to modern scientific understanding. Thus a toothache might be due to a malevolent ancestor or spirit; there was no concept of decay.

The *Zhouyi* describes many events that must have evoked intense emotion, but usually does not name the emotion directly. It simply describes the external events that evoke the emotions or the behavior that expresses them. This could be due to lack of suitable vocabulary at this early stage of development of the language, or reticence about referring to intense mental states. There is no indication in the *Zhouyi* of the now universal assumption of an "inner life."

The prognostic technical terms that I discuss in detail in Chapter 5, such as auspicious 吉 *ji*, beneficial 利 *li*, regret 悔 *hui*, or ominous 凶 *xiong*, only sometimes imply the emotions we would expect to be associated with them. Prognoses cannot be equated to emotions, for example:

16.3 Regret—tardiness will bring regret.

悔—遲有悔.

While a modern reader is likely to regard regret as an emotional state, in the *Zhouyi* the word functions more as a warning that unpleasant consequences will ensure, as in "You will regret being late because you might be punished." In this case there is no indication of shame or guilt, simply distress at unpleasant consequences. In the *Zhouyi* regret refers to disagreeable outcome, but not to the painful internal mental state.

Understanding regret in this way explains its usage in the following:

34.5 Losing the ram in Yi.
No regret.

六五喪羊于易. 无悔.

It is hard to see how someone losing property of significant value, as here livestock, would have felt no sorrow whatsoever. This makes sense when it is recognized that losing the ram would be expected to incur severe punishment, but for reasons not stated, the one who lost the ram gets away unscathed.

I have also translated 吝 *lin* as regret, though shame or frustration would be alternatives:

40.3 Carrying [possessions] on one's back while riding in a cart attracts the arrival of bandits. Divination: regret.

六三負且乘致寇至. 貞吝.

Here, too, the focus is not on the emotion, but on the harmful consequences of displaying one's possessions. There does not seem to be a underlying pattern determining whether *hui* or *lin* was chosen; it may having been habitual usage of different compilers or editors.

Mourning

Mourning rituals are found in all societies; those in early ones were often more elaborate, with behavioural expectations based on closeness of the relationship to the deceased. Grief was an inner state, but outward expression was socially required. Considering the large extended families and short life expectancies in early China, mourning must have been almost continuous.

Hexagram 30 離 *Li* Oriole has several lines indicating emotion; although some are related to mourning, this does not seem to be the meaning of the tag character. Since bird omens can fit almost any contexts, I have followed Rutt in translating as "oriole."[1]

> 30.3 An oriole at sunset.
> Not by drumming on an earthenware jar, but with a song.
> Thus, those of great old age make lamentation.
> Ominous.
>
> 九三日昃之. 不鼓缶，而歌.則大耋之嗟. 凶.

This resembles a well-known anecdote in the *Zhuangzi* in which the philosopher mourns the death of his wife by banging on a jar. Admonished for this, Zhuangzi justifies his behavior by observing that we arise from earth and then return to it; that is, life and death are inevitable as a natural cycle. Zhuangzi is suggesting that the simpler archaic mourning practices, as described here and in the *Zhouyi*, were more appropriate than the elaborate and wasteful funerary practices common even in early China, that simplicity and sincerity are more suitable than ostentation. The prognostic term "ominous" may refer to the oriole at sunset, rather than the expression of mourning. As a divination response, this would seem to be a warning of a death, but alternatively, could be read as a general recommendation of simplicity in ritual behavior.

Other images of emotional distress

Sudden catastrophic events are obvious causes of distress:

> 30.4 Happening suddenly—like a fire, like death, like abandonment.
>
> 九四突如其來-—如焚如，死如，棄如.

> 30.5 Weeping a flood of tears, as if grief-stricken, as if despairing.
> Auspicious.
>
> 六五出涕沱，若戚嗟若. 吉.

In 30.4 catastrophic events are listed, but not any emotional response; in contrast 30.5 indicates the emotion, but not the causative event. The weeping might be a reaction to the sudden event in the preceding line, but the auspicious prognosis might make sense in the context of mourning ritual in which showing grief is socially necessary. It is not certain however that these two line texts are related. The word 若 *ruo*, here translated "as if," indicates uncertainty as to whether grief is the cause of the apparent distress. I must confess that in my translation I suggested that the weeping was not significant in itself, but was merely an omen. Looking at it again, I think the mourning explanation is more likely. I may change my mind again.

The meaning of the passage remains uncertain; even Wilhelm-Baynes could not make sense of it, suggesting the weeping is due to "understanding the vanity of all things" (121). This is actually a Christian set phrase, as repeated with variants in *Ecclesiastes* and a common trope in homiletics. This world-weary sentiment seems out of place in the *Changes*, which includes many grim prognoses, but not overall pessimism.

Texts 30.3–5 are heterogeneous, suggesting that they were grouped together because about grief, but not constituting an underlying narrative.

Images of desolation and sterility

Images in these categories are among the most striking in the *Changes*.

Hexagram 48 井 *Jing* The Well has haunting images of the uncertain nature of early life. A properly functioning well was essential for village life and thus represents life-supporting abundance, but a dry or fouled one can threaten the survival of the village:

> 48.0 Can change the city; cannot change the well.
> There is no loss; there is no gain.
> Coming and going, to and from the well.
> The well is almost dried up; when they arrive does not have a well-rope and its jar is worn out. Ominous.
>
> 改邑；不改井．无喪无得．往來井．井汔至亦未繘．羸其瓶．凶．

A well symbolizes the fecundity of the earth to support life, while a dry or unusable well threatens life:

> 48.1 The well is muddy, not drinkable.
> By the old well there are no birds and beasts.
>
> 初六井泥，不食．舊井无禽

The following text seems like an arbitrary combination of phrases about wells, although it could mean that the undrinkable water is suitable for animals or crops, or that the king will somehow have the well restored:

> 48.3 The well has been drained. It cannot serve for drinking; our hearts are saddened.
> Can be used to draw water.
> The luminous king moreover grants his favor.
>
> 九三井渫不食。為我心惻。可用汲。王明。並受其福.

That the king is bright or luminous (王明 *wang ming*) suggests a supernatural figure, who might be capable of restoring the well.

The next line describes a functional well, reinforcing the importance of the well, in premodern times the center of small town life, along with markets:

> 48.5 The well is cold, a frigid spring for drinking.
>
> 九五井冽，寒泉食.

The last line combines two unrelated images:

> 48.6 To draw from the well, it must not be covered.
> Holding captives, begins auspiciously.
>
> 上六井收勿幕. 有孚元吉.

In this Hexagram, as with many in the *Zhouyi*, lines with favorable and unfavorable images are combined, presumably due to arbitrary placement by the compilers.

Hexagram 54 歸妹 *Gui* Marrying Maiden is considered in Chapter 10 on women and domestic life, but quoted again here because of the striking images of sterility:

> 54.6 The woman offers a basket; there is no fruit
> The official cuts a sheep, there is no blood.
> There is nothing beneficial.
>
> 上六女承筐无實. 士刲羊，无血. 无攸利.

Positive emotions and happiness

Most of the examples so far have had negative prognoses; this is not surprising, because divination is often sought to help prepare for impending dangers. It is not all gloom, however:

> 12.6 Inclined to bad.
> First bad; after, happy.

上九傾否．先否後喜

This might be moralistic advice that giving up being bad results in happiness. As a divination response, it would be useful for diviners using any method, who can interpret it as "Things may be bad now, but later will be happy," which usually pleases the inquirer. It is a safe sort of prediction as in all lives bad and good times alternate.

The following is an image of abundance, suckling pigs and fishes being essential for any Chinese banquet, then and now:

> 61.0 Suckling pigs and fishes, auspicious.
> Beneficial to ford the great river. Beneficial to divine.

豚魚,吉．利涉大川．利貞．

One of the best-known lines in the *Changes* is:

> 61.2 Cranes calling from the shady riverbank; their young answer.
> I have a good wine goblet; I will give to you generously.

九二鳴鶴在陰；其子和之．我有好爵；吾與爾靡之．

This simple but powerful image of friendship and abundance provides counterpoint to the images of sterility quoted above and similar images in 54.6, discussed below. It is not surprising that both abundance and deprivation would be present in a divination manual since, at least in theory, it must be able to predict all possible human situations, both auspicious and ominous.

Vocalizations

In this category I include production of sounds that are not language and are usually involuntary. Screaming and laughter are in this category. These can convey information to listeners, but this is not always the intent. They are often overflow phenomena, which may be accompanied by bodily movements. In the *Zhouyi*, descriptions of vocalizations are of particular interest because they are clues to emotions.

Wailing, tittering, giggling are common expressions of emotion in the *Zhouyi*. Sometimes the vocalizations are voluntary to comply with social expectations, as in this instance of mourning behavior:

19.5 Controlled wailing—proper for the great master. Auspicious.

六五知臨—大君之宜．吉

Other lines in this Hexagram also emphasize the importance of wailing:

19.2 Salty tears and wailing. Auspicious—nothing not beneficial.

九二咸臨．吉无不利．

19.3 Willingly wailing.
Nowhere beneficial.
Now sorrowful; There will be no blame.

六三甘臨．无攸利．既憂之；无咎

The word 憂 *you*, here translated as sorrowful, can also mean worry or anxiety. This is one of a limited number of early words naming an actual emotion or mental state. That tears and wailing could be auspicious seems peculiar, but here they seem to be ritual requirements at the death of one's parents or of a master. In this context, willingly wailing (in the sense of deliberate rather than involuntary) is not beneficial; genuine sorrow, however, will avert blame.

In the *Zhouyi*, laughing and tittering often express fear, but can also occur with relief. In Hexagram 51 震 *Zhen* Thunder, the same phrase 虩虩 *xixi* seems to express both:

51.0 Make offering. Thunder comes—frightening, frightening.
Laughing, chattering, ha ha ha.
Thunder shocks for a hundred li.
No spooning of the sacrificial wine.

亨．震來，虩虩．笑言啞啞．震驚百里．不匕鬯．

51.1 Thunder comes—terrifying, terrifying.
Afterwards, laughing, chattering, ha, ha, ha. Auspicious.

初九震來—虩，虩．後笑言啞啞．吉．

It seems unlikely that fear and relief would induce identical vocalizations; rather these were set expressions for extreme emotional outbursts. Such phrases are common in references to sacrifice, but occur in less extreme situations as well:

> 56.6 The bird tangles its nest.
> The Traveler first laughs, afterwards cries and wails.
> Losing a cow in Yi, misfortune.

上九鳥焚其巢．旅人先笑，後號咷．喪牛于易，凶．

Here different words are used, 號咷 *haotao*, but the meanings are similar. The bird tangling its nest is likely a metaphor for being stuck in a frustrating situation. The traveler's emotional turmoil might be due to the loss of the cow, although it is not certain that the third phrase refers back to the traveler in the second phrase. There are many such uncertainties in the *Zhouyi*, but they would probably not have interfered with its use as a divination manual. A diviner does not approach a text as do philologists or literary critics, who strive to discover the historically correct meaning; rather, the diviner devises a way to fit it to the inquiry.

Sometimes there are tears without specific explanation; here the prognosis does not fit the image.

> 19.2 Salty tears and wailing. Auspicious—nothing not beneficial.

九二咸臨．吉无不利．}}

Abnormal and involuntary bodily movements

Seemingly random or abnormal body movements, such as tremors or spasms, were commonly interpreted as omens in premodern cultures. Such movements are often disturbing to those witnessing them, as are physical anomalies and abnormalities of posture or gait.

Bodily movements and abnormalities functioning as omens in the *Zhouyi*, appear in Hexagram 27 頤 *Yi* Lower Jaw, which might be constituted of fragments of a more complete system of jaw divination. These omens can be considered a subset of physiognomy, the pseudo-science of divination by facial features.[2] This Hexagram describes several kinds of jaw movements and provides prognoses for them; as usual with omens, there is no apparent basis for why each jaw image is favorable or ominous.

The translation of 頤 *Yi* as jaw seems almost self-evident. Divination by facial features is well known and in the text the jaw images are directly associated with a prognosis, indicating that they are omens. Yet some exercised considerable ingenuity to make the passage more obscure. Rutt translates yi as "molars," but the term does not refer to this specific kind of tooth. An alternate translation is "nourishment," as used by Lynn (305–11) and Wilhelm-Baynes, who sometimes instead translate it as corners of the mouth (107–11).

All the texts, with the exception of 27.5, contain omens related to the jaw:

27.0 Divination auspicious according to observation of the jaw.
One's own mouth asking if it is full.

貞吉觀頤. 自求口實

The second phrase is amusing and must be a proverb referring to something about oneself that should be self-evident:

27.1 Leave at home your numinous tortoise
Observe my drooping jaw, ominous.

初九舍爾靈龜. 觀我朵頤, 凶.

The image of the tortoise is intriguing; the only related early text I have found is Zhuangzi's observation that a tortoise would prefer crawling in the mud to being dead but adorned with jewels. Such must have been used for decoration or divination, but I have not found any source that describes associated practices. The second phrase is a simple omen, as are the next two:

27.2 Twitching jaw.
Jaw: Going on an expedition, ominous.

六二顛頤. 拂經于丘. 頤征, 凶.

27.3 Stroking the jaw—ominous divination:
Nothing is beneficial.

六三拂頤—貞凶. 无攸利.

The most curious line text in this Hexagram is:

27.4 Twitching jaw, auspicious.
Tiger stares—glaring, glaring.
Craving—chasing chasing.
There will be no blame.

六四顛頤, 吉. 虎視—眈眈. 其欲, 逐逐. 无咎.

The description of the tiger's face is intended to be frightening, yet it is placed between two positive prognoses. The line could mean an escape from great danger, but nothing in the text supports this. The tiger face description is still used in colloquial Chinese to describe a facial expression showing extreme craving or greed. Thus it likely began as an oral set phrase with this possibly its first appearance in written form.

Taking the phrases together, this line text is clearly a warning about encountering greedy people. As so often with the *Changes*, commentators have proposed far-fetched meanings. Wang Bi, according to Lynn's translation, considered the tiger's ferocious expression to show one of high rank should regard his inferior (308). This suggests life in the Chinese bureaucracy could be harsh. Shaughnessy in his translation of the MWD version has the tiger looking sad, although nowhere else in the *Zhouyi* does an animal have facial expressions that show emotion (1996: 67). As with any image, the tiger's expression can have multiple meanings. The final line of this Hexagram is another jaw divination, although it seems separate from the second phrase:

> 27.6 According to the jawbone, harsh.
> Auspiciously beneficial to ford across the great river.
>
> 上九由頤, 厲. 吉利涉大川.l.

One could read this as advising crossing the river to escape a harsh situation, but this is not actually in the text. More likely it is another instance of arbitrary placing of phrases by compilers.

Notably, all the lines except 27.5 refer to jaws. These texts are somewhat different from usual physiognomy, 面相 *mian xiang*, because they are based on facial movements rather than fixed features. Divination based on the face has a certain logic, as it is the face that marks individuality and also reveals, to some extent, thoughts and emotions; we all make intuitive judgments based on facial appearances. However, the interpretation of jaw movements in this Hexagram do not indicate the observed person's state of mind, but are omens conveying prognoses.

In Hexagram 21 噬嗑 *Shi Ke* Biting and Chewing, jaw movement is described, but not as an omen:

> 21.2 Biting the flesh, the nose disappears.
> There will be no blame.
>
> 六二噬膚滅鼻. 无咎.

This might refer to eating a pig's head, a gourmet treat in Chinese cuisine; alternatively, it could describe amputation of the nose, a judicial punishment in early China:

38.3 Seeing a cart hauled by its ox.
Its man, heaven even cut off his nose.
Though without a beginning, it has an end.

六三見輿曳其牛掣．其人天且劓，无初，有終

Although amputation was a standard punishment, it is difficult to tell how commonly it was carried out, or even if many actually survived, given the likely consequences of severe bleeding and infection. The specific character for this punishment, 劓 *yi*, is not included in 21.2, although it does appear in 38.3 above and also in 47.5. Two other lines texts in this Hexagram refer to bodily punishment:

21.1 Shoes in the fetters; the feet disappear.

初九履校滅，趾．

21.6 Carrying on his shoulders a cangue, the ears disappear.

上九何校滅耳．

Since there were no tests to detect poisoning in the premodern world, fear of being murdered in this way was pervasive. The following could refer to this, or simply to eating meat that was spoiled:

21.3 Bites the soft dried meat; gets poisoned.
Slight remorse, but there will be no blame.

六三噬腊肉；遇毒．小吝，无咎．

Execution for alleged murder by poisoning or witchcraft was common; possibly more deaths were caused by false accusations than by actual poisoning.

There is only one favorable prognostication to relieve the overall gloom of this Hexagram, probably placed here by the compilers because it also involves biting:

21.4 Biting dried meat, obtains a bronze arrowhead.
Beneficial in difficulty—Divination auspicious.

九四噬乾胏，得金矢．利艱．貞吉．

Finding such objects as arrowheads or coins is often felt to indicate good fortune, as well as having actual value.

Abnormal bodily sensations and movements can be signs of disease; although in the *Zhouyi*, these are usually understood as omens, the following line may be an exception:

32.6 Trembling that endures is ominous.

上六振恆凶.

Movement disorders, which include essential tremor, Parkinson's disease, and a variety of other conditions, are reasonably common everywhere, so most people in early China would have seen individuals so afflicted. Here the tremor 振 *zhen* is ominous because it endures, suggesting it might have been recognized as a symptom of disease. It is plausible that some diviners and healers developed practical knowledge of the prognosis of various symptoms, without any actual understanding of the underlying disease process.

A line text that has puzzled many scholars is the following:

43.4 The buttocks have no skin; he walks with difficulty.
Leading a sheep, but regrets that it runs away.
Words are heard, but not believed.

九四臀无膚；其行次且. 牽羊悔亡. 聞言不信.

As often in the *Zhouyi*, a person, implicitly a stranger, is seen passing by; something about him (almost always) serves as an omen. This seems to be the case here. The lack of skin may not have been complete and must have been due to an injury—possibly a beating, but could just as likely be an abrasion from sliding down a hill or other rough surface.

A possible clue is offered in the following phrase from a different hexagram:

47.1 Buttocks obstructed by stumps and trees while entering into a deep and secluded valley.
Then three years no face-to-face meeting.

初六臀困于株木，入于幽谷. 三歲不覿

Walking through thick foliage could cause injuries that would have made movement painful, so that the person would be unable to pursue the sheep, hence the regret.

Disfigurement and mutilation

Accidental injuries must also have been common, not only in warfare, but in farming and other forms of strenuous labor. Here are examples:

> 38.1 Glimpsing a disfigured person, there will be no blame.

見惡人无咎.

The superstition that seeing a crippled or disfigured person is bad luck is common; recognition that they merit sympathy rather than disdain is quite recent. The term 惡人 eren can also mean an evil person, suggesting that bodily abnormalities were associated with evil.

> 38.3 Seeing a cart hauled by its ox.
> Its man, heaven even cut off his nose.
> Though without a beginning, it has an end.

六三見輿曳其牛掣. 其人天且劓. 无初, 有終

Here the unfortunate man, already subsisting by grueling labor, has had his nose amputated. The wording seems to imply his miseries were due to fate and thus suggest sympathy, something rare in the *Zhouyi*.

Another passage regarding mutilation, in this case even more severe, seems to have a happy ending, although the Chinese is ambiguous. Whether to punish or not is usually at the whim of those in power.

> 47.5 Cutting off the nose and feet is obstructed by one wearing vermillion, then calmly makes his statement.
> Beneficial to use for sacrificing to ancestors.

九五劓刖. 困于赤紱, 乃徐有說. 利用祭祀

While 38.3 seems to express sympathy and 47.5 seems to describe remission of the sentence, the propriety of harsh punishments is not questioned. Characteristic of pre-axial thought, society is taken as it is; there is no suggestion that it might be reformed.

While we find hints of sympathy in reference to the amputated nose and skinned buttocks, the *Zhouyi* does not comment upon the difficulties faced by these afflicted individuals. Rather than conclude that there was no compassion in early China, according to the *Lunyu*, Confucius states:

> When drinking with the others of the community, he waited until the elderly people with canes had left before leaving. (*Lunyu* 10.10; Watson 2007: 68)

This seems to be consideration for those with limited mobility, but could also be interpreted as deference to the elderly—or both. The *Zhouyi* demonstrates that this thoughtfulness was not universal. Likely not everyone possessed the refinement for which Confucius was exemplary.[3]

Bodily sensations

Not all omens are visual or auditory; some are internal sensations not due to ordinary stimuli. Everyone experiences such and unless painful or persistent, they tend to be ignored. Within the culture of divination random events are taken as having significance for the one experiencing them. Several such are grouped together in Hexagram 31 咸 *Xian* Sensation, arranged in anatomical order. The judgment text refers to choosing a woman, but the line texts are not gender specific.

Three line texts simply describe sensations of the sort that everyone experiences from time to time:

31.1 Sensation in one's big toe.

初六咸其拇.

31.5 Sensation in one's back.

九五咸其脢. 无悔.

31.6 Sensations in one's jaws, cheeks, tongue.

上六咸其輔, 頰, 舌.

Either prognoses were omitted by a copyist or it was left to the diviner to add the prognosis.

In contrast, 31.1 provides a more complete description:

31.3 Sensation in one's thigh. Grasping it while following. Going, regretted.

九三咸其股. 執其隨. 往吝.

Since the person is following, he (most likely) must have elected to walk with a group, but regrets doing so because he cannot keep up. As a divination response, this warns the inquirer to avoid activities that would strains one's ability.

Correlation of the body with the larger cosmos is fundamental to the pre-scientific correlative worldview and persists, for example, in contemporary astrology. That a sensation, twitch, or other change in a part of the body can be an omen connects the microcosm of the body to the overall life of the person and, further, to larger-scale events such as weather. On a still larger scale, macrocosmic events such as eclipses and earthquakes could be taken as heaven's judgment of the ruler.

Such beliefs persist because it is the nature of the mind to seek meanings in random events. While premodern cosmologies retain some appeal, being both fanciful and a way of ordering experience, in actuality, the enchanted universe was an anxious place because any event, even a twitch of one's toe, could portend disaster.

12

Hierarchy

Kings, Nobles, Commoners

Hierarchy is present in all societies, but in China it was the theoretical foundation of its civilization. In all important human interactions, rigid protocol dictated the proper behavior. The importance of living in accordance with the Dao, the proper way of things, was Confucius' major concern. Although not directly discussed as it was in the later *Lunyu*, references to social position appear frequently in the *Zhouyi*. When they offended those in power, transgressions of etiquette could be fatal. Even those of high rank were vulnerable—the *Spring and Autumn Annals* as well as the *Zuozhuan* frequently record executions of nobles. Zhuangzi famously advised someone who had been offered an official position to wash his ears and run away. Proximity to the powerful was hazardous; it subjected one to the whims of personages with the power of life and death. It is still true that offending the powerful can be dangerous, but retaliation tends to be less extreme, at least in democratic societies.

Divination was used frequently by people at all social levels, but as always with historical records, the doings of kings, as well as state and military affairs, were more likely to be recorded. The sheer number of inscribed oracle bones and fragments that survive—well in excess of 100,000—testify to the frequency of divination by the elite. For kings, no important event could be initiated without divining, often multiple times. The complex and expensive nature of such methods of oracle bone pyromancy or haruspicy made them the province of the affluent, although they were frequently accompanied by milfoil divination as well. Something like the *Zhouyi* was probably available for use, though likely in incomplete oral form, or manuscript fragments, for those at lower social levels. This is consistent with most, although not all, of the *Zhouyi* texts being concerned with ordinary events. Later, as the Ruist *Yijing*, it was frequently used by the literati, who were educated but not necessarily rich or powerful. It is often pointed out the character Yi 易 can mean "easy," which would make the title *Easy*

Classic 易經, which compared to oracle bone pyromancy it certainly was. Thus, it could be consulted as frequently as desired and without much preparation. Also important, although not often remarked upon, was its suitability for completely private consultation, in contrast to the public nature of pyromancy.

Although the *Zhouyi* makes frequent references to kings and nobles, we learn only a few details about their lives—they liked to hunt, they officiated at rituals and sacrifices, they married off daughters—but their policies, to the extent they had any, and their ways of maintaining power are not revealed to us. This suggests that whoever composed the *Zhouyi* could only observe the high-born from a distance and had limited knowledge of governance. In contrast, the centuries later *Zuozhuan* reveals much about the lives and machinations of the nobility, at least as the compilers imagined it.

The powerful tended to be capricious, so when they were favorably inclined, it was wise to take advantage of the moment; indeed, advancement could depend upon it.

> 17.1 The officials have changed their minds.
> Divination auspicious.
> Go out, engage, attain meritorious accomplishment.
>
> 初九官有渝． 貞吉． 出門，交，有功．

This and other images about hierarchy do not refer to the political matters at stake.

Respectful approach was essential, here covering the mouth so as not to breathe on his majesty:

> 2.3 Holding in the mouth a jade tablet.
> Can divine, perhaps in attending to the king's affairs.
> Though nothing accomplished, it has an end.
>
> 六三含章． 可貞，或從王事． 无成有終．

Obviously being on close terms with the powerful could be beneficial:

> 20.4 Observing the country's glory.
> Beneficial to be guests of the king.
>
> 六四觀國之光． 利用賓于王．

Serving the king, however worthwhile, was an endless undertaking;

> 6.3 Auspicious sometimes to follow the king's affairs for which there is no completion.
>
> 六三食舊德． 貞一厲終． 從王事无成．

While having high-ranking sponsors was important, much was expected in return, and rewards were not necessarily generous:

> 32.3 Not endless, their obligation.
> Perhaps offered delicacies.
> Divination: Stingy.

九三不恆，其德．或承之羞．貞吝

This suggests meager reward for effort expended.
Related advice, although less colorfully phrased, appears in the *Zhouyi*:

> 18.6 Instead of serving kings and lords,
> one seeks self-respect in following one's own affairs.

上九不事王侯。高尚其事

Revisiting this passage I feel that "self-respect" is anachronistic here. For 高尚 *gaoshang* nobility in the sense of refinement would be closer to the Chinese. This line is of particular interest as an early version of a theme that became explicit in Laozi, Zhuangzi, and the *Lunyu*: the refined person withdrawing rather than serve a government lacking in virtue.

On the other hand, sometimes serving the king was meritorious:

> 20.4 Observing the country's glory.
> Beneficial to be guests of the king.

六四觀國之光．利用賓于王．

Relationships with kings could be beneficial or burdensome, or even disastrous, so it is not surprising that divinatory advice would often be sought.

Success on the battlefield could be rewarded with high rank:

> 7.2 To situate troops in the center is auspicious and averts blame.
> The king three times confers rank.

九二在師中吉无咎．王三錫命

On the other hand, kings were notoriously capricious:

> 6.6 Disputation begins auspiciously
> It happened that given a big leather belt, on the same day three times it was taken away.

九五訟元吉．上九或錫之鞶帶，終朝三褫之．

The belt is a sign of rank, the bestowal of which was subject to the king's mood. A noble's anger could be deadly:

> 50.4 The cauldron's leg breaks
> overturning the duke's stew. His severe punishment—executed inside.
> Ominous.
>
> 九四鼎折足，覆公餗．其形渥，凶．

A contrasting outcome appears in Hexagram 39 蹇 *Ji An* Stumbling, in which approaching the king in a way that would normally be considered disrespectful is excused:

> 39.1 Going forth stumbling, on arrival, praised.
>
> 初六往蹇，來譽

The next line and final lines seem like paraphrases of this:

> 39.2 The king's minister—stumbling, stumbling, not bowing intentionally.
>
> 六二王臣蹇蹇．匪躬之故．

> 39.6 Going forth stumbling; arrival greatly auspicious.
> Beneficial to see the important person.
>
> 上六往蹇；來碩吉．利見大人．

Movements of the powerful, especially the king, would be watched anxiously, hence the reassurance in the second phrase:

> 37.5 The king goes to his household.
> Do not worry, auspicious.
>
> 九五王假有家．勿恤，吉．

Wars, as now, needed to be justified as righteous:

> 30.6 The king entering into a military expedition is praiseworthy.
> Chops off heads, having captured the detestable rebels.
> There will be no blame.
>
> 上九王用出征有嘉．折首獲匪其醜．无咎

Kings also officiated at sacrifice of captives following the victory:

17.6 Capture and tie them, then secure them with cords for the king to use as an offering on the west mountain.

上六拘係之，乃從維之王用亨于西山

Here the sacrifice commemorates a victory and further demonstrates the king's power over life and death.

In only one of the line texts referring to human sacrifice is the intended recipient named; it is Di 帝, usually translated as the high god. Di was a Shang deity, so this line is either of Shang origin, or a remnant of Shang belief before the Zhou replacement of Di 帝 with Tian 天 Heaven, was complete.

42.2 Perhaps advantageous—ten cowry shells for a tortoise.
Cannot overcome or avoid.
Long-lasting auspicious divination.
The king uses for an offering to Di (the high god), auspicious.

六二或益之十朋之龜. 弗克違. 永貞吉. 王用享于帝, 吉

The first two phrases seems to record the purchase of a tortoise using cowry shells as currency. The tortoise may have been used for some form of divination, or for soup, or both.

There were elaborate rules as to how kings and nobility were to be addressed; these also varied depending on family relationships. Luminous king was perhaps a polite form of indirect (third person) address:

48.3 (excerpt) The luminous king moreover grants his favor.

王明並受其福.

Although the character for king 王 *wang* appears 18 times in the *Zhouyi*, we are given only hints about royal lives and how they interacted with their subjects. We know they performed rituals and liked to hunt, as discussed in Chapter 15 on animal images. There may have been taboos against referring to the king. Even so, that paucity of details about kings suggests that the *Zhouyi* compilers had few sources available regarding royalty and were too low in rank to directly experience the life of the royal court. This is in contrast to the later *Zuozhuan*, which is gossipy in comparison.

The most vivid glimpse we get of a king's life is unexpected:

59.5 Spraying sweat, [the just-castrated stallion] utters a great cry.
Sprays the king's residence, Nothing blameworthy.

九五渙汗，其大號。渙王居, 无咎.

It is not clear whether the king was present for the horse's castration, but it was carried out close to his household, suggesting his life was not far removed from the gritty realities of agricultural life.

High-born women

Although references to women's lives have already been considered in Chapter 10, some mention of those who were part of the royal court is relevant here. Most striking is how much more frequently women were mentioned in the OBI than the *Zhouyi*. It is possible that women's agency began to decline after the onset of Zhou rule, but the few references are not sufficient to determine this. Clearly some had considerable power:

> 35.2 If advance, then sorrow.
> Divination auspicious.
> Receive now good fortune from the king's mother.
>
> 六二晉如, 愁如. 貞吉. 受茲介福于其王母

As in the West, marriages among the high-born were arranged to strengthen alliances. The decision was made by the father, not the daughter:

> 11.5 King Di Yi bestows his younger sister/cousin in marriage.
> For happiness, greatly auspicious.
>
> 六五帝乙歸妹. 以祉元吉.

This event, discussed in greater detail in Chapter 10, is historical and again indicates inclusion of Shang material in the *Zhou Changes*, since Di Yi 帝乙 (r. 1101–1076 BCE) was the penultimate Shang king. His successor, Di Xin 商帝辛; often referred to as King Zhou (r. 1075–1046 BCE), was the allegedly cruel ruler deposed by the Zhou.

Nobility

Early Chinese aristocratic titles are usually translated into English as their supposed equivalents in European feudalism, such as marquis and duke. I have followed this practice for lack of a better one, although the systems of nobility were quite different. All the Chinese titles tell us is that the person had high rank.

Early texts often assume rules of precedence, which are far from self-evident, as in the following:

62.2 Passes his grandparents; approaches his deceased mother.
Not reaching his prince, but encountering his minister.
Not blameworthy.

六二過其祖; 遇其妣. 不及其君, 遇其臣. 无咎

Although 其 *qi* can be masculine, feminine, or neuter, mourning seems to have been mainly the responsibility of sons, especially the elder, upon whom it incurred many obligations. Failure to carry these out could result in the ancestor harming the living, as well as social opprobrium. The above passage implies that there was a proper order of precedence to be followed in approaching ancestors' graves, but that it was violated. Since the mother is deceased and we can assume the grandparents were also, he probably did not follow the proper respectful order of approaching their graves. The next phrase was probably placed here because also about precedence in approaching people according to their relative rank. It seems that the person's rank was not high enough to meet the prince directly, but did give him the privilege of meeting the minister. It is unclear if the prince and minister were deceased or alive. For another interpretation see Kunst (362f). In any case, the failure to follow protocol was not severe enough to incur blame.

In China, one's fortunes depended on belonging to a group or unit that included some of high social status. What are termed "connections" in vernacular English were essential for advancement, and sometimes even for survival.

2.0 The upright person has somewhere to go. At first lost, he obtains a master. Beneficial.

君子有攸往. 先迷後得. 主利

Having somewhere to go is a set phrase, appearing four times in the *Zhouyi*. It seems to mean having a purpose in one's life. In the modern world, having a master would seem problematic, while in early China it was desirable, even essential.

The status of being a lord was granted by the king. A grant of nobility included land and people tied to the land, who would then be expected to be loyal to the king. But nobles who accumulated too much wealth and power could be tempted to rebel against the king, making enfeoffment decisions thorny:[1]

3.0 Begin with an offering; beneficial to divine.
Not useful if having to go somewhere
Beneficial to enfeoff lords.

元亨;利貞. 勿用有攸往. 利建侯.

The following probably represents an honor comparable to conferring noble status:

47.2 Obstructed from food and drink.
A vermillion ceremonial garment with seal arrives from a beneficial direction—is to be used for offering a sacrifice.
Going on an expedition—ominous, but not blameworthy.

九二困于酒食. 朱紱方來利—用享祀. 征—凶, 征凶无咎

What was permitted depended to a great degree upon social rank:

14.3 A duke can employ an offering to the son of heaven, but petty people must not.

九三公用亨于天子, 小人弗克

Hunting was a sport for nobility as well as royalty:

40.6 Using an arrow, the duke shoots a falcon high above the city wall, bagging it.
Nothing not beneficial.

上六公用射隼于高墉之上獲之. 无不利.

There is also recognition that noble privilege is limited:

15.1 The humblest and the high-born alike must wade to cross a wide river. Auspicious.

初六謙謙君子用涉大川. 吉

The prognosis of "auspicious" seems an arbitrary insert, not egalitarian social commentary.

To provide balance for this discussion of hierarchy, there are some lines that commend humility as a virtue. This theme was prominent in the *Lunyu*, later Ruist writings, and in the *Dao De Jing* and *Zhuangzi*. (This does not mean that actual behavior usually lived up to this ideal.) What is of interest is that humility, a virtue we associate with Confucius and Ruism generally, was appreciated as a character trait by as early as the time of the *Zhouyi*:

15.3 By laboring humbly, the high-born person has an auspicious outcome.

九三勞謙, 君子有終吉.

15.4 Nothing that is not beneficial about showing humility.

六四无不利撝謙.

While humility was the ideal, ordinary people were still apprehensive about appearing before those in authority, particularly when a favor was needed. This needed to be carefully timed so as to catch one's superior in a good mood, just as in the present day. The *Zhouyi* often advises if the time is right for this:

45.0 Beneficial to see the important person

利見大人

This set phrase appears several times, always positive. Curiously, it appears in connection with a dragon, sometimes an epithet for a distinguished or powerful person:

1.5 The dragon soaring in heaven. Favorable to see the important person

九五飛龍在天. 利見大人,

Shamans had been in and out of favor from the Shang onwards, making the history of their social status complex. Here the two mentioned as undergoing animal transformations are referred to as a "great person" *da ren* 大人 and an "upright person" *junzi* 君子, indicating they occupied positions of respect:

49.5 The great person undergoes a tiger change.
Before, prognosticates about the captives.

九五虎變. 未占有孚.

49.6 The upright person undergoes a leopard change.
The petty person changes his face.
For an expedition, ominous.
For a home, divination auspicious.

上六君子豹變. 小人革面. 征凶. 居貞吉.

Interpretation of the reference to the petty person is speculative, but perhaps means that the shaman can undergo a fundamental change but an ordinary person cannot.

These lines do not contain the word for shaman, 巫 *wu*, which is mentioned only once in the *Zhouyi*:

> 57.2 Kneeling at the low platform. Employ record keepers and shamans in large numbers. Auspicious, there will be no blame.
>
> 九二巽在牀下．用史紛若．吉，无咎．

This is obviously an important event with large numbers involved, but no details about the role of the shamans is included. There were different categories of practitioners of the supernatural with different skills and privileges.

While the *Zhouyi* often refers to social position, unfortunately it gives little information about social mobility.

13

Travel and Its Hazards

Archaeology and, more recently, DNA sequencing has shown that long before the jet age, many undertook to travel over long distances, despite it being slow, arduous, and dangerous. The *Zhouyi* references to travel indicate significant anxiety, not only about real dangers such as bandits but also supernatural ones. Safety of travel often depended on its direction; the *Zhouyi* frequently provides split prognoses indicating which directions are auspicious for travel and which ominous. Directionality was important for many other activities as well, such as sacrifices, and thus often specified in the OBI.

Here is a split prognosis related to travel:

2.0 In the west and south one obtains companions.
In the northeast one loses companions

西南得朋．東北喪朋

The consequences of travel in a particular direction are often stated, but not the underlying reason, which was likely only because the oracle said so.

Anxiety about leaving and returning home is apparent in a phrase still common on Chinese good luck posters, typically put up on the lunar new year and then left in place:

24.0 Coming and going there will be no infirmity.

出入无疾．

That this phrase, originally magical, has been transmitted for more than 3,000 years demonstrates that oral transmission can last for millennia. Posters with nearly identical phrases are available in Chinatowns throughout the world.[1]

Another line text combines directionality with another recurrent theme—the importance of having purpose, expressed as someplace to go:

40.0 Beneficial in the west and south.
If there is no place to set out to, their coming back is auspicious .

For having someplace to go, early is auspicious.

利西南. 无所往, 其來復吉. 有攸往, 夙吉.

This could mean that unless you have a destination in mind you should turn back, but if you do have a suitable one, you should not delay in starting out.

The following begins with the full four-word invocation; I have suggested that all actual *Zhouyi* divinations began this way, but the compilers did not feel it necessary to repeat it in each Hexagram. There does not seem any pattern as to which judgment texts include it and which do not.

3.0 Begin with an offering; beneficial to divine.
Not useful if having to go somewhere
Beneficial to enfeoff lords.

元亨;利貞. 勿用有攸往. 利建侯.

What is not useful is unclear; it seems to contradict the invocation that it is useful (beneficial) to divine, but nowhere else in the *Zhouyi* is the invocation contradicted. More likely what would not be useful was simply omitted from the text.

Some of the texts about travel are ordinary reassurances:

9.1 Returning along the road, what blame? Auspicious.

初九復自道, 何其咎. 吉.

The final line of Hexagram 9 小畜 *Xiao Chu* Small Livestock seems unrelated; unfortunately it is missing from the Shanghai Museum manuscript. The phrases make sense by themselves and a relationship can be proposed:

9.6 Now rains, now stops.
This place still holds potency.
The wife's divination is harsh.
Moon nearly full; for the cultivated person a long journey is ominous.

上九既雨既. 處尚德載. 婦貞厲. 月幾望; 君子征凶.

The phrases of this line text are suggestive, but together are not quite coherent. Weather, as now, greatly affected the ease of travel, yet rain was necessary for crops. The location has potential, despite the unreliability of rainfall. This might be for supporting crops, as suggested by Kunst and Rutt (Redmond 2017: 105), but the potency might be magical. The wife might be in danger because of the husband's being away, although this is not directly stated. The nearly full moon can be interpreted in so many ways that perhaps it is best left as mysterious. That the long journey is inauspicious for a cultivated person 君子 is one of several instances in which the prognosis is specific for a person of a certain rank. Outcomes based on character are also suggested in 11.0, 12.0, and 12.5. This trope may be an early form of the idea in later Chinese thought that the righteous thrive only in times of virtuous government.

Bandits were a much-feared hazard of travel:

5.2 Waiting on sand.
With a few words it ends auspiciously.

九二需于沙. 小有言. 終吉。

5.3 Waiting on the mud results in bandits arriving.

九三需于泥致寇至.

Taken together, these two line texts may mean that bandits were more likely to lie in wait in muddy areas where their victims cannot run fast. Sand, if hard-packed, would permit faster movement. Alternatively, the reference may be to a specific region infested by bandits.

Here is a seemingly banal line that conveys the fearful mind of the enchanted world of the ancients:

46.5 Divination auspicious for going up steps.

六五貞吉升階.

Even the most ordinary and trivial actions could be lucky or unlucky, which only divination could reveal. As usual with the *Changes*, there is no reference to spirits, but it seems likely that the concern here is the risk of offending the guardians of the staircase, who might be angered by the trespass. Such fears greatly complicated daily life because one needed to be wary not only of real dangers but of supernatural ones as well.

The *Zhouyi* does at times offer commonsense advice:

46.6 Going up in the dark, it is beneficial not to stop to divine.

上六冥升, 利于不息之貞.

The hazards of travel receive attention in Hexagram 56 旅 *Lu* The Traveler, beginning with an offering to win favor with whatever entities need to be appeased:

56.0 A small offering.
For travelers, the divination is auspicious.

小亨. 旅貞吉.

The subsequent lines are less sanguine, warning of specific dangers, particularly visible displays of wealth:

56.1 Travelers, their jades tinkling, tinkling.
Here they encounter calamity.

初六旅瑣瑣. 斯其所取災.

56.2 A traveler approaching his lodging holds his money close to the chest.
Obtains a servant boy, divines.

六二旅即次. 懷其資. 得童僕貞.

In an era when light and heat required fire, fatal conflagrations were common:

56.3 The traveler, lodging set on fire, loses his servant boy. Divination: harsh.

九三旅, 焚其次, 喪其童僕. 貞厲.

The traveler has escaped but not the servant boy; perhaps he had more confining quarters.

Travel, presumably for official purposes, was reimbursed, although carrying money in bronze coins, each of low value, must have been bulky, heavy, and not easily concealed:

56.4 The traveler at the resting place.
Obtains his traveling expenses in spade coins.
Our hearts not at ease.

九四旅于處. 得其資斧. 我心不快.

Taken together, these texts give a vivid sense of travel in early China as fraught with dangers, including accidents and robbery. We have no sense of it being pleasurable, but for a traveler divination would have been intended to help prepare for possible mishaps.

14

Human Sacrifice

Ritual Cruelty

Without question, the most unpleasant aspect of the *Book of Changes* is its frequent mentions of human sacrifice. These do not appear in the Ruist version and are little discussed in commentaries, including those by Western scholars. Most sources for early China avoid this subject, but given its prominence in the *Zhouyi* I have chosen to cover it in some detail. Archaeology has demonstrated that this "peculiar practice" was carried out with disturbing frequency in ancient China. While traditionally claimed to have ceased with the Western Zhou conquest of Shang c. 1046 BCE, the custom actually persisted for centuries more. The myth that it was abolished by the Zhou is part of the Ruist tradition that views the Zhou ascendance as restoration of ancient virtue. It must be noted that ancient China was not unique in practicing human sacrifice; the sacrifice of Iphigenia as ordained by a soothsayer in the *Iliad* shows that it was also practiced in ancient Greece.[1]

The *Zhouyi* usually does not provide the gory details of human sacrifice, but mainly describes the state of the victims just before the actual beheading. This contrasts with the description of the butchering of a ewe in Hexagram 23 剝 *Bo* Flaying, and the gelding of a horse in Hexagram 59 渙 *Huan* Spurting, suggesting some reticence when a human being is involved. The possible exception is Hexagram 52 艮 *Gen* Splitting, which describes splitting of a carcass, but does not indicate whether human or animal.

Human sacrifice can be defined as ritualized killing believed to be necessary for the welfare of society. So far as we can tell from early texts, including the *Zhouyi*, that ritual killing was a positive good for the flourishing of society was not questioned. Human sacrifice was not confined to the Eastern hemisphere, but was also practiced by the Aztecs and Mayans at the time of the Spanish conquest. While this shocked the Spanish invaders, it has been pointed out that the Inquisition also practiced human sacrifice. In providing violence for public viewing, the Roman games were a variant of human sacrifice. There is archaeological evidence of this practice from as early as the Stone Age.

For unknown reasons, human sacrifice was mainly practiced in agrarian societies with strong governments and relatively (for their era) developed cultures. The Shang and Western Zhou fit these descriptions. The victims, not surprisingly, tended to be from vulnerable groups: war captives as in the *Zhouyi*, children and elderly, criminals, weaker tribes (Bremmer 3f). Methods of killing were often cruel, suggesting sadism as an unacknowledged motivation. The sheer magnitude of homicidal ritual in Shang, with thousands of victims mentioned in the oracle bones and discovered in archaeological excavation, is horrifying (Barrett 2007: 235, et passim). Although it has been commonly claimed that human sacrifice ended with the ascent of the supposedly virtuous Zhou, archaeological evidence has shown that it continued, although gradually diminishing over subsequent centuries.

A related phenomenon is "following in death," in which retainers of deceased high-born individuals were buried with their master so as to serve in the afterlife. A variant of this is wives starving themselves to death after their husband's demise, or, in India, throwing themselves on his funeral pyre (*sati*).

Historical research on human sacrifice presents particular difficulties, not least because of its distressing nature, but also because of the unreliability of many sources. Accusations of human sacrifice, particularly of babies, were a common way to discredit enemies. The ancient Romans, whose games featured fights to the death for entertainment, hypocritically accused the early Christians of infant sacrifice. No actual first-hand evidence for this has ever been found. In general, allegations of ritual killing by one culture against another must meet with skepticism. The contrary problem exists with Chinese sources, which rarely mention the practice, because it could discredit the benevolence claimed by the Ruists. An example of what would now be called the "cover-up" of human sacrifice is Mencius' claim that "human sacrifice was simply the result of sporadic over-literal interpretations of the custom of burying life-like figures with the deceased" (Barrett 2007: 241).

Human sacrifice in the *Zhouyi* texts

That killing of innocents was felt necessary for the well-being of society now seems incomprehensible. I do not intend to belabor this unpleasant reality; in the present work I will confine discussion of human sacrifice to references in the *Zhouyi*. While human sacrifice was inflicted on different sorts of victims, all those referred to in the *Zhouyi* were war captives; obtaining them was a major motive for going to war. They seem to have been brought back so they could be sacrificed publicly; the frequency with which this is mentioned in the *Zhouyi* strongly suggests that it was a usual practice. Indeed, the *Zhouyi* is an important source for this aspect of early civilization.

The first mention of captives comes early in the *Zhouyi*:

5.0 Holding captives
Honorable offering for auspicious divination
Beneficial to cross the wide river.

有孚. 光亨貞吉. 利涉大川.

In context, it is the captives who were the offering; this is further reinforced by the presence of two characters, 亨貞 *heng zhen*, of the standard invocation, followed by auspicious 吉 *ji* that might be a near-synonym substituted for 利 *heng*. Given the presence of these characters, and the statement that the offering was to ensure a favorable divination, the question arises of whether human sacrifice was sometimes used to initiate *Zhouyi* divination. It seems implausible, however, that blood sacrifice would have been performed every time the *Zhouyi* was consulted. Killing would have made the divination procedure overly elaborate with several strong assistants necessary to restrain and behead the victims; nor do I know of any text suggesting human sacrifice in connection with *Zhouyi* divination. On the other hand, if a sacrifice were contemplated, the *Zhouyi* might have been consulted concerning whether it should be carried out. Some texts refer to divination by pyromancy and yarrow on the same occasion, although how the two methods were used together is unexplained. By the Song, and to the present day, the offering to begin *Yijing* divination has been lighting a single stick of incense. When this parsimonious ritual began is yet another unknown in the history of the Book.

It may be that the captives were "offered" to assure safe crossing of the wide river, rather than to initiate the divination. There would have been fear that the crossing would offend local spirits, but it seems unlikely that river crossing would require human sacrifice, unless for a particularly important event, such as an army traversing. Ultimately, the basis of decisions about human sacrifice, like the reasons for doing it at all, must elude us.

It is somewhat odd that the *Zhouyi*, in contrast to the OBI, never indicates the intended recipient of offerings. Blood sacrifice was always directed to particular entities; recipients in early China were usually deceased ancestors, or spirits.

Non-blood sacrifice, such as rituals, prayers, mantras, and dharani, were also directed to a particular spiritual entity. The reason for this omission in the *Zhouyi* is unclear. Possibly there was a taboo against mentioning some or all supernatural beings, or perhaps the compilers did not know.

The following line shows, not surprisingly, that captives had to be restrained to prevent their escape:

> 8.1 When holding prisoners, joining them together will avert blame.

> 有孚比之，无咎.

The blame to be averted might be the failure of the guards, or of the entities to whom the sacrifice was directed.

The following seems like an early reference to military intelligence with interrogation of captives, but the purpose would also have been to assert that they should not have stood up to the Zhou; that is, to display the power of the victors:

> 7.5 Fields with birds and beasts.
> Beneficial to seize captives to question. Blame averted.

> 六五田有禽. 利執言. 无咎.

The *Zhouyi* rarely describes states of mind, but in the following the fright of the captives is vividly described:

> 14.5 Fainting captives handed over, terrified. Auspicious.

> 六五厥孚交如威如. 吉.

Ritual aspects

Sacrifice was performed on particular occasions and at specific locations; the king was often, perhaps always, involved:

> 46.2 Captives are beneficial to use for Yue sacrifice.
> Nothing blameworthy.

> 孚乃利用禴. 无咎.

Rutt (337) suggests that the Yue sacrifice is a summer offering of vegetables, but the text states directly that captives are to be used; vegetables are not mentioned.

In context, the captives are probably the offering in the following:

46.4 The king carries out an offering at Qi mountain. Auspicious; there will be no blame.

六四王用亨于岐山. 吉，无咎.

Selection of victims

Hexagram 17 隨 *Sui* Pursuing has five line texts that give examples of how sacrificial victims were selected. The Wu Ding OBI often provide more detailed instructions, particularly specifying whether the victim should be human or animal, its positioning, and the ancestor to whom it was directed. The reasons for these are never stated, however.

In a few instances, the *Zhouyi* line texts do specify the traits to be used to select the victims:

17.2 Tying up the youths; letting slip the men.

六二係小子；失丈夫

17.3 Tying up the men; letting skip the young.
Pursue—obtain what is sought.
Beneficial divination for a home.

六三係丈夫；失小子. 隨有求得。利居貞

The final phrase implies that the sacrifice will help to protect the home, a common reason for sacrifice.

An even more peculiar selection criterion is head size:

20.0 Perform ablutions, but do not sacrifice the captives with big heads.

盥，而不薦有孚顒若.

This might be a physiognomic criterion or reference to a specific ethnic group thought to have bigger heads.

Another phrase seems to absolve the sacrificers of blame:

17.4 Pursue to have a capture.
Divination ominous.
Holding captives on the road for sacrifice, how could there be blame?

九四隨有獲. 貞凶. 有孚在道以明，何咎?

The following line indicates that sacrifice is not only not blameworthy, it is commendable:

> 17.5 Sacrificing captives is praiseworthy, auspicious.
>
> 九五孚于嘉，吉.

Procedures for sacrifice

The texts provide a few details about the final preparations for the sacrifice, but omit the sanguinary culmination.

The following line text provides instructions on preparing the victims, as well as specifying the sacrificer and the location:

> 17.6 Capture and tie them, then secure them with cords for the king to use as an offering on the west mountain.
>
> 上六拘係之，乃從維之王用亨于西山。

While archaeological excavation indicates that beheading was the most common method of killing, removal of the heart, as in Central American sacrifice, may have been practiced as well.[2]

One encounters occasional suggestions in anthropological literature that being a sacrificial victim may have been voluntary and honorable. This seems to me an attempt to revive the myth that early humanity lived in a state of harmony. To imagine that being sacrificed was truly voluntary seems delusional, especially given that we have no confirming reports from the victims. Even related practices like following in death or *sati* were more likely the result of extreme social pressure than free choice. History records many and diverse rationalizations for killing of innocents, most recently "ethnic cleansing." Scholars should be wary of rationalizations for such abhorrent practices.

As in the following, it is possible that some individuals did comport themselves bravely—they were soldiers, after all—but this does not mean they were offering themselves voluntarily, nor that they considered it an honor:

> 29.0 Holding captives tied together; their hearts are the offering.
> They walk with dignity.
>
> 有孚維；心亨. 行有尚.

Usually mentions of sacrifice have a prognosis of auspicious attached, obviously for the captors, not the victims.

As the following describes, an important goal of a successful military was taking of many captives:

> 35.1 If advance, will annihilate.
> Divination auspicious
> Ensnare captives in abundance.
> There will be no blame.
>
> 初六晉如, 摧如. 貞吉. 罔孚裕. 无咎.

These goals may not always have been met:

> 34.1 Strong feet for a military expedition.
> Ominous regarding captives.
>
> 初九壯于趾征. 凶孚.

The need for strong feet could be a general expression of the need for fitness, or an indication that the campaign will be conducted over rough terrain. That it is ominous for captives seems to suggest that the military operation will not be successful in taking captives, not the self-evident point that being captured would be ominous for the captives. Less likely, it could be a warning that many in the invading army would be captured.

The following line confirms that an important motive for human sacrifice was to display the power of the captors:

> 37.6 Holding captives who tremble as if in awe. Ends auspiciously.
>
> 上九有孚威如. 終吉.

Harshness similarly demonstrated the power of the captors:

> 38.4 Handing over captives, harshly, but not blameworthy.
>
> 交孚, 厲, 无咎.

The implication of the final phrase is uncertain. It could mean that treating captives harshly is not blameworthy, or that there is a limit to how harshly they should be treated.

The distress of the victims

Inquirers hope for good prognostications, while fearing the possibility of bad ones. The Ruist *Yijing*, particularly with the influence of Zhu Xi, tended toward being uplifting in the sense of serving the user for moral improvement. This is particularly apparent in the translation by Wilhelm-Baynes. In contrast, the ancient *Zhouyi* has an abundance of disturbing images, from beating children to castrating a stallion and butchering a ewe, to routinely decapitating war captives.

As an example:

9.4 Holding captives for blood sacrifice. They leave, shaking with terror as they go out.

六四有孚血. 去惕出.

In Wilhelm-Baynes this becomes:

If you are sincere, blood vanishes and fear gives way. (42)

Here, "sincere" *fu* has replaced its homonym "captives," the reference to blood is made to be a metonymy for anger, so that it means something like, "If one is sincere, anger will subside, and fear dissipate." This works, although slightly awkward,

How the texts about human sacrifice would have been interpreted during actual divination is particularly knotty; the inquirer is certainly not being enjoined to sacrifice captives, nor is there any evident connection between the victims and the person obtaining the divination. Of the human sacrifices in the *Zhouyi*, twenty-one are labeled as "auspicious" or "no blame." In a few cases the prognosis is ambiguous, but none are entirely unfavorable. The conclusion that sacrifice of captives was considered highly beneficial to the captors, and presumably others in their community, is unavoidable. (To be clear, I am not excusing the practice, nor do I believe it actually benefited ancient societies, even though they believed it did.)

What, then, are we to make of the inclusion in the *Zhouyi* texts of so many references to this repellent practice in texts used for divination? Clearly, the inquirer was not being advised to carry out or witness such sacrifices. If we momentarily set aside our repugnance, what comes across in most of these phrases is their auspicious prognoses. However, there were many benign images, such as bird calls, that were available to indicate a favorable outlook. Most likely the sacrifices of captives were included in the *Zhouyi* because they were major public events, serving to demonstrate the king's military might, to deter rebellions, and also, like the Roman games, as entertainment.[3] The expression of ultimate power, combined with the extreme emotions created, may have made the auspicious prognoses seem particularly significant. The inclusion of such material is best explained by compilers conceiving of their work as both as a "how to" manual and as an anthology of important divinations.

Sacrificial victims of higher social status may have been killed in less terrible ways; war captives had the lowest status and hence were subject to beheading, with the heads buried separately from the body (Barrett 2007: 252). All the sacrificial victims in the *Zhouyi* were in this category. The extreme distress of the captives at their impending violent demise is described in set phrases that use a few standard descriptive terms. The word I initially translated 臨 *lin* as "wailing" appears only in Hexagram 19, where it is the tag, also appearing in all of the line texts. This has been taken to refer to vocalization during mourning, but could possibly be the cries of captives about to be sacrificed. In context, several English words—not only wailing, but howling, moaning, etc.—capture the general meaning. On further reflection I think "lamentation" might be a better translation, as it indicates both emotion and vocalization, although the word for captives does not appear. Importantly, "lamentation" is attested as an archaic use by the *Shuowen Jiezi* 說文解字 (completed 100 BCE).[4]

Uncertainty remains, however. The modern meaning of 臨 *lin* is different—"to arrive" or "to be present"—but this can be set aside as it does not fit the context. A further possibility is as a variant in the MWD manuscript where the character is a homophone 林 *lin*, meaning forest (Shaughnessy 1997: 108 f).[5] In context "forest" makes some sense, but it seems more likely it is a phonetic substitution for 臨, meaning lamentation.[6] *Lin* can also be combined with "salty," 咸臨 *xian lin*, which I have translated as "salty tears."

Several set phrases are used to describe the vocalizations of extreme distress. A recurrent description is loud crying or wailing followed by laughter or tittering, 號咷而後笑 *haotao er hou xiao*:

> 13.5 Assembled, they first wail, then laugh.
> Great armies happen upon each other.
>
> 九五同人，先號咷而後笑． 大師克相遇。

Almost the same phrase occurs, although inverted, in the following:

> 56.6 The traveler first laughs, afterwards cries and wails.
>
> 旅人先笑，後號咷

Wailing as 號咷 *haotao* appears in both 13.5 and 56.6, as does the word I have translated as "laugh" 笑 *xiao*. Similar terms are 涕沱 *chuti* "weeping a flood of tears" and 涕洟 *ti yi* "weeping and snuffling":

30.5 Weeping a flood of tears, as if grief-stricken, as if despairing.
Auspicious.

六五出涕沱，若戚嗟若．吉．

45.6 Sighing, lamenting, moaning, tears and snuffling.
There will be no blame.

上六齎咨涕洟．无咎

Wailing is often followed by its seeming opposite 笑 *xiao*. Since in context this cannot mean laughing as an expression of positive emotion, it must refer to emotional overflow or so-called "nervous laughter"; thus "tittering" seems a better translation:

45.1 Holding of captives has not ended. Now disorderly, then assembled.
Wailing when grabbed by a hand, then tittering.
Do not sorrow, going will be not be blamed.

初六有孚不終．乃亂乃萃．若號一握為笑．勿恤，往无咎．

There does not seem to be any particular significance to which expressions of distress are used in a specific line text.

Mercy toward captives

The texts discussed so far suggest unmitigated cruelty to captives, though there are indications that a few participants in the sacrificial ritual may have felt regret:

42.5 Holding captives, kind heartedly. Do not put to questioning.
Begins auspiciously.
Holding captives kindly, shows our power.

九五有孚惠心．勿問．元吉．有孚惠我德．

Questioning of captives almost certainly included torture, yet here power is shown by refraining from cruelty, although it is not clear that the captives were ultimately spared.

Sometimes captives were released:

40.4 Release their thumbs with the arrival of friends of the captives.

九四解而拇朋至斯孚．

40.5 The nobleman is safe, having been released, auspicious.
Holding captive the petty people.

六五君子維有解, 吉. 有孚于小人.

This forms a brief, but coherent, narrative. The captives must have been tied together by their thumbs, possibly by putting cords through their hands. Powerful friends intervene to attain release of the nobles, but seem not to bother to rescue those of lower status.

Another line text suggests, by reference to a ritual bronze vessel, the *gui*, that sacrifices may sometimes have been part of a celebratory occasion:

41.0 Holding captives. Begins auspiciously. Nothing blameworthy can be divined.
Beneficial if having to go somewhere.
What is the use for a two-handled *gui*? It can be used for making offerings.

有孚. 元吉. 无咎可貞. 利有攸往. 曷之用二簋? 可用享。

The following lines, except for the last one, is a set description of the captives' distress. Presumably, they were grabbed by the hand to be taken to the place of sacrifice.

45.1 Holding of captives has not ended. Now disorderly, then assembled.
Wailing when grabbed by a hand, then tittering.
Do not sorrow, going will be not be blamed.

初六有孚不終. 乃亂乃萃. 若號一握為笑. 勿恤, 往无咎.

The final phrase can be read as some participants feeling sorrow for the victims and, not wanting to witness the killing, being permitted to leave the area. This may be wishful thinking on my part, as the *Zhouyi* has many set phrases about going and coming.

Captives were not always killed:

55.2 Fully covered with their straw mats.
At midday, see the dipper.
Going results in doubts and indisposition.
Holding captives, letting them out is favorable. Auspicious.

六二豐其蔀. 日中見斗. 往得疑疾. 有孚發若. 吉.

Here releasing the captives is declared to be favorable, but it is unclear if this is an act of mercy, or based on divination.

Hexagram 58 兌 *Dui* Exchange shows that sometimes captives were exchanged rather than killed:

58.2 Captives exchanged, auspicious
Regret goes away.

九二孚兌. 悔亡.

However, agreements between mutually hostile adversaries could easily fall apart:

58.3 The exchange arrives, ominous.

六三來兌.

58.4 The palaver is not cordial.

九四商兌未寧.

The bitterness of those involved has a terrible result:

58.5 Captives flayed with harshness.

九五孚于剝有厲.

Being skinned alive is one of the most painful methods of execution.

The final line seems out of order; it would make more sense after 58.3, describing extended negotiations that end badly.

58.6 Drawn out exchange.

上六引兌

Tanning leather or revolution?

Hexagram 49 革 *Ge* Tanning Leather has attracted much interest because of the Wilhelm-Baynes translation of the tag, *Ge*, as "revolution."[7] In the Western Zhou, *ge* meant tanning leather or, by analogy, transformation. There was nearly constant warfare in early China, but not, to my knowledge, revolutions in the sense of being ideologically motivated.

In the *Zhouyi*, the word 革 *ge* serves as a metaphor for physical change, not political or social change. As translation of *ge* as the tag, "Tanning Leather" fits the context better than "Revolution" because 49.1, 49.2, and 49.3 refer to use of leather to bind captives:

49.3 For an expedition, ominous, divination harsh.
Binding with leather, speak three times while approaching the captives.

九三征凶貞厲。革言三就有孚.

That in the *Zhouyi* 革 *ge* simply meant "leather" is further supported by the MWD version, which uses the character 勒 *le* meaning binding or bridle (Shaughnessy 1997: 129, 311). Thus there is no evidence in the *Zhouyi* that *ge* carried an implication of social transformation or revolution; such abstractions came much later. The virtuous Zhou's conquest of the decadent Shang, a part of the mythology of the *Yijing*, was justified not as social transformation but as *restoration* of virtuous government in accordance with the mandate of heaven.

In their discussion of the *Ge* Hexagram, Wilhelm-Baynes comment on political revolutions as extremely grave matters. One of the most quoted lines from their version is:

Fire in the lake: the image of Revolution. (637)

The first phrase is based on the names of the trigrams that make up the hexagram, in which that for fire is below that for lake. The line achieved fame as the title of a best-selling 1972 book on the Vietnam War by Frances FitzGerald, *Fire in the Lake: The Vietnamese and the Americans in Vietnam*. Disappointingly, the book does not otherwise mention the *Changes*.

All but the final two lines of the *Ge* Hexagram refer to captives or tanned hide, the leather serving to restrain the captives. The emphasis of the texts, including the judgment, is on the captives rather than the leather:

49.0 On a *si* day, sacrifice captives.
Begin with an offering, beneficial to divine.
Regrets go away.

已日乃孚．元亨利貞．悔亡.

The captors (presumably) are instructed to speak three times to the captives, presumably a ritual verbal formula:

49.3 For an expedition, ominous, divination harsh.
Binding with leather, speak three times while approaching the captives.

九三征凶貞厲。革言三就有孚.

The utility of yellow cow hide for binding also appears in reference to pigs:

3.2 To grasp it, use yellow ox's hide. Nothing can succeed in getting it off.

六二執之用黃牛之革. 莫之勝說

Clearly, binding with leather was a usual practice.

The final two lines of Hexagram 49 are unrelated to the lines that precede them, being about shamanic impersonations of a tiger and a leopard; accordingly they are considered in Chapter 15.

Other violence

While sacrifice is the most commonly mentioned occasion for violence in the *Zhouyi*, there are a few other instances, for example:

> 50.4 The cauldron's leg breaks, overturning the duke's stew. His severe punishment—executed inside. Ominous.

九四鼎折足，覆公餗. 其形渥，凶.

This concise anecdote gives a sense of the irritability of those in power and the danger of serving them. The translations of Rutt (273) and Shaughnessy of MWD (149) also refer to killing, while those of Lynn (455) and Wilhelm-Baynes (196) refer instead to "misfortune." According to the latter, Confucius interpreted this line as an example of how "Weak character coupled with ... heavy responsibility ... will seldom escape disaster" (196). This is a reasonable way to read the line; it replaces the execution with "disaster," which leaves it open to milder prognostications, but in doing so places the blame on the unfortunate subordinate who handled the *ding*. Interpreting in this way absolves the duke's cruel exercise of his arbitrary power.

Attempts to rationalize human sacrifice

While objectivity is essential in the study of history, this should not mean being value-neutral. In the preceding discussion I have confined myself to the textual references to human sacrifice in the *Zhouyi*. I have not attempted to explain the existence and centuries-long persistence of this repugnant ancient practice; for me it is beyond explanation. Efforts to account for it can come dangerously close to justification. Particularly repellent are speculative theories that purport to show that killing innocents had social utility. This is a hypothesis that creates a dangerous slippery slope, as does much of so-called evolutionary psychology. To illustrate this I quote the conclusion to an article in the *Atlantic* by Laura Spinney in which she speculates on reasons for human sacrifice. Commenting on the case of a 10-year old Andean girl walled up in a mortuary tower in 1598 as a sacrifice, but fortunately rescued by a Spanish mine worker, she draws a rather odious conclusion:

> The big-data approach to history has already provided a fascinating glimpse into the roots of social complexity. To return to the case of the Andean girl rescued by the Spanish miner, the data suggest that the modern world sprang from belief systems like this—but that those systems might never have come to be if earlier peoples hadn't buried children alive. (Spinney, 2018)

"Big data"—like "AI," or "5G," or "meta"—is a buzz word denoting a new tech innovation, not necessarily understood by the writer, who uncritically repeats the apocalyptic rhetoric of the IT industry. The quotation suggests the possibly that the modern world exists only because of child sacrifice, and that this can be proven by "big data"—that is, by computers. Computers can do many things, but justifying one of the most terrible practices of ancient humanity is not one of them.

This sort of pseudo-evolutionary theorizing derives from a misunderstanding of the unverifiable principle of "survival of the fittest." The assumption is that just as living species depend on a selective advantage, all social behavior exists because it somehow maintains the viability of the society. While this is certainly what the sacrificers believed, when we study the societies that practiced human sacrifice, we discover that they either abandoned the practice, sometimes from external pressure, or the entire culture became extinct. Thus it is difficult to argue on historical grounds that human sacrifice benefited society.[8]

15

Animals in Early China

Given the ubiquitous presence of animals, their importance for humans, and their often intriguing behavior, it is not surprising that animal images occur frequently throughout the *Zhouyi*. In ancient times, animals were essential for farm labor, especially horses, camels, and water buffalo, as well as providing an essential source of dietary protein. In contrast to the modern idea of species conservation as an ethical value, attitudes and treatment of animals in the premodern world were entirely concerned with their utility for humans, including ways that may seem bizarre and cruel to moderns.

The descriptions of animals in the *Zhouyi* are of particular historical interest because they are naturalistic, in contrast to works like the *Classic of Mountains and Seas* in which the animals are imaginary combinations of heads and bodies:

> There is an animal on this mountain that looks like a horse, but it has a white head and stripes like a tiger, and a scarlet tail. It makes a noise like the crooning of a human being ... If you wear some of it in your belt, it will help you to have children and grandchildren. (Birrell 1999)

Nothing remotely this fanciful appears in the *Zhouyi* in which the only mythical animals mentioned are dragons, appearing only six times (Hexagrams 1 and 2). Most often animals are interpreted as omens, although their behavior is described realistically. Some, notably geese, seem to have been appreciated aesthetically, as in Hexagram 53. Animals were killed not only for food but also as sacrificial offerings to appease transcendent beings, particularly ancestors. It was simply assumed that sacrifices were necessary for the success of ordinary activities and also for the welfare of society generally.

Appreciation of animals

Despite routine killing of animals on a daily basis, some people in early China had kindly feelings for them, as evidenced in a famous, though much later, passage in the *Lunyu*:

> Zigong wanted to do away with the sacrificial sheep at the first-of-the-month announcements to the ancestors. The Master said, Si (Zigong) you care about the sheep, I care about the ritual. (*Lunyu* 3.17; Watson 2007: 28)

Zigong was not the only one troubled by violence against animals. Mencius observes that the cruel butchering of animals is bound to elicit sympathy, but his advice is for the cultivated person to stay out of the kitchen, lest his appetite be spoiled. In both instances, sympathy for the animals is something to be overcome; it is not a sign of virtue.

In much of the premodern world food insecurity was pervasive and meat or fish were needed for adequate nutrition; adequate food supply took precedence over any concern for animal rights. A millennium later, some branches of Buddhism came to favor vegetarianism, particularly monastic orders in China, but this was far from universal.[1]

In what follows, discussions are organized by species, but not completely consistently, as some Hexagrams mention more than one kind of animal.

Birds as omens

Birds are the most commonly seen and heard wild animals because their of their ability to fly. There is also an apparently randomness to when they appear and call out, which makes them a natural choice as omens. These can be quite simple:

16.1 A bird calls. Prepare—ominous.

初六鳴. 豫凶.

Here the bird call is an omen of possible impending misfortune and has no deeper meaning. There is no clear pattern determining when bird calls are auspicious and when they are unfavorable:

30.2 Yellow oriole—greatly auspicious.

六二黃離, 元吉.

30.3 An oriole at sunset . . .
Ominous.

九三日昃之 . . . 凶

12.4 Has been a decree. There will be no blame.
Cultivated field with orioles—prosperity.

九四有命. 无咎. 疇離一祉。

While there is no obvious link between the decree and the field with orioles, both are positive—a ruler declaring indulgence and a fertile field with birds.

It may seem confusing that similar images, such as bird calls, can have quite different prognostic meanings, but divination is inherently arbitrary. Here, for example, in 30.2 the oriole is auspicious, while in 30.3 it is associated with lamentation for the dead. This does not necessarily mean that the sound of the oriole is similar to the sound of lamentation, it is simply a combination of related images: sunset and old age. Oriole, a rather speculative translation for 離 *li*, was proposed by Rutt (235, 306, 485).

While most omens in the *Zhouyi* are mentioned only once within a particular Hexagram, in a few the image is developed over several lines. In Hexagram 36 明夷 *Mingyi* Calling Pheasant and Hexagram 53 漸 *Jian* Gradual Approach, there are multiple omens based on pheasants and wild geese flights respectively. Translation of 明夷 *mingyi* as "calling pheasant" is the consensus of Kunst, Shaughnessy, and Rutt, as I have previously discussed (Redmond 2017:212). This Hexagram is clearly about shooting a bird; not recognizing this creates such absurdities as "Darkening of the light injures him in the left thigh" (Wilhelm-Baynes 141).

The two sets of bird omens are organized differently. With the pheasant both the calls and the movements are described, but with the geese, only the directions of flight are mentioned. The pheasant references contain a simple narrative: the bird reveals itself by its call, then swoops down and is struck in the heart with an arrow. Wounded, it first rises, then falls to earth. The archer is the king or one of his party; in divinatory terms, the killing of the pheasant indicates the complete success of the hunt and the prowess of the king.

The wild geese omens in Hexagram 53 漸 *Jian* Gradual Approach do not form a narrative sequence in the manner of Hexagram 36; instead they enumerate several types of landforms that wild geese might fly toward. It is not the geese themselves, but their directions, that determine the prognosis. Typical of omen texts, it is not self-evident why a particular flight direction is auspicious or inauspicious.

Rather than an organized system of bird omens, those in the *Zhouyi* have an ad hoc quality; flights of geese, and perhaps other birds, were likely a standard method of divination, but with the diviner deciding the prognosis on the spot. Despite the frequency of omens in the *Zhouyi*, we do not have evidence of systematic omen interpretation in early China. Two other divination manuals, now lost, were said to have been in use during the Shang and might have contained other sorts of omens, but we know nothing about these works save their alleged existence.

What is perhaps most curious about the geese flight omens is their contrasting prognoses:

> 53.1 Wild geese gradually approach toward the river bank.
> For the small child, harsh.
> Words without shame.

初六鴻漸于干. 小子厲. 有言無咎.

Two lines suggest possible use for the geese; in the other cases they serve only as omens:

> 53.2 Wild geese gradually approach toward the boulders. Food and drink—joy, joy, auspicious.

六二鴻漸于磐. 飲食衎衎, 吉.

One can guess that some of the geese were served at the banquet.

The last line mentions use of their feathers for ritual:

> 53.6 Wild geese gradually approach toward the land. Their feathers can serve
> for ritual ceremonial use, auspicious.

上九鴻漸于陸. 羽可用為儀, 吉.

Although feathers have been commonly used for rituals to the present day, there is no other mention of them in the *Zhouyi*.

Two lines from this Hexagram include some of the most vivid images in the *Zhouyi*, all concerning sterility or loss:

> 53.3 Wild geese gradually approach toward the land.
> The husband on campaign does not come back.
> The wife, pregnant, does not give birth, calamitous.
> Beneficial to repel the enemy.

九三鴻漸于陸. 夫征不復. 婦孕不育, 凶. 利禦寇.

53.5 Wild geese gradually approach toward the hill.
Wife after three years not pregnant. In the end nothing successful or auspicious.

九五鴻漸于陵. 婦三歲不孕. 終莫之勝吉.

Of interest, four of the lines (53.0, 53.1, 53.3, 53.5) refer to children, women, or infertility; one wonders if reproduction was somehow associated with geese, but, if so, the basis for this association is not apparent.

Related images are found in Hexagram 45 歸妹 *Gui* Marrying Maiden:

54.6 The woman offers a basket; there is no fruit
The official cuts a sheep, there is no blood.
There is nothing beneficial.

上六女承筐无實 . 士刲羊, 无血. 无攸利.

As divinatory responses, these lines must have been extremely disturbing, although a diviner could manipulate the words of any prognostic text into something quite different from their apparent literal meaning.

Hunting

Hexagram 36 明夷 *Mingyi* Calling Pheasant recounts the successful hunting of a pheasant by the king. While some of the lines seem out of order the narrative is clear: the pheasant's call is heard, it is shot with an arrow that enters its heart through its left side; it first rises then falls to earth.

The sighting is mentioned in the first line text, which also describes its movement:

36.1 Calling pheasant in flight, swooping down on its wings.

初九明夷于飛, 垂其翼.

This may be an omen, but is also the game for the king's hunting party, which is alerted to its presence by its call:

36.3 Calling pheasant during the king's southern winter hunt.

九三明夷于南狩.

The pheasant is wounded with an arrow, although the line recounting this precedes the above:

> 36.2 Calling pheasant.
> Wounded in the left thigh.
>
> 六二明夷．夷于左股．用拯馬壯，吉．

Lines that seem out of order are common in the *Zhouyi*; scribes may not have thought that it was important to maintain narrative order.

The killing of the bird is described graphically and would have served to uphold the king's potency as well as providing a meal:

> 36.4 Enters into the left flank, snaring the calling pheasant's heart.
> Through the gate into the courtyard.
>
> 六四入于左腹，獲明夷之心．于出門庭．

> 36.6 Not bright, but dim.
> First rises toward the heavens, afterwards to the earth.
>
> 上六不明晦．初登于天，後入于地

Only one line text provides a prognosis; this may have been a usual bird call omen, placed here because it contains the tag character, 明夷 *mingyi*:

> 36.5 Jizi's calling pheasant—a beneficial divination.
>
> 六五箕子之明夷—利貞．

As in many cultures, in the *Zhouyi*, hunting was a royal recreation that also served for the king to demonstrate his might. Kings did not always hit the game, however:

> 8.5 Appearing together for the king to employ to drive out game from three directions.
> Misses the birds and animals in front.
> The people of the region are not admonished. Auspicious.
>
> 九五顯比王用三驅．失前禽．邑人不誡．吉．

Presumably, locals were conscripted as beaters to drive out the game for the king, but on this occasion he missed. The final phrase suggests that it would not be unusual for a king to blame his subordinates for his own failures.

Wild animals

In ancient times when most land was still covered with forest, sightings of wild animals would have been frequent and their movements familiar.

Animal movements, especially unusual ones, were commonly regarded as omens:

> 43.5 A wild goat very determinedly runs through the middle. There will be no blame.
>
> 九五莧陸夬夬中行, 无咎.

As so often the case with the *Zhouyi*, it is not clear how the prognosis follows from the omen. Here is an even more obscure combination:

> 3.3 Immediately a deer, alone and without caution approaches into the midst of the forest.
> The upright person soon gives up—going on would be shameful.
>
> 即鹿無虞, 惟入于林中. 君子幾不如舍一往吝.

The first phrase describes anomalous behavior on the part of an animal, a common sort of omen. Deer favor dense forest to hide from predators, including human ones, yet here the animal carelessly enters an open area. The oddity of this behavior would be easily noticeable in an era when wild animal sightings were common. It might be due to the animal being injured or ill, but in the *Zhouyi* it not the cause of the behavior that is of interest, but rather its significance as an omen; although not stated in the text, it would have been provided by the diviner. The second phrase is unexpected because giving up it is contrary to the common advice to push ahead tirelessly:

> 1.3 The upright person strives energetically all day long.
> Vigilant day and night, thus averting blame.
>
> 九三君子終日乾乾. 夕惕若厲. 无.

Lines 3.3 and 1.3 taken together imply the fundamental idea of the *Book of Changes*—that what actions are proper is a function of the conditions applying at that moment. This idea, inherent in the *Zhouyi*, became fundamental in philosophical Daoism: flourishing in life depends on according with the Dao, the particular nature of each moment.

The fox's tail and the last two hexagrams

The last two Hexagrams in the received order, 63 既濟 *Ji Ji* Already Across The River and 64 未濟 *Wei Ji* River Not Yet Crossed, are of particular interest both for their imagery and for the *Xiangshu* interpretations of the line patterns, which form part of the rationale for change to be considered as a positive attribute of existence, to be discussed below.[2]

That it is a fox that is crossing is stated in 64.0, but implied in 63.1 and 64.1. The main images in both versions are the fox wetting its tail, a ribbon being trailed, and fording of a river. There is also mention of a military campaign:

> 63.3 The high ancestor (king Wu-ding) defeated Guizong, the demon land, in the course of three years.
> Petty people are not to be utilized.
>
> 九三高宗伐鬼方，三年克之．小人勿用．

The military image is almost the same in the subsequent Hexagram:

> 64.4 Divination auspicious, regret passes away.
> Zhen used a military expedition against Guifang, the devil land.
> In three years got his reward from the great country.
>
> 九四貞吉，悔亡．震用伐鬼方．三年有賞于大國．

Several of the standard prognoses are attached: no blame, nothing is beneficial, regret, auspicious, regret passes away. While it is tempting to weave all of these images and prognoses into a single narrative, they make more sense as two overlapping narratives: a fox crossing a river and a military action. Not all the phrases in these two Hexagrams fit these themes, however.

Here are the images related to the fox:

> 63.1 Trailing a ribbon.
> Dips its tail. There will be no blame.
>
> 初九曳其輪．濡其尾．无咎．

> 64.2 Trailing a ribbon. Divination auspicious.
>
> 九二曳其輪．貞吉．

Together these suggest that the ribbon was somehow stuck to the fox. Alternatively it could be part of military costume, but this is less likely, as the ribbon does not appear in the lines about military action.

> 64.0 The fox, when nearly across the river wets its tail. Nothing is beneficial.
>
> 亨小．狐，汔濟，濡其尾．无攸利．

> 64.1 Wets its tail. Regret.
>
> 初六濡其尾. 吝.

The prognosis is unfavorable in both lines. Since the *Zhouyi* never ascribes thoughts or feelings to animals, regret in 64.1 is the prognosis of the omen, not the emotion of the fox.

The remaining lines of Hexagram 64 have military associations, possibly historical (Rutt 359f).

> 64.3 Not yet across, for an expedition, ominous.
> Beneficial to ford the great river.
>
> 六三未濟, 征, 凶. 利涉大川.

This is one of the seemingly contradictory prognoses so common in the *Zhouyi*. Perhaps the army not yet being completely across makes it vulnerable, so needs to finish crossing the river.

The next line is anticlimactic as it is the last line of the entire *Zhouyi/Yijing* in the received order:

> 64.6 Wetting one's head. Holding captives, losing them, truly.
>
> 上九有孚; 于飲酒. 无咎. 濡其首. 有孚失是

Most likely, the line was placed in this Hexagram because it contains wetting 濡 *ru*, the same character as 'wetting" of the tail.

Overall, the imagery is about crossing a river, whether by a fox or an army. In each instance those crossing encounter setbacks, as represented by getting wet, although presumably minor ones. Thus as divination responses these lines can be applied metaphorically to many situations.

The Images and Numbers (*Xiangshu*) interpretation of the last two hexagrams

Although the present work is concerned with the early meanings of texts, as reconstructed over the past century, I include here discussions of Hexagrams 63 and 64 as understood in the Images and Numbers *Xiangshu* 象數 school of *Changes* interpretation; this system emphasized interpretation by line and trigram positions. Although these appear in the *Ten Wings*, they receive no mentions in the *Zhouyi* texts. Flourishing in the Han dynasty, this school added the metaphysical speculation based on yin and yang that has been associated with the *Changes* ever since. It is useful to discuss this in relation to the last two hexagrams, which fit this scheme particularly well:

Looking at Hexagrams 63 and 64 beside each other, it is apparent that both are reduplicated trigrams, water over water and fire over fire, respectively, making the line patterns reciprocals of each other. According to the yin-yang theory, 63 is correct because all yang lines are in yang (odd-numbered) positions, while the yin lines are in yin (even-numbered) positions. This also fits the tag, which means crossing complete. In contrast, 64 represents incompleteness because all the lines are in the incorrect position. It might seem that 63 is better because all the lines are in the correct position, but this was interpreted as a static situation and thus unfavorable, In contrast, Hexagram 64, with the tag meaning not yet complete, was dynamic as each line could change, providing many possibilities.

These sorts of mathematical oddities attracted some of China's brightest minds to devote themselves to working with hexagram patterns, Shao Yong 邵雍 (1011–77) being the most renowned. Much ingenuity was expended in this sort of analysis, thus enriching the creativity of students and practitioners of the *Xiangshu* school. While many of the proposed relationships of line patterns to texts now seem strained, a few, such as the image of the fox crossing the river, could be another source for the complete/incomplete interpretation of the last two Hexagrams.

Although I have some mathematical background, for me the efforts to find deep meanings in the hexagram arrangements are little more than mental gymnastics. To the extent that the patterns of lines within a hexagram model society or the cosmos, it is because these were projected onto them. Remaining agnostic about any mystical or metaphysical profundity of the hexagrams allows us to consider what their interpretive history tells us about the culture of traditional China. While this is not the subject of the present work, it is worthy of study in its own right.[3]

Domestic animals

The importance of pigs

Archaeological excavation has established that pork has been a major part of the Chinese diet from the Neolithic period or even earlier; pork dishes continue to be essential to its cuisine. The contribution of pigs to Chinese civilization was extolled by Mao Zedong, who termed them "fertilizer factories on four legs" and encouraged their rapid breeding. Famously, his favorite dish was red-braised pork belly, still a very popular dish among Chinese.

Because pigs are omnivorous, breed quickly, and are not fastidious about their living conditions, they are easy to raise. Their movements often seem random and thus were often regarded as omens (Rutt 326, 332). Given their nutritional and divinatory importance, their mention in the *Zhouyi* is unsurprising.

Characters for pig or piglet (遯*dun*, 豕 *shi*, 豚 *tun*)appear seven times in the *Zhouyi*; all but one them in the line texts of Hexagram 33 遯 *Dun*, suggesting a system of divination based on pigs' appearance or condition. As usual with the *Zhouyi* texts, the relation of the prognosis to the image seems arbitrary, as here:

> 33.1 Piglet's tail.
> Harsh, do not use if having to go somewhere.
>
> 初六遯尾. 厲, 勿用有攸往.

This, like many of the *Zhouyi* texts, seems to be a record of a divination. Perhaps someone seeing a pig's tail took it to be a warning against traveling, then it was passed along orally until it somehow ended up in the *Zhouyi*. If this hypothesis is correct, much of the *Zhouyi* seems to record ordinary events that were taken to be omens and remained in collective memory; in modern internet jargon, they are "memes."[4]

As previously emphasized, *Zhouyi* texts are "split" conditionals in that the prognosis is favorable for certain people, but not for others:

> 33.3 Bound up piglet.
> Will have harsh illness.
> For raising livestock and male and female servants, auspicious.
>
> 九三係遯. 有疾厲. 畜臣妾, 吉.

Here the harsh illness applies to the inquirer, not the piglet. Although being bound up on the way to market is certainly harsh, there are no divinations for animals in the *Changes*.

As with most omens, piglets can be auspicious, or not:

33.4 A good piglet, for the upright person, auspicious.
For the petty person, not.

九四好遯，君子，吉．小人，否．

Most images with food animals are favorable:

33.5 Excellent piglet. Divination auspicious.

九五嘉遯．貞吉．

33.6 A fat piglet. Nothing not beneficial.

上九肥遯．无不利。

In 61.0 Suckling pigs and fishes, auspicious.
Beneficial to ford the great river. Beneficial to divine.

豚魚,吉．利涉大川．利貞．

44.1 Tied to a bronze spindle, divination auspicious.
If having to go somewhere, ominous observation.
A weak pig can be captured as it paces back and forth.

初六繫于金柅，貞吉．有攸往，見凶．羸豕孚蹢躅．

Pigs can be vicious and even catching one in a pigpen can be challenging, so that the tethered or weak pig would suggest an easily obtained meal.

Horses

Like pigs, horses were ubiquitous in early China and so often appear in the *Zhouyi*. They were domesticated very early and essential to warfare as early as the Shang.

A common form of set phrase describes them as ranked for a formal occasion, as in Hexagram 3 屯 *Tun* Gathering:

3.4 Horse carts ranked for the proposed wedding.
Going is auspicious; Nothing not beneficial.

六四乘馬班如求婚媾．往吉．无不利．

In a related image, the horse is decorated for the festive occasion:

2.4 Adorned in white, a white plumed horse.
Not bandits invading, but a wedding.

六四賁如皤如白馬翰如. 匪寇婚媾.

While 3.4 describes a happy occasion, not all references to horses are positive:

3.6 Horse carts ranked.
Weeping, tears of blood flowing unceasingly.

上六乘馬班如. 泣, 血漣如

Blood in discharge from the eyes, haemolacria, is a real condition due to irritation or tears in the conjunctiva, but it is rare and its relation to emotion or stress seems to be purely symbolic. Although it seems possible that horses' eyes could be irritated by the soil stirred up by battle, or even from blood spurted on them, I have not found any veterinary reference to this condition in horses. Thus the image is probably purely metaphorical to suggest having endured extreme adversity, such as in battle.

The importance of horses, including as a store of wealth, is indicated in Hexagram 35 晉 *Jin* Advance:

35.0 Bestowed upon Marquis Kang were numerous horses.
They became abundant, mated three times a day.

康侯用錫馬蕃. 庶, 晝日三接.

The first line shows that skill in animal breeding was highly valued. That the horses were gifted, presumably by the king, suggests that Marquis Kang was of high rank, whose loyalty was important to the king. This image is also an obvious allusion to male potency and fecundity.

Most of the line texts of this Hexagram refer to advancing, presumably why the horse image was placed here. These may have been part of a system for military divination:

35.6 "Advance!" Use horns to hold together the military expedition to attack the city.
Harshness auspicious, not blameworthy.
Divination: regret.

上九晉! 其角維用伐邑. 厲吉, 无咎. 貞吝.

In this context the following rather odd image seems like a warning not to attack too slowly:

35.4 Advancing like a squirrel
Divination harsh.

九四晉如鼫鼠. 貞厲.

Livestock was an important store of value in early civilization; lost or escaped domestic animals would have represented significant economic harm for farmers:

38.1 Regret goes away
Losing one's horse, do not pursue it. Naturally, it will return.

初九悔亡. 喪馬勿逐. 自, 復.

Gelding a stallion

Castration of stallions to make them more tractable for use as working animals is an ancient practice that continues to the present day. Other domestic animals subjected to this include bulls, rams, and boars, whose meat is inedible unless they are castrated before maturity. Recently, short-acting anesthesia has come into use, but even today, this is impractical outside the developed countries. Animal farming is inherently cruel. The castration procedure was almost as dangerous for the humans involved as for the animal, as vividly described in Hexagram 59 渙 *Huan* Spurting, which has a particularly dramatic narrative structure:

59.1 Use to geld a robust horse, auspicious.

初六用拯馬壯, 吉.

59.2 Spurts, bolts away with the device on.
Regret goes away.

九二渙, 奔其机悔亡.

59.3 Spurting onto their persons. No regret.

六三渙其躬, 无悔.

9.4 Spurting onto those assembled, greatly auspicious. Spurting onto a knoll, not a smooth place as one would expect.

六四渙其羣，元吉．渙有丘，匪夷所思．

59.5 Spraying sweat, it utters a great cry.
Sprays the king's residence, Nothing blameworthy.

九五渙汗，其大號。渙王居，无咎．

59.6 Spurting its blood, sets out to get far away.
Nothing blameworthy.

上九渙其血，去逖出．无咎．

This Hexagram forms an orderly narrative and is one of the most dramatic in the *Zhouyi*. Unusually for the *Zhouyi*, it is emotionally intense; the suffering of the animal and implied danger to the workers come across vividly. Finally, each line of the narrative includes a prognosis; all are auspicious (吉) or indicate no blame or regret (无咎). This might be attributable to the relief felt when this dangerous procedure has been successfully completed without injury to the men performing it and perhaps that ritual requirements, though unstated, have been met. For a modern reader, it is a reminder of the rawness of agricultural life.

Cows, sheep, and oxen

Given their importance, the breeding and care of domestic animals was a common subject for divination:

30.0 Beneficial to divine; make offering. For breeding cows, auspicious.

利貞' 亨．畜牝牛，吉．

For a farm family, an animal would be a significant part of their net worth, hence their loss might be catastrophic:

25.3 Unexpectedly, calamity. Their tied up ox—someone walked by and took it. Disaster for the country person.

六三无妄之災―或繫之牛行人之得．邑人之災．

Since animals, both domesticated and wild, were ubiquitous sights, they commonly served as images:

> 26.4 Bull-calf in its pen; horns held by a board.
> Greatly auspicious.
>
> 六四童牛之牿. 元吉.

Presumably the board was to render the animal harmless in preparation for sale or sacrifice, as discussed below.

There is at least one example of use of an animal body part as an amulet or medicine, a common practice in many societies, as rabbits' feet were in the United States when I was growing up:

> 26.5 Castrated boar's tusk, auspicious.
>
> 六五豶豕之牙, 吉.

Castration would have resulted in the tusk being smaller and softer, but the magical significance of this is obscure.

Other domestic animals

While pigs and horses are the most often mentioned, other domestic animals make appearances. The ram images of Hexagram 34 大壯 *Da Zhuan* Great Strength seem to be proverbs, or at least intended to convey lessons about the limitations of brute strength; they could serve as omens as well:

> 34.3 The petty person uses strength; the cultivated person uses deception.
> Divination harsh.
> A ram getting his horns entangled in a fence wearies his horns.
>
> 九三用壯;用罔. 貞厲. 羝羊觸藩羸其角.

This begins with the set contrast of petty people 小人 *xiao ren* to cultivated people 君子 *junzi*; these are often translated into English following Wilhelm-Baynes as "inferior man" and "superior man," as in 34.3:

> The petty person works through power.
> The superior man does not act thus. (134)

"Inferior man" sounds snobbish in English; I have used "petty person" instead in the sense of the English idiom "small-minded," implying poor character, which I take to be the meaning of the Chinese in this context.

It might seem that the ram's getting its horns stuck is a metaphor for use of strength rather than intelligence. Yet his strength ultimately enables him to get loose, so it seems that the animal does not serve as a metaphor for the petty person. This is further suggested by the subsequent line text:

34.4 Divination auspicious—regrets will go away.
Fence breaks, [the ram] is not weak.
Strength like a big cart's undercarriage.

九四貞吉─悔亡. 藩決不羸, 壯于大輿之輹.

34.6 Like a ram getting its horns caught, it cannot pull back, cannot go forward.

羝羊觸藩. 不能退. 不能遂

This phrase as I have translated it is a simile, suggesting it was a set phrase to describe being stuck in a situation.

Animals could escape or be stolen:

34.5 Losing the ram in Yi.
No regret.

六五喪羊于易. 无悔.

Livestock was a major store of wealth, so its loss could be devastating. Here there is no suggestion that the ram will return; no regret must mean that the person responsible will not be punished, but we do not learn why. As a divination response, it could mean the inquirer made a significant mistake but escaped adverse consequences.

In the following, loss of an animal is regretted:

43.4 Leading a sheep, but regrets that it runs away.
Words are heard, but not believed.

牽羊悔亡. 聞言不信.

The final phrase suggests that excuses were not accepted. (The obscure first phrase of this line text, omitted here, referring to buttocks without skin 臀无膚, is discussed in Chapter 8 and in Redmond 2017: 245.)

Hunting

Hunting was the sport of the high-born. Although the less privileged must have killed animals for food, this is not mentioned in the *Zhouyi*. Beaters were used to drive out the game for the king to kill with bow and arrow; this was not only for recreation but also to demonstrate his masculine prowess. To miss would have been embarrassing for the king and could possibly weaken his hold on power.

Capturing animals or hitting a bird with an arrow was highly auspicious:

40.2 In the field catch three foxes and find a bronze arrow, divination auspicious.

九二田獲三狐得黃矢，貞：吉.

40.6 Using an arrow, the duke shoots a falcon high above the city wall, bagging it.
Nothing not beneficial.

上六公用射隼于高墉之上獲之．无不利.

Butchering

Killing of animals for food or as offerings must have been a frequent sight in the ancient world, in contrast to the modern world where it is kept out of sight. As described in the *Zhouyi*, division of the carcass seems to have been carried out in a prescribed order. In the skinning of a ewe described in Hexagram 23 剝 *Bo* Flaying, each step has an attached prognosis. Recent archaeological excavation has established that extensive animal sacrifice was carried out in early China, but extispicy, divination by inspection of the liver, is rarely mentioned in early texts. Since the meat of sacrificial animals was consumed, there may not have been an absolute distinction between sacrificial killing and killing for ordinary consumption.

While seemingly economically wasteful, when a large animal was sacrificed, a mass feeding of the cooked meat was generally served to those in attendance. The best portions went to the those of highest rank; this meant fatty meat, which is higher in calories and thus desirable in conditions of food insecurity or high energy expenditure, as associated with physical labor.

Cutting up the carcass seems to have been done in ritual order; possibly this counteracts the ominous prognostication:

23.1 Flaying a ewe from the foot.
Set aside the ominous divination.

初六剝牀以足．蔑貞凶.

23.2 Flaying a ewe to determine.
Set aside the ominous divination.

六二剝牀以辨．蔑貞凶。

The relation of the prognoses to the cutting of the carcass is not clear. Possibly this is a ritual which includes divination; it might also be that the procedures are themselves auspicious or ominous:

23.3 Flaying is without blame.

六三剝之无咎．

23.4 Flaying a ewe's skin. Ominous.

六四剝牀以膚．凶．

Taken together, 23.3 and 23.4 constitute a split prognosis. Depending on which line was drawn, the outlook would have been without blame, or ominous. There is no contradiction here, as inquirers would have received one or the other lines, not both, as the divinatory response. Split inquiries were also characteristic of the OBI, in which questions were phrased in the form of pairs of possible outcomes: "this week it will rain" and "this week it will not rain." It seems to have been assumed that asking the question in both ways would provide a more accurate divination.

This rather graphic description of flaying the ewe shows the matter-of-fact approach to killing animals for human use. Starting at the foot was probably for ritual reasons, but may also have been the most practical means to remove the skin intact, as it would have value. Careful butchering to harvest all usable parts of the animal would have been important in a near-subsistence economy. Skinning, butchering, and rendering (extracting by-products such as grease) would have been frequent sights in early farming societies.

Hexagram 52 艮 *Gen* Splitting also contains quite explicit lines about butchering. Although the tag came to mean, as in the Wilhelm-Baynes translation, Keeping Still or Mountain, the character *gen* does not have these meanings in any other text. The normal character for mountain is 山 shan, which is obviously unrelated. Rutt provides an interesting history of the peculiar etymological speculations regarding *gen*, which he translates as "cleaving," concluding that none are very convincing, while demonstrating that "keeping still," the Ruist meaning, was not the early one (344).

In the Mawangdui version, the tag character is the homophone 根, translated by Shaughnessy as "stilling" (59, 293), as he also translates the tag of the received text (2014: 125). In his translation there is no direct indication of divining by body part, only the usual prognostic terms that recur in most line texts. Although both Rutt's and Shaughnessy's translations suggest that it is a human victim being split, it could refer to an animal, since the text is not specific. Ritual slaughter continues in a few areas of China and Vietnam; in Islam and Orthodox Judaism halal and kosher regulations dictate methods of slaughter for animals to be consumed as food.

The procedures seem to progress in a prescribed order:

52.0 Splitting its back, not getting into the body.
Will not be blamed.

艮其背，不獲其身. 无咎.

52.1 Splitting the feet. There will be no blame. Long-term beneficial divination.

初六艮其趾. 无咎.

52.4 Splitting the trunk. There will be no blame.

六四艮其身. 无咎

52.5 Splitting the jaws.
Words have the proper order. Regret goes away.

六五艮其輔. 言有序. 悔亡.

That words have their proper order suggests ritual recitation during the splitting of the carcass.

Another line suggestive of ritual requirements is:

52.6 Complete splitting is auspicious.

上九敦艮吉.

This indicates that the procedure must be carried out to completion.

As here translated, Hexagram 52 is thematically consistent, all lines referring to splitting the victim. Several lines have prognoses attached, but these seem to refer to acts of dividing the body; there is no indication that the body parts serve for divination, making it unlikely that this is primarily a description of haruspicy. However, one line does describe exposure of internal organs:

52.3 Splitting the lower back. Breaking open the spine.
Harsh—the heart smokes.

艮其限. 列其夤厲. 熏心.

The inside of a body is wet. In cold weather moisture would evaporate, then quickly condense, giving the impression of smoke. It is possible, but not certain, that the vapor released from opening the body is the reason for the harsh prognosis. There are, however, no similar bodily omens in the *Zhouyi*.

This is a particularly gruesome hexagram, yet the Ruist meanings as rendered into English by Wilhelm-Baynes retain no trace of this:

Six in the fourth place means:
Keeping his trunk still.
No blame.

The translators' commentary on this text is "Keeping the back at rest means forgetting the ego. This is the highest stage of rest" and goes on to explain the passage in terms of psychological development, "leading in the end to the complete elimination of egoistic drives" (201–3). The anachronisms of "forgetting the ego" and the back as being "the highest state of rest" can be blamed on the Jung-influenced translators, but would probably seem unremarkable to psychologically oriented readers in the West.

Fish

Surprisingly, considering the importance of fish in China, both as imagery and as food, they receive only two mentions in the *Zhouyi*. The following image now seems unflattering, but probably was not so intended in the Western Zhou:

23.5 A string of fishes to favor the palace ladies.
Nothing not beneficial.

六五貫魚宮人寵. 无不利.

In China this was interpreted to represent abundance, the usual meaning of fish, but also the colored scales were metaphors for the parade of brightly attired palace women.

In an era without refrigeration, food must have frequently spoiled before consumption:

44.2 The sack holds fish
Nothing blameworthy, but not beneficial for guests.

九二包有魚. 无咎, 不利賓.

Perhaps the species of fish was not appealing as food, or was not quite fresh.

Animals dangerous to humans

Curiously, animal predators are mentioned in only two hexagrams: 10 履 *Lu* Treading and 49 革 *Ge* Tanning Leather. In Hexagram 10, tigers get their tails stepped on; in some lines the tiger bites, but in others the feckless stepper is not bitten. This is another instance of split prognostication in which the same action is auspicious in one line, but ominous in another. In Hexagram 49 *Ge* the tiger and leopard are virtual; shamans undergo transformation to take on the characteristics associated with these animals:

49.5 The great person undergoes a tiger change.

九五大人虎變.

49.6 The upright person undergoes a leopard change.
The petty person *Changes* his face.

君子豹變. 小人革面

Oddly, while both use 變 *bian* to refer to the animal transformation, the petty person's facial change is designated by the title character 革 *ge*. Since the primary early meaning of *ge* was tanning, one wonders if the line once referred to the "leathery" appearance caused by sun and wind exposure in those who labor outdoors, such as farmers and fishermen.[5]

While shamanistic elements would seem appropriate in an early divination manual, these lines, together with the mentions of dragons in *Qian* and *Kun*, are the only explicitly shamanistic elements in the work. Later *Zhouyi* divination as practiced by literati seems not to have been shamanic, being conceived as consulting the recorded wisdom of ancient sages, rather than entering another reality. Although we cannot rule out diviners seeming to enter a trance state while using the *Zhouyi*, so far as I am aware there is no textual evidence for this. Fu Xi 伏羲, the apocryphal discoverer of the trigrams, was depicted in later art as wearing a leopard skin while gazing at the back of a tortoise which bears the

Luo Shu 洛書 magic square (or, sometimes, the trigrams), but the only basis for this in the *Zhouyi* is 49.6 quoted above.

Animal magic

Hexagram 18 蠱 *Gu* Disease From Excessive Sex is of particular interest, its diverse interpretations all revelatory of dark aspects of early culture. The tag *gu* could refer to improper sexual activity, shamanistic spell casting, deadly poison, intestinal worms, and venomous insects. Line texts 1 through 5, in my reading, refer to pre-scientific beliefs about parental behavior, particularly sexual excess, having effects on the child (Redmond 2017: 137–42). Even now, knowledge of effects of parental behavior and health on the offspring is incomplete, with some still of the opinion that intercourse during later pregnancy can temporarily decrease blood flow to the fetus.

The tag 蠱 *gu* of Hexagram 18 is the graph for "insect" tripled, over a component meaning dish or container. In the MWD manuscript it is 16 *gu*, an archaic character translated as "branch" by Shaughnessy (1996: 68f, 295), but I would suggest this is a phonetic substitution, or perhaps a euphemism, as *gu* has distinctly unpleasant connotations.

The poison designated by 蠱 *gu* was made by putting venomous animals, such as insects and snakes, together in a container to fight each other. The last one left alive was pulverized to prepare what was believed to be a particularly malevolent poison.[6] Even though *gu* was a myth, accusation could lead to gruesome execution—beheading with the heads displayed on poles. The ghosts of these unfortunate individuals were also termed *gu*. Although it had many other black magical associations such as a love charm, *gu* mainly referred to various forms of malevolence.

Knowledge of disease patterns and etiology was negligible, certainly not sufficient to distinguish poisoning (or curses) from disease as a cause of death. Thus allegations of malevolent magic or poisoning were impossible to refute. Almost certainly far more people were executed because of false accusations than died of actual poisoning. This is an example of the socially detrimental aspect of divination—to make accusations of supernatural harm; as to whether the *Zhouyi* was used to adjudicate such charges we have no evidence. Besides this hexagram, the *Zhouyi* has no other definite references to witchcraft or sorcery. In addition to these gruesome meanings, in the Zhou dynasty *gu* could also mean sexual attraction or seduction, similar to the English word "enchantment." Its meaning of improper sexual misbehavior fits the context of the Hexagram 18 texts, while those related to poisoning or violence do not:

> 18.2 Undoing illness caused by the mother, one must not be too strict.
>
> 九二幹母之蠱。不可貞。

> 18.3 In undoing illness caused by the father,
> There will be regrets but no culpability.
>
> 九三幹父之蠱。小有悔。无大咎。

> 18.4 Be generous and indulgent toward illness caused by the father, because excessive zeal would bring shame
>
> 六四裕父之蠱。往見吝。

While divination sometimes helped clarify decisions, it could also, as with witchcraft accusations, be extremely disruptive to social order. Whether on balance divination was positive for individuals and society or harmful, it was central to premodern consciousness.

The mystique of the tortoise

Although a tortoise seen in a river by Fu Xi is central to the myth of the origin of the *Changes*, this did not save them from ritual use in oracle bone divination, nor from being made into soup. Oracle bone divination was still performed in the Western Zhou, but the *Zhouyi* makes only one reference to tortoises in the *Zhouyi*, a rather obscure one, which is adjacent to a jaw movement omen:

> 27.1 Leave at home your numinous tortoise
> Observe my drooping jaw, ominous.
>
> 初九舍爾靈龜. 觀我朵頤, 凶.

Wilhelm-Baynes translate the line similarly, although with the drooping now transferred to the presumed inquirer:

> You let your magic tortoise go;
> And look at me with the corners of your mouth drooping.
> Misfortune. (108f)

This misses the significance of the involuntary bodily movements, such as twitches, as omens. Rutt (320, citing Waley A134) suggests that that the twitching jaw is that of a sacrificed animal. This seems dubious to me. Not everything in the *Zhouyi* is about blood sacrifice and, more importantly, there are abundant other examples of using involuntary movements as omens. This phrase suggests a magical tortoise shell 靈龜 *ling gui* used for divination but carefully looked after, rather than subjected to the destructive process of pyromancy. There are other references in early texts to tortoise shells being kept for magical or divinatory purposes, for example, Zhuangzi:

> I have heard that in Chu there is a spirit-like tortoise-shell, the wearer of which died 3000 years ago, and which the king keeps, in his ancestral temple, in a hamper covered with a cloth. Was it better for the tortoise to die, and leave its shell to be thus honored? Or would it have been better for it to live, and keep on dragging its tail through the mud?[7] (Watson 1968: 137)

Obviously, the animal would prefer to live. This is evidence of magical tortoise shells, but nothing about how they were used, unfortunately.

Taken together, the two *Zhouyi* phrases might be saying, in effect, "Do not use your magic turtle for this divination; use the twitching jaw (as an omen) instead." This is one of very few references to the actual practicalities of divination.

The *Zhouyi* tells us much about the interactions of humans with animals, but without sentimentality. Food animals were essential to human survival. Knowledge of the behavior of wild animals served for hunting, but also as omens for divination.

16

Warfare

In the ancient world, divination was employed for virtually all important military decisions. In ancient Greece and the Middle East, haruspicy was the preferred method, sometimes to the point of seriously depleting the livestock. Given that warfare was almost continual in ancient China, it is likely there were manuals, or at least orally transmitted methods, for military divination, but none have survived, to my knowledge. Two works on strategy have been frequently translated into English, notably the *Thirty-six Stratagems* and *The Art of War*. The origins of both are obscure and their textual history is complex. The former seems to be a collection of oral apothegms that could easily be used for divination, possibly in a different format.

It may seem puzzling that life-or-death decisions were made, at least in part, by a random method, especially because it must have been obvious that the advice was often wrong. This was usually blamed on insufficient skill of the diviner, rather than on the method itself. Often, repeated divinations were made, but knowing which to follow would be inherently problematic.

The most fundamental reason for use of divination was, I suggest, not because of a preference for superstitious thinking, but because knowledge of causality was sparse. Such life-or-death matters as rainfall for crops, fertility, safety of travel, and disease were largely unpredictable and uncontrollable. Early society provided scant protection from impoverishment, banditry, invasion, and the whims of the powerful. Divination was a way of trying to increase control over these and other uncertainties. Military strategy and tactics were also high-stakes activities requiring decisions to be made despite insufficient information.

The *Zhouyi* does contain some texts that could be used for military divination, but they cover only a few situations. This suggests that they recorded historical events, rather than providing a comprehensive system dedicated to tactics and strategy. Hexagram 7 師 *Shi* Troops, or the Army, is mainly about military matters, all but 7.0 and 7.6 containing the word 師 shi meaning troops. (The same word occurs in five other hexagrams: 11.6, 13.5, 15.6, 16.0, and 24.6.) Three of the lines are about positioning soldiers:

> 7.1 The troops go out in accord with the regulations.
> Not good! Ominously not good!
>
> 初六師出以律. 否臧！凶臧！

> 7.2 To situate troops in the center is auspicious and averts blame.
> The king three times confers rank.
>
> 九二在師中吉无咎. 王三錫命.

> 7.4 Ranking troops on the left averts blame.
>
> 六四師左次无咎.

These texts suggest that positioning troops, the most critical tactical decision, could be based on which of three line texts was randomly selected. It does not seem plausible that military decisions were made so simplistically, but I am not aware of any sources for what, if any, role the *Zhouyi* played in military decisions.

The next line would appear to be correct for any military engagement:

> 7.3 Some troops will be carried as corpses, ominous.
>
> 六三師或輿尸. 凶.

The next line is more specific:

> 7.5 Fields with birds and beasts.
> Beneficial to seize captives to question. Blame averted.
> The eldest son commands the troops.
> The younger son carts the corpse. Divination ominous.
>
> 六五田有禽. 利執言. 无咎. 長子帥師. 弟子輿尸. 貞凶.

The first phrase has been interpreted by Rutt and others as an abundance of animals to provide food for the troops (Redmond 2017: 97). It might be a set phrase to indicate sufficiency in contrast with 48.1, "By the old well there are no birds and beasts." However, it has no necessary connection to the remaining phrases. Line 7.5 contains a reminder about the desirability of taking captives, an obsessive theme in the *Zhouyi*. The final two phrases are more specific, first distinguishing the roles of the elder and younger son in this battle, the latter being to cart a corpse. Rutt suggests this is an historical reference to the final defeat of the Shang, suggesting that King Wu had the corpse of his father, King Wen, carried into battle (300). This may be a topos as it resembles the (much later) legend of the Spanish general hero Rodrigo Díaz de Vivar "El Cid" (c. 1043–99) whose corpse was supposedly set on his horse in full armor to encourage his troops.

Here is an ambiguous military divination from the *Zhouyi*:

> 24.6 Getting lost while returning, ominous.
> There will be a disaster unforeseen.
> Marching the troops ends with a great rout.
> For their country's ruler, ominous.
> For ten years, not capable of a military expedition.

> 上六迷復. 凶. 有災眚. 用行師終有大敗. 以其國君, 凶. 至于十年, 不克征.

This is ambiguous as to whether the enemy or the inquirer's troops will be routed. In this it resembles what is perhaps the most famous divination in classical literature, that recounted by Diodorus as given at Delphi to King Croesus. The king was told that if he crossed the Halys River, a great empire would be destroyed. Croesus invaded, only to realize too late that it was his empire that was to be destroyed. Historical sources are indefinite as to what actually happened, but it serves to illustrate the slipperiness of divination, allowing the apparent meaning to change when the outcome is not as expected.

Another military reference is almost too obvious:

> 34.1 Strong feet for a military expedition.
> Ominous regarding captives.

> 初九壯于趾征. 凶孚.

The first phrase could be advice to conscript soldiers with strong feet, an obviously desirable physical attribute. This sort of phrase can baffle readers of the *Book of Changes*, unless they recognize that, despite its formidable reputation, not every fragment of text is profound. The second phrase probably does not refer to the ominous plight of the captives, but that of the captors; that is, the battle will not result in taking enough captives.

The next text that uses the character *shi* (troops or army) is one that resists clear translation:

11.6 The city wall collapses into the moat.
Do not use the army; one's own city declares the order.
Divination—regret.

上六城復于隍. 勿用師；自邑告命. 貞一吝.

The first two phrases seem to be a unit, possibly referring to an historical event. The advice is to avoid using the army to repair the wall, but instead rely on the people of the city. A reason for not using the army might be that they would not be available to defend against attack, or even that they might take over the city. No doubt other explanations could be advanced. As is usual with the *Zhouyi*, the obscurity is due to paucity of details; nothing suggests a hidden or esoteric meaning.

I have translated the tag of Hexagram 13 同人 *Tong Ren* simply as Assembling, although it could be rendered as "assembling men," or simply 'assembling people," but in the context of lines 13.3, 13.4, and 13.5, it is troops that are being assembled. Lines 13.0 and 13.6 could relate to preparing for a campaign and subsequent sacrifice to celebrate victory. Wilhelm-Baynes' translation of the tag as Fellowship with Men, in giving a generally optimistic tone to the texts, downplays the military implications which are quite evident in the Western Zhou text.

The judgment begins with a set phrase, "Beneficial to cross the great river," but in context it seems to refer to a crucial step in a military campaign. It is followed by a modification of the standard invocation.

13.0 Assembling in the wilderness, making offering.
Beneficial to cross the great river.
Beneficial for the upright person to divine.

同人于野, 亨. 利涉大川. 利君子貞.

The first line text partially parallels the judgment, something unusual in the *Zhouyi*:

13.1 Assembling at the gate; there will be no blame.

初九同人于門；无咎.

In the following line assembling is done regretfully, probably to commemorate those killed in combat and also to gain the support of the ancestors for the upcoming military action:

13.2 Assembling at the ancestral temple, regretfully.

六二同人于宗, 吝.

The next three lines carry out the military theme:

> 13.3 The forces ambush from the thicket.
> They climb the high hill, but for three passings of Jupiter, not achieved.

九三伏戎于莽．升其高陵，三歲不興

A passage of Jupiter is about one solar year on earth; this is one of very few indications of duration in the *Zhouyi*. It suggests that the military operation involves recurrent attacks over several years. This might be another historical reference.

The action recounted in the next line has a different barrier—a wall rather than a hill—but similarly obstructs the troops:

> 13.4 War chariots at their city wall attack but unable to overcome. Auspicious.

九四乘其墉弗克攻．吉．

The next line contains the set phrase, wail, then laugh, presumably expressing fear as the battle is about to commence:.

> 13.5 Assembled, they first wail, then laugh.
> Great armies happen upon each other.

九五同人，先號咷而後笑．大師克相遇。

The word I have translated as laughing or tittering, 笑 *xiao*, also appears in 45.1, 51.0, 51.1, and 51.6; in all of these it is a reaction to a stressful situation, usually extreme, such as being about to be sacrificed. Presumably it represents what in English is termed "nervous laughter." However, the word is a set term regularly applied to captives about to be killed, so it may not describe their actual behavior.

The final line of this hexagram suggests a victory celebration, although it could have been placed here simply because it fits the theme; the various warfare references are not necessarily from the same military action:

> 13.6 Assembling at the outskirts to sacrifice to heaven.
> Nothing to regret.

上九同人于郊．无悔．

In conclusion, the *Zhouyi* contains many texts about military action, some of which probably refer to historical events. It does not, however, provide a comprehensive system for military divination.

17

Optical Imagery

The Diagrams

While the purpose of the present work is to elucidate the texts of the *Book of Changes*, it must be acknowledged that it is the unique hexagrams that initially captivate readers and tempt some to delve more deeply into the ancient work. Of the many divination texts that circulated in the ancient world, only the *Changes* continues to be read and quoted, almost certainly because of the numinous aura of its visual element. Many theories have been advanced to explain the figures but none are definitive, despite the exegetical efforts of Chinese literati over two millennia and three centuries of scholarship in the West, beginning with Bouvet and Leibniz. Claims to have deciphered the true meanings of the hexagrams continue to appear, yet no single interpretation has established itself as definitive.

Despite the many ingenious theories, the hexagrams have no intrinsic meanings. In contrast, the *Zhouyi* core texts do have meanings, however ambiguous or obscure. Although all lines have a text assigned to them, these do not fix the meaning of the associated line or hexagram. Aside from a few linear markings on Neolithic ceramics, we have no records of the development of the figures. Nor are there any extant sources that describe how they came to be combined with the texts. The most plausible explanation, although less appealing than the mythology of Fu Xi and the early Zhou culture heroes, is that the figures began as a system for selecting the texts that constituted the correct response to an inquiry. Lines were recursively selected by yarrow sorting or coin toss, and the attached texts were the response. At some point, when the book came to be regarded as a repository of the wisdom of high antiquity, it was a short mental leap to assume that the figures recorded this wisdom. A more detailed account of hypotheses of the origin of the *Changes* is provided by Richard J. Smith (2007: 7–18).

The *Ten Wings*, thought to be of Warring States origin and declared canonical by Emperor Wu 劉徹 (r. 141–87 BCE), frequently mention use of line and trigram positions, often based on the hierarchical society of their time. This approach was the basis of the *Xiangshu* school that predominated in the Han and was also fundamental in the philosophies of the Song so-called "Neo-Confucians," notably Zhou Dunyi, Cheng Yi, and Zhu Xi.

Sima Qian (*c.* 145–*c.* 86 BCE) 司馬遷 the "Grand Historian," author of most of the 史記 *Shiji* Book of History, refers to several of the *wings*, stating that they were known to Confucius (Rutt 364), but he does not describe their contents. Thus we have no sources for the early development of the *Xiangshu* method. As it is most unlikely that this complex system existed when the core texts were composed, it seems that the hexagrams were created *before* meanings were attributed to them. This contrasts to virtually all other religious or metaphysical diagrams, such as Hindu yantras, Buddhist mandalas, or Daoist talismans, which were based on pre-existing belief systems. Images tend to engender more images and this has been the case with the hexagrams, which inspired a rich variety of diagrams meant to illustrate the underlying metaphysics. While essential to the *Xiangshu* mode of interpretation, they were not excluded by the *Yili* school.

Here I will interject a personal note regarding my mode of experiencing the ancient classic. When I am in China discussing the *Yijing*, I am usually asked if I belong to the *Xiangshu* or *Yili* school, something I am never asked in the West. Thinking about how to answer this question led me to recognize that the hexagrams and texts work for different cognitive temperaments; for me the *Yili* seems to fit naturally, while the metaphysical elaborations and the mathematical conundrums of the *Xiangshu* do not. My appreciation of the diagrams is aesthetic rather than philosophical. In using the *Changes* for divination, I instinctually rely on the texts and only make use of line or trigram positions when the texts do not seem to be fully responsive to the situation inquired about.

The diagrams function projectively like Rorschach ink blots, commentaries only tell us about the commentator. What most interests me is figuring out what the words meant when they were set down 3,000 years ago and what they can tell us about ancient life and thought. Yet it cannot be denied that it is the visual element that creates the character of the classic; for this reason, a brief consideration is relevant here. A more detailed discussion can be found in Smith (2008:62–88, 113–32).

The circular black-and-white yin-yang symbol (Figure 2) is instantly recognized throughout the world, even by those who have never heard of the Chinese classic. It ingeniously blends the early meanings of yin and yang as shade and brightness with their later metaphysical significance. The curved

Figure 2. The most frequent yin-yang diagram. Public domain via Wikimedia Commons.

dividing line elegantly represents the reciprocal waxing and waning of the two forces. The dots of the opposite color in some versions show that yin and yang each contain the genesis of the other. The broad appeal and recognition of this symbol is shown by its availability as a unicode emoji ☯ (U+262FYIN YANG).

Often the yin-yang symbol is depicted surrounded by the eight trigrams; in this form it is termed the *bagua* 八卦.

The Song dynasty (960–1279 CE) was a time of great philosophical, artistic, and scientific activity in China. The predominant philosophy was a re-visioned form of Ruism termed 道學 *Dao Xue* Study of the Way. Zhou Dunyi 周敦頤 is generally credited with founding this school, while Zhu Xi, considered China's second most important philosopher after Confucius, broadened it by incorporating elements of Daoism and Buddhism. The resulting synthesis dominated Chinese thought until the early twentieth century. As the philosophy became more complicated, so did the diagrams. This trend reaches its extreme in the numerological meanderings of Shao Yong 邵雍 (1011–77 CE), whose work was more admired than understood. Fortunately, the works of two of the important Song philosophers of the *Yijing*, Cheng Yi 程頤 (1033–1107 CE) and Zhu Xi, are now available in excellent translations (Adler 2020 and Harrington

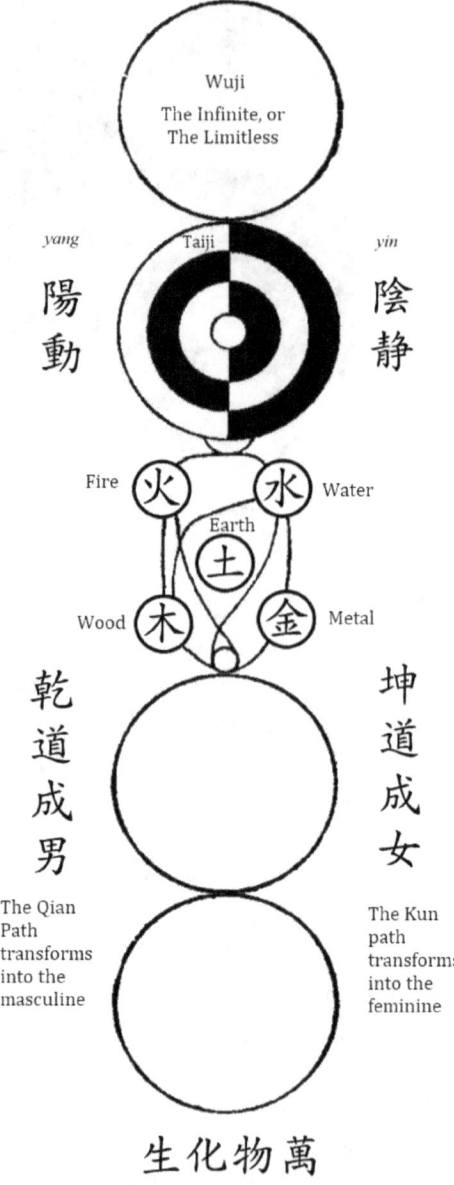

Figure 3. The Supreme Ultimate in one of its many variants. Public domain via Wikimedia Commons.

2019 respectively), making them accessible to those without knowledge of their difficult Chinese.

It is important to bear in mind that the complex theories of the Song philosophers were developed 2,000 years after the core text, so that they can cause confusion when one attempts to apply them to the reconstructed early text, although they are related to the *Ten Wings*, particularly the *Dazhuan* and *Shuogua*.

While the yin-yang and *bagua* diagrams discussed above present basic *Yijing* metaphysics in fairly direct form, those of the Song scholars were far more elaborate. The most common of these is the Supreme Ultimate 太極 *tai qi*, devised by Zhou Dunyi 周敦頤 (1017–73 CE), shown in Figure 3 in its simplest form.

This diagram adds the characters of the five phases 五行 *wu xing*, nearly as important in Chinese metaphysics as yin-yang. Sometimes erroneously translated as the "five elements," these are stages of processes, not constituents of matter. The systems of two and five components never fit together very well and their addition to the diagram creates only a visual connection.

Zhu Xi further developed alternating light and dark patterns into even more complicated images, but all were based on the underlying metaphysics of yin and yang with patterns of alternating black and white. This indicates that the two forces pervade all phenomena, but does not establish a conclusion that Chinese philosophy is dualistic, because contrary assertions are frequent, as in the Laozi, Chapter 42:

> The Dao engendered One; the One engendered two; the two engendered three; the three engendered the ten thousand things . . .

道生一，一生二，二生三，三生萬物

Yin-yang and *bagua* imagery spread to many cultures adjacent to China, often mixed with other religious imagery, as shown in a Tibetan diagram (Figure 4), which also incorporates the *Luo Shu* magic square, the trigrams, the animal zodiac, and Buddhist symbols. The original describes it as a "mystical tablet," an example of the exoticism associated with *Yijing* diagrams that constitutes much of their appeal.

An interesting question, which I have not seen addressed, is the extent to which the cross-cultural popularity of these images is independent of their metaphysical meanings. My impression is that they have primary visual appeal, as I suggest do the star of David, the cross, the crescent moon, as

Figure 4. A Tibetan assemblage of symbols both Chinese and Vajrayana Buddhist. From Waddell (1865) *Buddhism of Tibet or Lamaism*. Public domain via Wikimedia Commons.

well as the glyphs of astrology, thankas, Egyptian hieroglyphs, and many other images that appeals beyond their symbolism. Corporate logos function similarly.

These diagrams, with many variations, have appeared in many modern publications, in both Chinese and Western languages. A massive compilation in three folio volumes, based on a Qing dynasty compilation, is Zhu (1995).

It was on a diagram of Shao Yong that the hexagrams first arrived in the West (Figure 5). The missionary Joachim Bouvet, SJ, noticed the similarity of the two kinds of lines to the binary numbers system and sent a copy to Gottfried Leibniz, with whom he was acquainted. (Binary notation indicates all numbers as sequences of zero and one, analogous to the broken and solid line types of the *Book of Changes*.) It should be noted that while Leibniz was intrigued by the Chinese figures, he had discovered the binary number system before seeing them. The *Book of Changes* has inspired many things, but not the invention of computers.

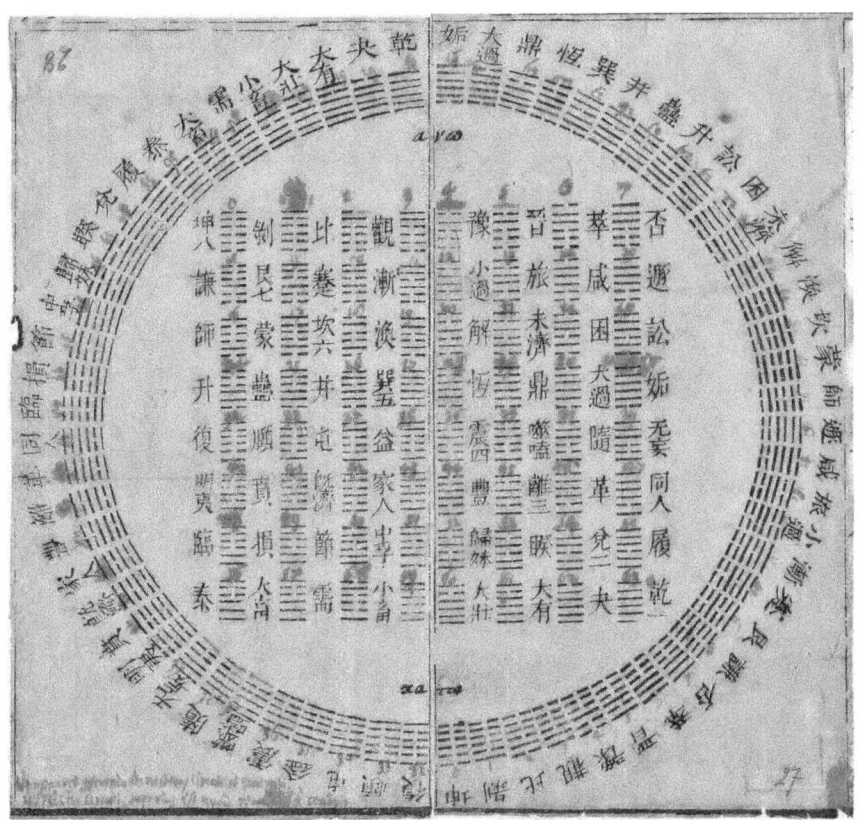

Figure 5. The diagram of Shao Yong that introduced hexagram arrays to the West. Public domain via Wikimedia Commons.

Part Four

Final Reflections

Not long ago, I had the privilege of discussing my own translation of the *Zhouyi* with Richard J. Smith, one of the leading Western scholars of the *Book of Changes*. He had kind words for my version, but also observed that there can never be a final or definitive translation of the *Book of Changes*. This is a sobering admonition for a translator who, whether admitting it or not, aspires to creating the ultimate, definitive translation. It is, however, absolutely correct. First, there is the problem of conveying the style of the original in language that will seem natural to contemporary readers. Then there are the technical issues, such as selecting between multiple possible meanings, all of which make sense to varying degrees. Parsing—deciding which words belong together to make a phrase—is laborious, but essential to make the ancient text readable. A reader must make similar choices but without facing the irrevocability that writing inflicts.

Philology, like economics, is a dismal science, not because of scarcity, but because the closer one reads, the more problematic a text becomes. Yet it is in these struggles that the subtleties of the work become apparent. One asks, if only subconsciously, "If I were living in the Western Zhou, how would I understand these texts that seem like word jumbles?"

Paradoxically, much of the important scholarship on the *Changes* over the last hundred years has been carried out by those intending to debunk it, beginning with the Chinese Doubting Antiquity Movement, followed by the Christian missionary-translators, Canon McClatchie, James Legge, and Richard Rutt. Equally paradoxically, it was another missionary, Richard Wilhelm, whose felicitous adaptation (not quite a translation) made it a world classic.

The *Book of Changes* has always promiscuously consented to multiple ways of reading and translating; otherwise, it could not have held meaning for so many people over so long. Depending on one's view, this is a bane or a blessing. For those who see ambiguity as something to be resolved, it is an intellectual challenge; their work is to restore the meanings as precisely as possible. For more casual readers who need not be inhibited by literal meanings, it can inspire flights of fancy.

Recent interest in the classic has tended in these two different directions. In popular culture it has been imagined to contain quantum mechanics, depth psychology, self-help, stress management, and other recent preoccupations. Sometimes these perspectives do provide insights, notably Carl Jung's Foreword to Wilhelm-Baynes, but more often these distract from the actual Chinese book. The comparisons to science do show that some modern ideas have ancient antecedents; however, these supposed similarities are metaphysical, not scientific. They belong to the history of philosophy, not that of science.

The other direction of Changeology, as two collaborating scholars have quaintly termed this field (Zhang and Fu 2008: 81 et passim.), has been to move back in time, applying recent discoveries in archaeology and historical linguistics to reconstructing the early meanings; it is these advances that have inspired the present work.

I can imagine a middle ground between the psychological and philological approaches—comparing ancient ways of human coping with those of the present. The *Zhouyi* was practical, advising how to act, or not act, in a problematic situation. Modern advice, at least for the well-off, tends to recommend attitude change, such as stress management or, lately, mindfulness. These methods, together with other practices such as psychotherapy and, sometimes, medication, assume that mental change is an important means of addressing human difficulties. Jung's approach was to make the *I Ching* a means of accessing the unconscious, and thus facilitating self-understanding. This has antecedents in Buddhism and the works of the Daoist philosophers Laozi and Zhuangzi; much earlier, Zhu Xi, like Jung, used the *Changes* as a method of self-examination, but moral rather than psychological. In its early phase, however, the *Zhouyi* was not particularly psychological, or even philosophical, but practical, at least in the context of Bronze Age life. And here is the ultimate fascination of the Chinese classic—that it has been able to accommodate 3,000 years of transformations in how humans understand themselves and their world. It is unlikely that the ancient sages actually existed, but if they did, they were onto something.

Appendix

Table 1. *Zhouyi* prognostic terms © Geoffrey Redmond

CHINESE	PINYIN	ENGLISH	SELECTED EXAMPLES:
FAVORABLE PROGNOSES			
利	li	beneficial, usually referring to an action to be taken	4.1
不利	bu li	not beneficial	9.0
无不利	wu bu li	nothing not beneficial	6.0
吉	ji	favorable, auspicious (lucky)	31.2
貞吉	zhen ji	divination auspicious	2.0
光	guang	honorable, bright	5.0
UNFAVORABLE PROGNOSES INCLUDING NEGATIONS			
貞厲	zhen li	divination harsh	35.4
凶	xiong	ominous	3.5
貞凶	zhen xiong	divination ominous	60.6
悔亡	hui wang	regret vanishes	
吉凶	ji xiong	auspicious or ominous (In *Dazhuan*, not *Zhouyi*)	
吝	lin	shame, remorse, regret	3.3
无咎	wu jiu	no blame, or blame averted (often refers to supernatural blame)	7.2
其咎	qi jiu	what blame?	9.1
吉无咎	ji wu jiu	auspicious for averting blame	7.2
悔	hui	regret	6.3, 18.3
无悔	wuhui	no regret	25.4

NOTE: Prognostic terms appear throughout the *Zhouyi*. It is not unusual for a favorable prognosis to be attached to what seems an unfavorable situation, and vice versa. This table is intended to provide quick reference; these prognostic terms are discussed in detail in Chapter 4. The translations of these terms are my own, but should be uncontroversial.

APPENDIX.

Glossary of Names and Specialized Terms

Most entries are in the order: English—*pinyin*—Chinese character. This is different from the main text, but I believe it will be most helpful to non-Chinese readers in finding entries. Those without standard English equivalents are listed alphabetically by italicized pinyin, followed by the Chinese character and then the English translation. For words not based on Chinese, no Chinese equivalents are provided.

People important in *Changes* commentarial history are included; living scholars are mentioned in the Acknowledgments. Many early Chinese dates are uncertain; I given usual dates but in the interest of brevity have avoided discussions of controversies.

Agonistic. Argumentative or aggressive in character. Originally referred to sports competition in ancient Greece. Early philosophical texts in Greece and China, such as those of Plato and Confucius, are agonistic in structure.

Axial Age, Axiality. A theory proposed by the German-Swiss psychiatrist and philosopher Karl Jaspers (1883–1969) that a fundamental transformation of consciousness occurred in several ancient societies in the mid-first millennium BCE. This was characterized by the beginnings of reflection on human nature and the cosmos, together with the rise of abstract philosophy, cosmology, and principle-based ethics. Perhaps most prominent is the sense of human life as unsatisfactory and in need of transformation. The *Zhouyi* is pre-axial while the Ruist *Yijing* is post-axial.

Confucian Classics *Wujing* 五經. Five very early works apocryphally attributed to Confucius; these formed the basis of literati education until the Song. They include the *Yijing*, as well as Classic of Poetry *Shijing* 詩經; the Book of Documents *Shujing* 書經 or *Shangshu* 尚書; the Book of Rites *Liji* 禮記 and the Spring and Autumn Annals *Chunqiu* 春秋. A sixth classic, that of music, *Yuejing* 樂經, was supposedly lost, although some scholars doubt that such a work ever existed.

Confucius. *Kongzi* 孔子 (561–479 BCE). The pre-eminent philosopher of China, still revered, if less often read. Apocryphally assigned authorship of several of the ancient classics including the *Ten Wings* of the *Yijing* and the *Spring and Autumn Annals*.

Core text. The four components that made up each section of the early *Zhouyi*: hexagram, tag (title), judgment text, and the six numbered line texts (seven in Hexagrams 1 and 2). In effect it is, *Book of Changes* without the later canonical *Ten Wings* commentaries.

Dazhuan 大傳 or ***Xi Ci*** 繫辭 (Wings 1 and 2). Usually translated as the *Great Treatise* or the *Great Commentary*, and sometimes as Commentary on the Appended Phrases. This is the most intellectually sophisticated section of the *Yijing*, containing much of its philosophical and cosmological content. It has been much quoted and highly influential throughout Chinese intellectual history.

Figurism. A theological doctrine mainly advocated by early Jesuit missionaries that explicated the Chinese classics as consistent with Christianity. The French-born Joachim Bouvet, SJ Bai Jin 白晋 or 白進 (1656–1730) lived in China for much of his life, participating in geographical and astronomical activities, but also devoting himself to study of the *Yijing*, attempting to find in it traces of the Christian revelation.

Fu Xi. 伏羲 The mythical first ruler of China credited with the many cultural essentials from hunting and fishing to music. According to a much quoted line in the *Dazhuan*, Fu Xi devised the trigrams based on observation of heaven and the natural world.

In an alternative version, he discovered them on the back of a tortoise.

Geng Day. 庚. The seventh day of the ten-day week of the Chinese calendar.

Guodian Chu Bamboo Strips. *Guodian Chujian* 郭店楚簡. A cache of bamboo manuscripts that has been much studied since being unearthed in 1993. Of late Warring States origin, these do not include the *Book of Changes*, but contain several references to it.

Hemerology. Divination to select favorable dates for important actions, still widely practiced in China. The earliest extant sources for ancient hemerology are manuscripts unearthed in Hubei from a tomb dated to 217 BCE.

Hexagram and **trigram**. These terms originated in the West to designate the six line and three line diagrams respectively. The Chinese term for these figures, *gua* 卦, refers to both trigrams and hexagrams. The English term "hexagram" is ambiguous because it can refer to the six-line figures, but also to the entire unit associated with a specific hexagram also comprising the include tag (title), judgment text, and the six numbered line texts. To disambiguate, I refer to the six line figures themselves with lower case h—"hexagram"—and to entire chapters with upper case H—"Hexagram".

Hexagram Text. Also referred to as Judgment Text, this is the first text portion associated with each hexagram. It precedes the line texts and is unnumbered. These seem to have a separate, later, origin than the line texts. Only in their Ruist reading can these be considered to summarize the meanings of the associated hexagrams and line texts.

I Ching. The title of the *Book of Changes* in the older Wades-Giles Romanization, commonly mispronounced by non-Chinese speakers as "eye-ching." It has been replaced by the more phonetic pinyin Romanization as *Yijing*.

Images and Numbers School. *Xiangshu* 象數. Interpretive school that based interpretation on the trigram and hexagram line positions with little consideration of the associated texts. This became dominant in the Han but continued to be influential even with the rise of the text oriented *Yili* 義理 school. During the Song dynasty the *Xiangshu* reached an extreme degree of elaboration with the work of Shao Yong 邵雍 (1011–77).

Jaspers, Karl. (1883–1969) German-Swiss psychiatrist and later philosopher who proposed the notion of the Axial Age.

Judgment Text. Synonymous with Hexagram Text.

Junzi. 君子 This originally meant prince. Wilhelm-Baynes translated this phrase as "superior man," although the Chinese has no reference to gender. In its traditional use it would nearly always have referred to males, but nothing in the actual texts precludes reading it as gender-neutral. Originally a title of rank, under Ruist influence it became a term for a virtuous person. Wilhelm-Baynes render this as "superior man," but is more appropriately translated as "upright person," which better conveys its moral connotation and avoids the snobbish implication.

Line Texts. *Yao* 爻. This is the usual term for the six (seven in Hexagrams 1 and 2) numbered lines of text following the judgment text. These are highly paratactic and vary in coherence.

Literati. *Wenren* 文人. The scholar class educated in the classics, often as a qualification for office. While the *Yijing* was important in their education, they followed the received meanings, not the early ones that had been largely forgotten by the time literary education became widespread.

Luo Shu. 洛書. A magic square of nine elements in which all rows add up to 15. In some versions this is what Fu Xi saw on a turtle shell that inspired his creation of the trigrams. This is part of later mythology; no reference to it appears in the *Zhouyi*.

Lunyu. 論語 The more accurate Romanization of the title of the **Analects.** Although not one of the five classics, it consists of teachings attributed to Confucius, usually in the format of conversations with his followers. While it was almost certainly compiled centuries after the life of the Master, it is generally thought to accurately represent his thought.

Mawangdui. (MWD) 馬王堆 lit. the "Horse King Mound." The site of important archaeological discoveries in the early 1970s. This included a cache of important manuscripts from the Western Han, including an early *Changes* manuscript written on silk. The MWD version differs from the received version in the ordering of the Hexagrams and many of the tags; there are many textual variants, but only a few are substantive. Included in the manuscript are supplementary texts with some resemblance to the *Ten Wings*.

Neo-Confucianism. The usual, but misleading, translation of *Dao Xue* 道學 lit. Study of the Way, a synthesis of Ruism with elements from Daoism and Buddhism. Zhou Dunyi 周敦頤, invented the diagram referred to as the Supreme Ultimate, but Zhu Xi was the most influential philosopher of this school.

Omens. These are chance happenings interpreted as having prognostic significance. Most are quite ordinary events, such as bird calls or animal sightings, but could evoke fear when taken to be unfavorable. When omens apply to the entire society, they can also be referred to in English as signs. Much of the text *Book of Changes* consists of omens.

Oracle bone inscriptions. (OBI) *Jiaguwen* 甲骨文. The earliest known Chinese writings; most are from the Shang, but a few date from the early Zhou. The inscriptions were engraved and then brushed on tortoise plastrons or ox scapulae; rarely other animal bones were used. Unlike the *Zhouyi* texts, some OBI contain names of diviners and annotations as to whether the prognostication turned out to be correct.

Parataxis. Placement of clauses adjacent to each other without connectives, subordination, or narrative relationship. It is common in ancient texts and has been a conscious literary mannerism in modern ones.

Polysemy. The property of a word, or of a phrase or image, to have multiple meanings, often unrelated. Homophones, in contrast, are different words that have the same sound. Both are common in Chinese.

Practitioners and Scholars. These terms refer to two contrasting approaches to reading and using the *Book of Changes*. Practitioners use it in their lives as a source of practical guidance and spiritual wisdom. This often involves use of simple rituals such as coin tosses to select the hexagrams that are taken to apply to inquiry. Many practitioners, although not all, accept the traditional accounts of the book's origin, such as discovery of the trigrams by Fu Xi, authorship of the texts by King Wen and Zhou Gong, and of the *Ten Wings* by Confucius. Scholars are primarily interested in the *Changes* as an historical document and study its textual history critically rather than mythologically. Some scholars, including myself, use it for divination in order to understand its actual use.

Ruism. 儒家 The Chinese word for the cultural elements usually (mis-)translated as "Confucianism," a word that does not exist in Chinese. Using the same root are: **Ruists** 儒家 *Rujia* Confucians; **Ruist (or Confucian) Philosophy** *Rujia Sixiang* 儒家思想. Referring, for example, to "Confucian" interpretations of the *Yijing*, as much of what is attributed to the classic has no precedent in the Master's supposed works, or any other source that can be reliably attributed to him. For this reason I have referred to this cluster of ideas as *Ruism*.

Shanghai Museum bamboo manuscript. (*c.* 300 BCE) The earliest, but unfortunately unprovenanced, version of the *Changes*. It includes the hexagrams and for the most part, resembles the received version.

Shangshu. 尚書 *Book of Documents*, a collection of speeches by notable ancient figures that was considered one of the five *Confucian Classics*.

Spring and Autumn Annals. Chunqiu 春秋 One of the five so-called Confucian classics, of particular interest as it was considered to contain Confucius' actual views of statecraft.

Song Neo-Confucian Scholars of the *Yijing*. In the Song so-called Neo-Confucianism (Chinese *Lixue* 理學 School of Principle) added to the complexity of Ruist thought by incorporating ideas derived from Daoism and Buddhism, which they nevertheless opposed. Several Song philosophers influential in the development of this school also made important contributions to study of the *Yijing*, *Yi Xue*.

Cheng Yi. 程頤 (1033–1107 CE) Cheng Yi simplified the metaphysics of the *Xiangshu* school by emphasizing yin-yang relationships.

Shao Yong. 邵雍 (1011–77 CE). Shao Yong developed complex numerological systems for interpreting the *Yijing*.

Zhu Xi. 朱熹 (1130–1200 CE). The most influential "Neo-Confucian," Zhu Xi made extensive use of the *Yijing* for his personal ethical development. In this sense his approach foreshadowed the approach of Carl G. Jung who regarded the Chinese classic as a means for psychological self-understanding.

Ten Wings. *Shi Yi* 十翼. Canonical commentaries included in the received *Yijing*, but composed centuries later than the core text, probably late Warring States or early Han. Despite their apocryphal attribution to Confucius, they are stylistically diverse. Although traditionally considered to explicate the core text, they contain much material of much later origin and hence are not helpful in understanding the early meanings.

Ten Wings **Contents.** While nominally consisting of ten units, three (1 and 2; 3 and 4; 5 and 6) are seemingly arbitrarily divisions of the same text into two sections.

    Wings 1 and 2. Commentaries on the Judgment (Hexagram) Texts. *Tuanzhuan* 彖傳 has brief quotations from each Hexagram, but places emphasis the meanings of the trigram positions.

    Wings 3 and 4. 象傳 *Xiangzhuan*. Both sections combine *Daxiang* 大象 Greater Images and *Xiaoxiang* 小象 Lesser Images. *Daxiang* indicates the positions of the constituent trigrams and their implication for princes, while *Xiaoxiang* provides brief glosses on each line text, with some references to line types and positions.

    Wings 5 and 6. The Great Commentary (or Treatise) *Dazhuan* 大傳, also referred to as the Commentary on the Appended Phrases 繫辭傳 *Xi Ci Zhuan*.

    Wing 7. Commentary on the Words 文言傳 *Wenyan Zhuan*. A collection of fragments commenting on Hexagrams 1 Heaven *Qian*, 乾 and 2 Earth *Kun* 坤.

    Wing 8. Explanation of the Trigrams *Shuogua Zhuan* 說卦傳. The second most influential Wing after the *Dazhuan*, which its first section somewhat resembles. The remainder itemizes trigram correlations.

    Wing 9. Sequence of the Hexagrams *Xugua Zhuan* 序卦傳. Brief statements on 61 of the 64 hexagrams, supposedly explaining their ordering.

    Wing 10. Assorted or Miscellaneous Hexagrams *Zagua Zhuan* 雜卦傳. Consists of short phrases purported to summarize the meanings of 56 of the Hexagrams. Although suitable for divination, these otherwise add little to understanding of the texts.

Wang Bi. 王弼 (226–49) A brilliant scholar of the Three Kingdoms period who tragically died at the age of 23 during an epidemic, Wang Bi wrote a commentary that was influential in restoring use of the texts in *Yijing* interpretation. Associated with the *Yili* school, he also continued to use line positions.

Warring States. *Zhanguo* 戰國 (475–221 BCE) The second phase of the Eastern Zhou Dynasty *Dongzhou* 東周, during which the major schools of philosophy developed. Sometimes compared to the Athens of Socrates, Plato, and Aristotle, although the philosophies are quite different.

Western Zhou Dynasty. *Xi Zhou* 西周 (1046–771 BCE) (estimates of exact dates vary slightly). The era of the *Zhouyi*'s compilation, although it incorporates earlier material.

Wilhelm-Baynes. Common abbreviation for the *I Ching* translation by Richard Wilhelm and Cary F. Baynes with the inflential Foreward by Carl G. Jung..

Wu Ding. 武丁 The *Yin* 殷 (later Shang) king under whose his reign the first extant OBI were produced. Dating of his reign has been the subject of a complex controversy. The tomb of his second (of many) wives, 婦好 Fu Hao, was discovered intact at the former Yin capital near Anyang 安陽 . She is mentioned in the OBI and was a successful general.

Yao 爻. Hexagram line.

Yarrow. (Milfoil) *Shi* 筮. Divination by randomly sorting yarrow sticks to select a hexagram.

Yijing. 易經 When used specifically, this refers to the core text together with the *Ten Wings*.

Yili. 義理 The school of *Changes* interpretation based mainly on the texts, although not excluding consideration of line patterns. It is particularly associated with Wang Bi (226–249).

Yin-Yang. 陰陽. The best known concept of Chinese metaphysics, according to which phenomena are explained as due to the interaction of two basic forces. These developed many correlations besides female and male, but in earliest usage referred to bright and shady. Yin appears only once in the *Zhouyi*, in line 61.2, referring to a shady riverbank; yang does not appear at all.

Zhou Dynasty Founding and *Yijing* Mythology. The *Zhouyi*, lit. *Zhou Changes*, has been associated with the Zhou conquest of Shang in 1046 BCE, traditionally held to have restored virtuous government. Several of the conquering Zhou family were credited with creation of the final form of the classic. The persons are historical but their roles in creating the classic are almost certainly mythical:

Wen Wang. 文王 lit. Literary King. According to tradition he was imprisoned by the evil last king of Shang, Zhou Wang 紂王, for three years. During his enforced leisure, he combined the trigrams into hexagrams, simplifying interpretation for non-sages. The title of king was an honorific conferred posthumously as it was his son, King Wu, who conquered the Shang to establish the Zhou.

Wu Wang. 武王 lit. Martial king. Conquered the Shang to become the first ruler of the Western Zhou dynasty.

Zhou Gong. 周公. Duke of Zhou. The brother of Wen Wang and supposed author of the line texts. A culture hero, he was considered a paragon of virtue because he served as regent for Wu Wang's younger brother without seizing power, although the actual historical record is less clear about this. In a much-quoted passage of the *Lunyu*, Confucius laments no longer dreaming of the Duke of Zhou.

Zhouyi. 周易 or *Changes of the Zhou* refers to the text as it existed in the early Western Zhou dynasty. This has been reconstructed based on archaeological discoveries and advances in historical linguistics. It contains only the hexagrams and the core texts. Especially in China, *Zhouyi* is often an alternate term for the *Yijing*.

Zhouyi Hexagram Chart In Received Order

(Based on Wikipedia with corrections and hexagram tags replaced by my translations. The tags have been translated in many ways; rationales for my translations are explained in the commentaries of my 2017 translation.)

1 乾 Qian Heaven	2 坤 Kun Earth	3 屯 Tun Gathering	4 蒙 Meng Neophytes
9 小畜 Xiao Chu Small Livestock	10 履 Lu Treading	11 泰 Tai Great	12 否 Fou (Pi) Bad
17 隨 Sui Pursuing	18 蠱 Gu Disease from sex	19 臨 Lin Wailing	20 觀 Guan Observing
25 無妄 Wu Wang Unexpected	26 大畜 Da Xu Large Livestock	27 頤 Yi Lower Jaw	28 大過 Da Guo Big Mistake
33 遯 Dun Piglet	34 大壯 Da Zhuang Great Strength	35 晉 Jin Advance	36 明夷 Ming Yi Calling Pheasant
41 損 Sun Decrease	42 益 Yi Advantage	43 夬 Guai Determination	44 姤 Gou Meeting
49 革 Ge Tanning Leather	50 鼎 Ding Bronze Cauldron	51 震 Zhen Thunder	52 艮 Gen Splitting
57 巽 Xun Kneeling	58 兌 Dui Exchange	59 渙 Huan Spurting	60 節 Jie Segment of Time

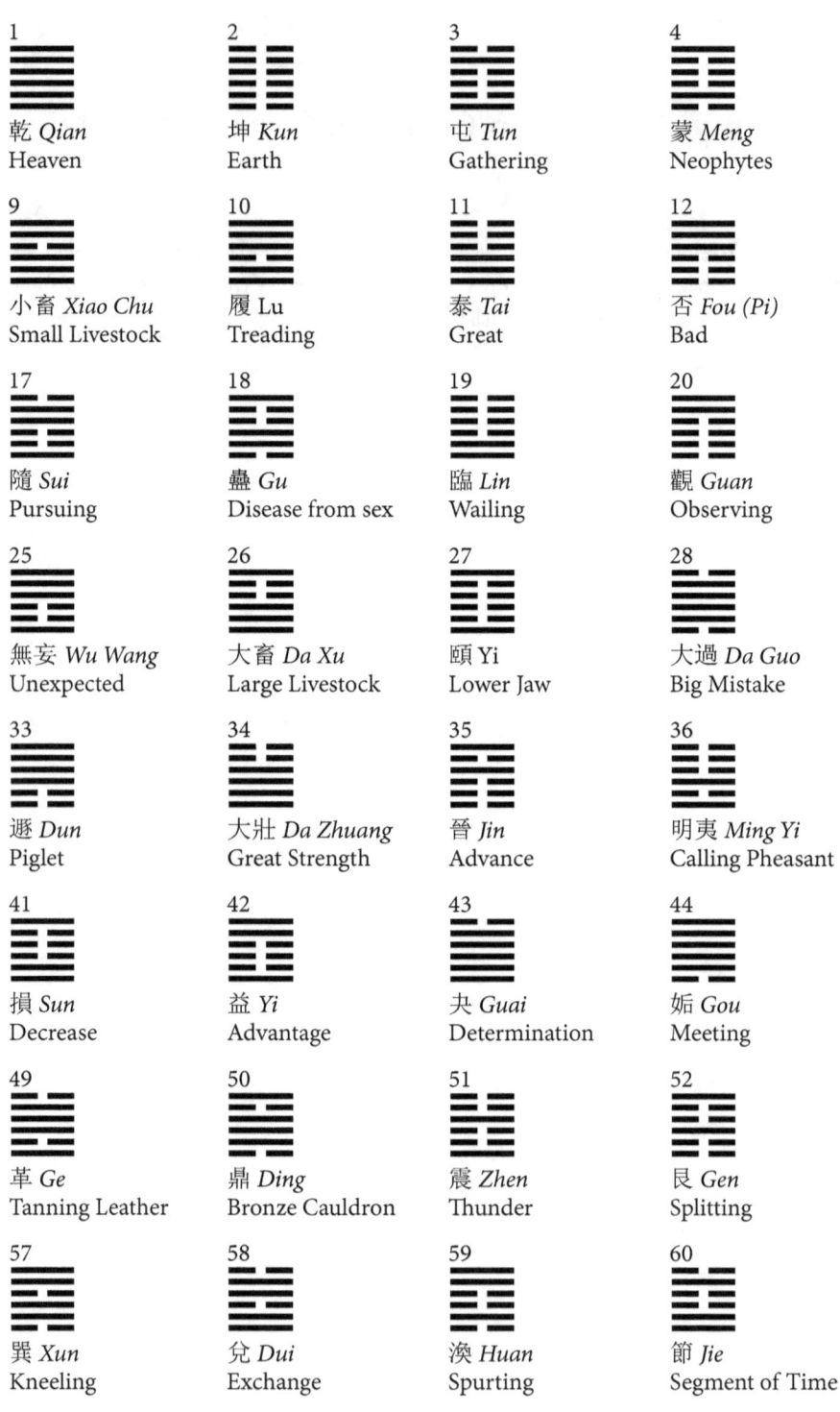

5 需 Xu Waiting	6 訟 Song Dispute	7 師 Shi Troops	8 比 Bi Joining
13 同人 Tong Ren Assembling	14 大有 Da You Abundance	15 謙 Qian Humble	16 豫 Yu Preparation
21 噬 Shi Ki Biting and Chewing	22 賁 Bi Adornment	23 剝 Bo Flaying	24 復 Fu Return
29 習坎 Xi Kan Numerous Pitfalls	30 離 Li Oriole	31 咸 Xian Sensation	32 恆 Heng Enduring
37 家人 Jia Ren Family Members	38 睽 Kui Opposition	39 蹇 Jian Stumbling	40 解 Xie Release
45 萃 Cui Assembling	46 升 Sheng Going Up	47 困 Kun Obstruction	48 井 Jing The Well
53 漸 Jian Gradual Approach	54 歸妹 Gui Mei Marrying Maiden	55 豐 Feng Fullness	56 旅 Lu Traveler
61 中孚 Zhong Fu Captives Within	62 小過 Xiao Guo Small Mistake	63 既濟 Ji Ji Already Crossed River	64 未濟 Wei Ji River Not Yet Crossed

Hexagram Finder

	☰	☳	☵	☶	☷	☴	☲	☱
☰	1	34	5	26	11	9	14	43
☳	25	51	3	27	24	42	21	17
☵	6	40	29	4	7	59	64	47
☶	33	62	39	52	15	53	56	31
☷	12	16	8	23	2	20	35	45
☴	44	32	48	18	46	57	50	28
☲	13	55	63	22	36	37	30	49
☱	10	54	60	41	19	61	38	58

Notes

Introduction

1 The Chinese word translated as "hexagram" is 卦 *gua*, which refers to both hexagrams and trigrams. Unfortunately, in English usage the word hexagram is ambiguous because it can refer to both the six-line figure and to the entire chapter associated with it, which also includes the tag (title), the judgment text, and the six- or seven-line texts. In an effort to disambiguate, I use lower case "hexagram" to refer to the figure and "Hexagram" to refer to the entire chapter.
2 For those interested in how divination might work, I have provided a detailed discussion in a previous publication; see Redmond and Hon 2014: 19–36.
3 With the renewed popularity of the *Yijing*, innovative selection procedures continue to appear. These include eight-sided dice with a trigram on each facet, choosing colored beads with eyes closed, polarity of magnets, and serial subtraction of the number 6 from a larger randomly chosen number, such as license plates, bank balances, or airline flight numbers.

1 Engaging with the Archaic Text

1 The *Lunyu* has also been rearranged in the supposed "original" order. This can be useful for providing a fresh look at this renowned classic, but deprives readers of the experience of the text as it was throughout China's intellectual history. See E. Bruce Brooks and A. Taeko Brooks 1998, also Qian Ning transl. Tony Blishen 2011.
2 These comments refer to historical development and are not formulated as a comparison of literate and non-literate societies in the modern world.
3 Several systems have been used to select the relevant line within the hexagram. Usually this is an "old" or changing line, which also indicates a second Hexagram. If there are no changing lines, the judgment line applies. Many other systems have been used, all based on selecting elements of sets of six with two possible values. Many commentators, beginning with Gottfried Leibniz, have noted that this uses numerical patterns of the binary system; this later became the basis of digital computing.
4 For detailed consideration of these arguments see Bellah and Joas 2012.

5 By minimal or descriptive axiality I mean setting aside likely unanswerable questions such as why these intellectual changes happened at particular times and particular places, nor do I imply that its forms were invariant. As I shall explain, axiality is useful for categorizing the content of early texts, but by itself is not a comprehensive account of intellectual history.
6 A comprehensive discussion of the *Chunqiu* is that of Nylan (2001: 253–306). Confucius clearly played an important role in the beginnings of ethical thought in China, although his exact contribution is unclear; he was unquestionably influential, but also served as a convenient figure to personify Chinese moral culture.
7 It is plausible, although not certain, that in the *Zhouyi* 德 *de* could mean virtue as well as power. Shaughnessy's transliteration of the Shanghai Museum strip has the same character for virtue, although the preceding two characters of the phrase are different (2014: 76). The character 德 *de* appears also in 9.6, where it seems to refer to power, and 32.5, where it could mean either power or virtue in context.

2 Divination

1 The literature on divination by both practitioners and scholars is vast. Some recent works that can give an idea of the range of beliefs and practices in both the ancient and modern worlds are Annus 2010; Baumann 2008; Berglund 1990; Cicero trans. Falconer 1923; Johnston 2008; Kalinowski 2003; and Koch. 2010.
2 The misogynistic side of divination is evident in the archetype of the eccentric old woman with arcane knowledge, as exemplified by T. S. Eliot's Tarot card diviner in *The Wasteland*, Madame Sosostris. Here, as often, the archetype of the diviner involves sexual ambiguity, as Eliot took the name from a transvestite character in Aldous Huxley's novel *Chrome Yellow*.
3 A sense of the extreme intricacy of Chinese metaphysics is quickly apparent upon perusing Joey Yap's 1,029-page *The Chinese Metaphysics Compendium* or the historically organized *Zhouyi Tushhuo Zhonghui*, spanning 2,301 pages in three volumes. It is hard to see anything more than historical interest in these today, but they demonstrate the immense effort and imagination applied to this sort of speculation. Joseph Needham suggested that one reason science in China did not develop as it did in the West is that the yin-yang and *wu xing* metaphysics seemed to provide a complete account of phenomena. Yin and yang still have appeal for describing subjective experience, although they supplement science rather than competing with it.
4 An *I Ching* reader might refer to solid and broken lines, concluding that "the Oracle tells us that travel is inauspicious"; a mother might say, "I love you and want the best for you"; a therapist could comment, "What I hear you saying is . . ."

5   For those with more serious interest in the *Book of Changes* there is an excellent website with diverse materials and perspectives: http://www.biroco.com/*Yijing*/links.htm
6   To be clear, I have little sympathy for such "psychic" or alternative practices when they promote such things as herbs or talismans to cure cancer, or astrology to decide how to invest one's life savings. The more important the inquiry, the more wary one needs to be about divination.
7   Murders seemingly motivated by bizarre belief systems were part of the dark side of the 1960s: the mass suicide at Jonestown, Charles Manson's celebrity murders, and the self-named Son of Sam caused widespread shock and fear; Roman Polanski's 1968 film *Rosemary's Baby* turned psychotic violence into entertainment.

4   Divinatory Prognostic Terms

1   McLuhan, although an intellectual exhibitionist, was a serious scholar of evolution of human communication. Here he alludes, I think, to early cultures for whom causality was entirely mysterious and thus nothing, even rain, could be reliably foreseen.
2   Rutt was an Episcopal missionary, then a Bishop in the Church of England, then a Roman Catholic priest. He was completely transparent about his religious convictions, and criticized the *Zhouyi* from this framework (Redmond 2017: xxxiii f).
3   When the *I Ching* rose to bestsellerdom in the 1960s counterculture, the frequency of "no blame" seemed amusing to many readers and was mentioned ironically in *The Illuminatus! Trilogy*, a once popular satirical novel by Robert Shea and Robert Anton Wilson: "World War III is probably imminent . . . with the sickness vibrations of Hexagram 23 [PO Splitting Apart or Flaying; a hexagram destruction or killing] . . . as probable as thermonuclear overkill. No blame. 'My ass, no blame,' Hagbard raged" (1975: 24). As satire this is rather weak; mention of the *I Ching* seems to have been to show readers that the author is hip.
4   Lynn's translation is longer, but otherwise nearly identical (50).

5   The Grammar of the *Zhouyi*

1   For a brief but informative explanation of parataxis from the point of view of a teacher of creative writing, see Constance Hale 2013.
2   For more detailed discussion of later moralistic meanings of this phrase, see Bernardo 2012: 267.
3   For a detailed discussion of this important character in the *Changes*, see Bernardo 2012: 150, 272.

4. Both Freudian and Jungian psychotherapy made use of dream images, and so can be considered oneiromancy in scientific guise, showing how, despite efforts to debunk it, divination finds its way back into human consciousness.
5. We do not know when the idea of changing lines developed; it is present in the *Zuozhuan*, suggesting that it may have originated in the Spring and Autumn, but this is not conclusive.
6. The positive conception of change in the *Yijing* contrasts with *aniccca*, the concept of impermanence in Buddhism, which did not arrive into China until much later.
7. Rutt credits the eminent Chinese expert Li Jinchi 李鏡池 (1902–75) as the source of his first three categories.
8. The judgment texts containing this phrase in full or partial form are 1.0, 3.0, 4.017.0, 19.0. 25.0, 26.0, 36.0, 31.0, 32.0, 33.0, 34.0, 45.0, 49.0, 53.0, 62.0, 63.0, 64.0. The line texts in which it appears are 36.5 and 41.2.

6 Rhetoric and Forms of Expression

1. Shang Shu 堯典 *Canon of Yao*. https://ctext.org/shang-shu/yu-shu. Accessed March 11, 2022.
2. I have quoted the *Shangshu* only as an example of formal rhetoric. The textual history of the *Shangshu* is exceedingly complex, making it of limited use in determining the historical development of Chinese rhetoric.

7 The Nature of Omens

1. Wikipedia 2023, "Terror Management Theory." https://en.wikipedia.org/wiki/Terror_management_theory#Terror_management_health_model. Accessed January 5, 2023.
2. In the modern world pre-scientific ideas of protection are partially replaced by scientific medicine, but also by the wellness movement that has been endlessly inventive in proposing remedies for the human condition.
3. A search on Etsy turned up 85,645 hits for this word. The items listed as useful for manifestation include herb teas, essential oils, jewelry, remote psychic healing, and casting of spells—all available with a few clicks.

9 Joys and Hazards of Daily Life

1. Estimates of average life expectancy in early China range from mid-twenties to thirties, with women's being shorter due to deaths in childbirth, and perhaps less able

to obtain food and other necessary resources. Only about half of live-born children survived to adulthood.
2   The most useful translation is Unschuld 2003.
3   Fu Hao 婦好 d. 1200 BCE, wife of Wu Ding 婦好, was buried with 755 jade objects and nearly 500 bone hairpins.

10 Women's Lives

1   Most famous, or notorious, were Empress Wu Zetian 武則天 (624–705 CE) of the Tang and the Qing so-called "Empress Dowager" 慈禧太后 Cixi Taihou (1835–1908), whose reign was followed by the last emperor, Pu Yi 溥儀 (1906–67).
2   That this rule has recently lapsed may be because the one-child policy left many families with only daughters to attend to ancestors. When my wife and I visited her ancestral village in Hainan some years ago, firecrackers were set off to announce her arrival to the ancestors, an honor previously reserved for male progeny.
3   The two components mean woman and broom respectively, consistent with assignment of domestic tasks to women.
4   In the instances I know of in Hong Kong, each wife maintained a separate household with her own children; the half-siblings had little contact with each other.

11 Emotions and the Body

1   Rutt based "oriole" on a conjecture of Gao Heng. Several other possibilities have been suggested; the MWD manuscript has a different character translated by Shaughnessy as "net." See Redmond 2017: 188; Rutt 322f; Shaughnessy 1997: 312f. Unfortunately, there is no definitive evidence for any of these putative renderings. However, since most omens are simply a pretext for the prognostication, the remainder of the line text can usually be understood by itself.
2   Many other bodily features parts have been used for divination in China and other cultures, including shape of the breasts and examination of feces. In these cases divination can be a pretext for what would otherwise be unacceptable.
3   General recognition that those with disabilities merit special consideration is an innovation of the twentieth century. As late as the nineteenth century in England, tricking blind people into bumping into walls was considered funny. The first comprehensive legal protection, the Americans with Disability Act, become law only in 1990.

12 Hierarchy

1. Enfeoffment is an English term for conferring noble rank with an associated grant of land and the workers bound to it. It could placate powerful rivals to the throne, but also increase their military resources.

13 Travel and Its Hazards

1. Such a poster adorns the front door of our home, and so far our coming and going has been mostly, if not entirely, without difficulty.

14 Human Sacrifice

1. For a cross-cultural consideration of this regrettable aspect of early humanity, see Bremmer 2007.
2. Archaeological evidence from Central America indicates three methods of removing the heart: from below the diaphragm, between the ribs, or by splitting the sternum. The first method, and possibly the second, would not leave evidence in the form of skeletal injury (Tiesler and Olivier 2020). Thus the frequency of heart extraction in Chinese human sacrifice is uncertain.
3. That public executions had entertainment value is illustrated by the last one to take place in America, which was in 1936; it attracted 20,000 spectators. Despite this, public sensibility was changing and disgust at the spectacle led to cessation of the practice, which was abolished in France at about the same time.
4. "Wailing" or "keening" are the suggestions of Kunst (276f) and Rutt (314). The latter is a paraphrase, because "keening" refers specifically to traditional Gaelic funereal chanting.
5. Hexagram 19 in the received version, but 36 in MWD.
6. For further discussion of manuscript variants in excavated texts, see Shaughnessy 2014: 92 et passim.
7. This had particular appeal in the 1960s, at the height of the *I Ching*'s Western popularity, because many youth had fantasies of being revolutionaries, at least to the extent of wearing Che Guevara T-shirts.
8. Some extend the definition of human sacrifice to include other forms of killing under the pretext of benefiting society, such as capital punishment and "ethnic cleansing."

15 Animals in Early China

1. Full disclosure: I have been vegetarian for more than 30 years, for both religious and humanitarian reasons. Yet for most of humanity this has not been an available choice. In conversations I have had with horse and cattle breeders, they show some affection for their animals, but do not express regret over their ultimate fate. The cruel confinement of animals in modern factory farming shows that maltreatment continues.
2. In the MWD version these Hexagrams have the same tag characters, but are not consecutive, being numbers 22 and 54 respectively. The fox image is essentially the same in both versions. Shaughnessy's translation of the tag is similar to Wilhelm-Baynes as "Already completed," and "Not yet completed." These tags can refer to crossing the river by the fox, or, less directly, by soldiers, or more abstractly, to any passage of life.
3. Useful sources on the *Xiangshu* school include Nielsen 2003 and Liu Dajun 2019.
4. Richard Dawkins introduced the concept of "memes" in his 1976 book, *The Selfish Gene*. In analogy to genes, memes are units of information with survival value in a culture, although not necessarily true. The term has come to be used in other senses as well, such as "meme stocks."
5. The "leathery" appearance of the facial skin is biochemically entirely different from the tanning of an animal skin.
6. Most venoms are proteins; these are destroyed in the stomach, making them non-toxic if ingested. The actual extent of attempted *gu* poisoning is uncertain. Deaths from natural causes could easily be attributed to poisoning.
7. https://ctext.org/text.pl?node=2826&if=en&show=meta

Bibliography

Adler, Joseph A. transl. 2002. *Introduction to the Study of the Classic of Change (I-hseuh ch'I-meng)*. Provo, UT: Global Scholarly Publications.
Adler, Joseph A. transl. 2020. Zhu Xi. *The Original Meaning of the Yijing: Commentary on the Scripture of Change*. New York: Columbia University Press.
Adler, Joseph A. 2022. *The Yijing: A Guide*. Oxford: Oxford University Press.
Anthony, Carol K. and Hanna Moog. 2002. *I Ching: The Oracle of the Cosmic Way*. Stow, MA: Ichingbooks.
Argüelles, José. 1984 *Earth Ascending: An Illustrated Text on the Law Governing Whole Systems*. Boulder, CO: Shambala.
Ayton, Peter, Anne J. Hunt and George Wright. 1989. "Psychological Conceptions of Randomness." *Journal of Behavioral Decision Making*, 221–38.
Barrett, T. H. 2007. "Human Sacrifice and Self-Sacrifice in China: A Century of Revelations." In *The Strange World of Human Sacrifice*, ed. Jan N. Bremmer, pp. 237–57. Leuven-Paris-Dudley: Peeters.
Bauer, Wolfgang. 1979. "Chinese Glyphomancy (ch'ai-tzu) and Its Use in Present-day Taiwan." In Sarah Allan and Alvin P. Cohen, eds. *Legend, Lore, and Religion in China: Essays in Honor of Wolfram Eberhard on His Seventieth Birthday*, pp. 71–96. San Francisco: Chinese Materials Center.
Baxter, William H. and Laurent Sagart. 2014. *Old Chinese: A New Reconstruction*. Oxford and New York: Oxford University Press.
Bellah, Robert N. and Hans Joas. 2012. *The Axial Age and Its Consequences*. Cambridge, MA: Belknap Harvard.
Bernardo, Daniel. 2012. *YiJing (I Ching): Chinese/English Dictionary with Concordance and Translation*. United States: Self-published.
Birdwhistell, Anne D. 1989. *Transition to Neo-Confucianism: Shao Yung on Knowledge and Symbols of Reality*. Stanford, CA: Stanford University Press, 1989.
Birrell, Anne, transl. 1999. *The Classic of Rivers and Seas*. London and New York: Penguin Books.
Boltz, William G. 2005. "The Composite Nature of Early Chinese Texts." In Martin Kern, ed.
Bremmer, Jan N., ed. *The Strange World of Human Sacrifice* Leuven-Paris-Dudley: Peeters, 2007.
Brooks, E. Bruce and A. Taeko Brooks. 1998. *The Original Analects: Sayings Confucius and His Successors. A New Translation and Commentary*. New York: Columbia University Press.

Callender, Craig. 2013. *The Oxford Handbook of Philosophy of Time*. Oxford and New York: Oxford University Press.

Capra, Fritjof. 4th edition 1999. First published 1975. *The Tao of Physics: An Exploration of the Parallels Between Modern Physics and Eastern Mysticism*. Fourth Updated Edition. (35th Anniversary). Boston, MA: Shambhala.

Cassirer, Ernst. 1923. Transl. 2021 Steve G. Lofts. *The Philosophy of Symbolic Forms*, Vol. 1. London and New York: Routledge.

Cerquiglini, Bernard. 1999. *In Praise of the Variant: A Critical History of Philology* Baltimore, MD: Johns Hopkins University Press (Parallax: Re-visions of Culture and Society).

Cheng, Kat Hung Dennis. 2023. "The Philosophy of Change and the Metaphor of Body: From the *I Ching* (The Classic of Changes) to Wenxin diaolong (Carving the Dragon with a Literary Heart)." *Literature and Theology* 37(2). Oxford: Oxford University Press.

Cook, Constance. 1998. "Myth and Fragments of a Qin *Yi* Text: A Research Note and Translation." *Journal of Chinese Religions* 26: 135–43.

Cook, Constance. 2006. *Death in Ancient China: The Tale of One Man's Journey*. Leiden: Brill.

Cook, Constance. 2013. "The Pre-Han Period." In T. J. Hinrichs and Linda A. Barnes, eds, *Chinese Medicine and Healing*. Cambridge, MA and London: Belknap Press of Harvard University Press.

Cook, Constance and Zhao Lu. 2017. *Stalk Divination: A Newly Discovered Alternative to the I Ching*. New York and Oxford: Oxford University Press.

Cook, Richard Sterling. 2004–6. *Classical Chinese Combinatorics: Derivation of the* Yijing *Hexagram Sequence*. Berkeley, CA: Sino-Tibetan Etymological Dictionary and Thesaurus Project Monograph 5.

Cook, Scott. 2012. *The Bamboo Texts of* Guodian: *A Study and Complete Translation*. Vols I and II. Ithaca, NY: East Asia Program, Cornell University.

Dick, Philip K. 1962. *The Man in the High Castle*. Various editions

Dickens, Charles. 1954. *Hard Times*, Book 1, Chapter 8. Various editions.

Richard Dawkins, 1976. *The Selfish Gene*. Oxford: Oxford University Press.

Eliot, T. S. "Hamlet and His Problems." *The T. S. Eliot Collection: Collected Poems and Essays*. Kindle ed. Bybliotech 2015 www.2492f

Elman, Benjamin A. 2001. *From Philosophy to Philology: Intellectual and Social Aspects of Change in Late Imperial China*, Second edition. Los Angeles, CA: UCLA Asian Pacific Monograph Series.

Eno, Robert. 2009. "Shang State Religion and the Pantheon of the Oracle Texts." in *Early Chinese Religion. Part One: Shang through Han*. Vol. I, pp. 41–102. Leiden: Brill.

Feng, H. Y. and J. K. Shryock. 1935. "The Black Magic in China Known as Ku". *Journal of the American Oriental Society* 553: 1–30.

Farnsworth, Ward. 2010. *Farnsworth's Classical English Rhetoric*. Boston, MA: Godine.

Field, Stephen L. 2008. *Ancient Chinese Divination*. Honolulu: University of Hawaii Press.

Field, Stephen L. 2015. *The Duke of Zhou Changes: A Study and Annotated Translation of the Zhouyi* 周易. Wiesbaden: Harrassowitz Verlag.

Fingarette, Herbert. 1998. *Confucius: The Secular as Sacred*. Long Grove, IL: Waveland Press.

Fiskejö, Magnus, ed. 2004. "Reconsidering the Correlative Cosmology of Early China." *Bulletin of The Museum of Far Eastern Antiquities*, Stockholm.

FitzGerald, Frances. 1972. *Fire in the Lake: The Vietnamese and the Americans in Vietnam*. New York: Little, Brown and Company.

Flad, Rowan K. 2008. "A Multiregional View of the Development of Oracle Bone Divination in Early China." *Current Anthropology* 49: 403–37.

Flusser, Vilem. 2018. *Language and Reality*. Roderigo Maltez Novaes transl. 1963 Portuguese edition (*Lingua e Realidade*). Minneapolis, MN: University of Minneapolis Press.

Geaney, Jane. 2004. "Guarding Moral Boundaries: Shame in Early Confucianism." *Philosophy East & West* 54: 113–42.

Goldin, Paul R. 2020. *The Art of Chinese Philosophy: Eight Classical Texts and How to Read Them*. Princeton, NJ: Princeton University Press.

Guo Moruo. 1940. *Zhouyi de goucheng shidai* 周易的構成時代 (The Ages of the Formation of the *Zhouyi*). Shanghai: Shangwu yinshuguan

Guo Moruo. 1982. *Guo Moruo quanji. Lishi bian* 郭沫若全集 (The Collected Writings of Guo Moruo: Historical Writings). Beijing: Remin chubanshe.

Hadot, Pierre and Michael Chase, transl. 2004. *What is Ancient Philosophy?* Cambridge, MA: Belknap; Harvard University Press.

Harbsmeier, Christoph. 1998. *Science and Civilization in China. Vol. 7, Part I: Language and Logic*. Cambridge: Cambridge University Press,

Hacker, Edward. 1993. *The I Ching Handbook: A Practical Guide to Logical and Personal Perspectives from the Ancient Chinese Book of Change*. Brookline, MA: Paradigm Publications.

Hale, Constance. 2013, August 7. "There's Parataxis, and Then There's Hypotaxis". *The Chronicle of Higher Education Blogs: Lingua Franca*. https://www.chronicle.com/blogs/linguafranca/2013/08/07/parataxis-and-hypotaxis/ Accessed September 5, 2022.

Harper, Donald and Marc Kalinowski, eds. 2017. *Books of Fate and Popular Culture in Early China: The Daybook Manuscripts of the Warring States, Qin, and Han*. Leiden: Brill.

Harrington, L. Michael. 2019. *The Yi River Commentary on the Book of Changes*. Cheng Yi. New Haven: Yale University Press.

Hart, David Bentley. 2019. *The New Testament: A Translation*. New Haven, CT: Yale University Press.

Hatcher, Bradford. 2009. *The Book of Changes: Yijing, Word by Word*. Vols I and II. http. hermetica.info, United States: Self-published.

Hillman, James. 1996. *The Soul's Code: In Search of Character and Calling*. New York: Ballantine Books.

Hon, Tze-ki. 2005, *The Yijing and Chinese Politics: Classical Commentary and Literary Activism in the Northern Song Period 960–1127*. Albany, NY: State University of New York Press.

Huang, Alfred. 1998. *The Complete I Ching: The Definitive Translation by the Taoist Master Alfred Huang*. Rochester, VT: Inner Traditions.

Huang, Shih-shan Susan, 2012. *Picturing the True Form: Daoist Visual Culture in Traditional China*. Cambridge, MA: Harvard University Asia Center for the Harvard-Yenching Institute.

Hunter, Michael and Martin Kern. 2018. *Confucius and the* Analects *Revisited: New Perspectives on Composition, Dating, and Authorship*. Leiden and Boston: Brill.

Instituts Ricci. 2003. *Apercus de Civilization Chinois: Les Dossiers du Grand Ricci*. Paris and Taipei: Instituts Ricci–Desclee de Brouwer. (Also available in Pleco, although not entirely complete.)

James, William. 1902. *The Varieties of Religious Experience: A Study in Human Nature*. London: Longmans & Greene. (Many recent editions.)

Jung, C. G. 1960. *Synchronicity: An Acausal Connecting Principle*. Princeton, NJ: Princeton University Press.

Kan Lifeng. 2011. In M. Schipper et al., 117–33.

Keightley, David N. 1985. *Sources of Shang History: The Oracle-Bone Inscriptions of Bronze Age China*. Berkeley, CA: University of California Press.

Kennedy, George A. 1999. *Classical Rhetoric and Its Christian and Secular Tradition from Ancient to Modern Times. Second Edition, Revised and Enlarged*. Chapel Hill, NC and London: University of North Carolina Press.

Kern, Martin, ed. 2005. *Text and Ritual in Early China*. Seattle, WA and London: University of Washington Press.

Kunst, Richard. 1985. *The Original* Yijing*: A Text, Phonetic Transcription, Translation, and Indexes, with Sample Glosses*. Ann Arbor, MI: University Microfilms International.

Legge, James, transl. 1899. *The Yi King. The Sacred Books of the East*. Vol. XVI. Reprinted New York: Dover 1963. Also available at Legge, James, transl. 1865. *The Chinese Classics*. Vol. III. *The Shoo King*. [*Book of Documents* or *Shangshu*] Reprint Taipei: SMC Publishing 1994. (See also Chinese Text Project. ctext.org *Ancient Texts*. Xi Ci 1 and 2. and ctext.org/shang-shu/marquis-of lu-on-punishments.)

Lewis, Mark Edward. 1999. *Writing and Authority in Early China*. Albany, NY: State of New York Press.

Li Dingzuo 李鼎祚. 1988 reprint, *Zhouyi jijie* 周易集解 (Collected commentaries on the *Changes* of the Zhou Dynasty). Taipei: Shangwu yinshuguan.

Li Jingchi 李镜池. 1978. *Zhouyi tanyuan* 周易探源 (A Study of the Origins of the *Zhouyi*). Beijing: Zhonghua shuju.

Li Jingchun 李景春. 1961. *Zhouyi zhexue yuqi bianzhengfa yinsu* 周易哲学与其辩证因素 (The Philosophy of the *Zhouyi* and Its Elements of Dialectical Method). Jinian: Shangtong renmin chubanshe.

Li, Feng and David Prager Branner. 2011. *Writing & Literacy in Early China: Studies from the Columbia Early China Seminar*. Seattle, WA and London: University of Washington Press.

Li, Ling. 1990. "Formulaic Structure of Chu Divinatory Bamboo Slips." *Early China* 15: 71–86.

Li, Shen 李申 and Guo Yu 郭#t11. 2004. *Zhouyi Tusho Zonghui* 周易图书总汇 (Collection of Diagrams of the *Zhouyi*). Shanghai: Huadong shifan daxue chubanshe.

Li, Wai-yee. 2007, *The Readability of the Past in Early Chinese Historiography*. Cambridge, MA: Harvard University Asia Center.

Liao Mingchun 廖明春. 2001. *Zhouyi jingzhuan yu yixue shi xinlun* 周易经传与易学史新论 (New Studies of the Core Text and Commentarial Materials of the *Zhouyi* and the History of the *Yi Learning*). Jinian: Qilao shushe.

Liu, Dajun. 2019. Transl. Zhang Wenzhi. *An Introduction to the Zhouyi (Book of Changes)*. Ashville, NC: Chiron Publications.

Liu Guozhong. 2016. Transl. Christopher J. Foster and William N. French. *Introduction to the Tsinghua Bamboo-Strip Manuscripts*. Leiden: Brill.

Loewe, Michael. *Divination, Mythology and Monarchy in Han China*. Cambridge: Cambridge University Press.

Lu, Xing. 吕行 1998. *Rhetoric in Ancient China Fifth to Third Century B.C.E.* Columbia, SC: University of South Carolina Press.

Lynn, Richard John. 1994. *The Classic of Changes: A New Translation of the I Ching as Interpreted by Wang Bi*. New York: Columbia University Press.

Lurie, Alison. 2001. *Familiar Spirits: A Memoir of James Merrill and David Jackson*. New York: Viking.

Marshall, S. J. 2001. *The Mandate of Heaven: Hidden History in the* I Ching. New York: Columbia University Press.

McClatchie, Rev. Canon Thomas. 1872. "The Symbols of the Yeh King." *The China Review* 1.3: 151–63.

McClatchie, Rev. Canon Thomas. 1876 transl. *A Translation of the Confucian* 易經 *or the "Classic of Change" With Notes and Appendix*. Shanghai: American Presbyterian Mission Press. Reprint Taipei: Cheng Wen Publishing Company, 1973.

McKenna, Dennis J. and Terence McKenna. 1975. Revised 1993. *The Invisible Landscape: Mind, Hallucinogens, and the I Ching*. New York: Seabury.

McLuhan, Marshall. 1962. New edition 2011. *The Gutenberg Galaxy: The Making of Typographical Man*. With new essays by W. Terrence Gordon, Elena Lamberti, and Dominique Scheffel-Dunand. Toronto: University of Toronto Press.

Melzer, Arthur N. 2014. *Philosophy Between the Lines: The Lost History of Esoteric Writing*. Chicago, IL: University of Chicago Press.

Merrill, James. 1992. *The Changing Light at Sandover*. New York: Knopf.

Ming Dong Gu. 2005. *Chinese Theories of Reading and Writing*. Albany, NY: State of New York University Press.

Mungello, D. E. 1989. *Curious Land: Jesuit Accommodation and the Origins of Sinology*. Honolulu: University of Hawaii Press.

Needham, Joseph. 1956. With the research assistance of Wang Ling. SCC Vol. 2 *History of Scientific Thought*. Cambridge: Cambridge University Press.

Nielsen, Bent. 2003. *A Companion to* Yi Jing *Numerology and Cosmology*. London: Routledge Curzon.

Nylan, Michael. 1993. *The Canon of Supreme Mystery by Yang Hsiung: A Translation of the T'ai Hsuan Ching*. Albany, NY: State University of New York Press.

Nylan, Michael. 2001. *The Five "Confucian" Classics*. New Haven, CT: Yale University Press.

Nylan, Michael and Thomas Wilson. 2010. *Lives of Confucius: Civilization's Greatest Sage Through the Ages*. New York: Crown Archetype.

Ong, Walter J. 2002 [1982]. *Orality and Literacy: The Technologizing of the Word*. 30th Anniversary edn. With additional chapters by John Hartley. London and New York: Routledge.

Ong, Walter J., SJ. 2004. *Ramus: Method, and the Decay of Dialogue: From the Art of Discourse to the Art of Reason*. Chicago, IL: University of Chicago Press.

Ong, Walter J. and Thomas J. Farrell. 2002. *An Ong Reader: Challenges for Further Inquiry*. New York: Hampton Press.

Palmer, Martin and Confucius. 2014. *The Most Venerable Book (Shang Shu)* UK: Penguin

Parry, Milman. 1971. *The Making of Homeric Verse: The Collected Papers of Milman Parry*, ed. Adam Parry. Oxford: Oxford University Press.

Pines, Yuri. 2002. *Foundations of Confucian Thought: Intellectual Life in the Chunqiu Period, 722–453 B.C.E.* Honolulu: University of Hawai'i Press.

Pines, Yuri. 2009. *Envisioning Eternal Empire: Chinese Political Thought of the Warring States Era*. Honolulu: University of Hawai'i Press.

Qian Ning, transl. Tony Blishen. 2011. *The New Analects: Confucius Reconstructed, A Modern Reader*. China: Better Link Press (city unspecified).

Ramey, Joshua. 2016. *Politics of Divination: Neo-liberal Endgame and the Religion of Contingency*. London: Rowman and Littlefield.

Raphals, Lisa. 2008–9. "Divination in the Han Shu Bibliographic Treatise." *Early China* 32: 1–43.

Raphals, Lisa. 2014. *Divination and Prediction in Early China and Ancient Greece*. Cambridge: Cambridge University Press.

Redmond, Geoffrey. 2008. *Science and Asian Spiritual Traditions*. Westport, CT: Greenwood Press.

Redmond, Geoffrey. 2017. *The I Ching (Book of Changes): A Critical Translation of the Early Text*. London: Bloomsbury Academic.

Redmond, Geoffrey and Tze-ki Hon. 2014. *Teaching the I Ching (Book of Changes)*. Oxford: Oxford University Press.

Rohsenow, John S. 2002. *ABC Dictionary of Chinese Proverbs*. Honolulu: University of Hawaii Press.

Rutt, Richard. 1996. *The Book of Changes (Zhouyi): A Bronze Age Document.* Transl. with an Introduction and Notes. Richmond, UK: Curzon.

Said, Edward W. 1979. *Orientalism.* New York: Vintage

Sawyer, Ralph D. 2004. *Ling Ch'i Ching: A Classic Chinese Oracle.* Boulder, CO: Westview Press.

Schaberg, David. 2001. *A Patterned Past: Form and Thought in Early Chinese Historiography.* Cambridge, MA: Harvard University East Asia Center.

Shangwen, Zhang and Fu Huisheng. 2008. *The Zhou Book of Changes.* Hunan: Peoples Publishing House.

Shaughnessy, Edward. 1983. *The Composition of the Zhouyi.* Ann Arbor, MI: UMI Dissertation Services.

Shaughnessy, Edward L. 1991. *Sources of Western Zhou History: Inscribed Bronze Vessels.* Berkeley, CA: University of California Press.

Shaughnessy, Edward L. 1993. "The Duke of Zhou's Retirement in the East and the Beginnings of the Minister-Monarch Debate in Chinese Political Philosophy." *Early China* 18: 41-72.

Shaughnessy, Edward L. 1994. "I Ching 易經 (Chou I周易)" In *Early Chinese Texts: A Bibliographical Guide*, ed. Michael Loewe. Berkeley, CA: Society for the Study of Early China and Institute of East Asian Studies, University of California.

Shaughnessy, Edward L. 1995. "The Origin of a *Yijing* Line Statement." *Early China* 20: 223-40.

Shaughnessy, Edward L. 1997a. *I Ching, the Classic of Changes: The First English Translation of Newly Discovered Second-Century B.C. Mawangdui Texts.* New York: Ballantine Books.

Shaughnessy, Edward L. 1997b. "'New' Evidence on the Zhou Conquest." In *Before Confucius: Studies in the Creation of the Chinese Classics*, pp. 31-67. Albany, NY: State University of New York Press.

Shaughnessy, Edward L. 1999a. "Calendar and Chronology." In *The Cambridge History of Ancient China: From the Origins of Civilization to 221 B.C.*, ed. Michael Lowe and Edward Shaughnessy, pp. 19-29. Cambridge: Cambridge University Press.

Shaughnessy, Edward L. 1999b. "Western Zhou History." In *The Cambridge History of Ancient China: From the Origins of Civilization to 221 B.C.*, ed. Michael Lowe and Edward Shaughnessy, pp. 292-351. Cambridge: Cambridge University Press.

Shaughnessy, Edward L. 2001. "The Fuyang *Zhou Yi* and the Making of a Divination Manual", *Asia Major, Third Series* 14 (2): 7-18.

Shaughnessy, Edward L. 2006. *Rewriting Early Chinese Texts.* Albany, NY: State University of New York Press.

Shaughnessy, Edward L. 2007. Review of Zheng Jixiong 鄭吉雄. Yi tuxiang yu Yi quanshi 易圖象與易詮釋. Dongyawenming yanjiu congshu 東亞文明研究叢書 [Volume] 6. Taibei: Taida Chuban Zhongxin.

Shaughnessy, Edward L. 2014. *Unearthing the Changes: Recently Discovered Manuscripts of the Yi Jing (I Ching) and Related Texts.* New York: Columbia University Press.

Shea, Robert and Robert Anton Wilson. 1975. *The Illuminatus! Trilogy: The Eye in the Pyramid, the Golden Apple, Leviathan*. New York: Dell.

Škrabal, Ondřej. 2019. "Writing Before Inscribing: On the Use of Manuscripts in the Production of Western Zhou Bronze Inscriptions." Online before publication. Cambridge: Cambridge University Press. Accessed December 20, 2020.

Smith, Richard J. 2008. *Fathoming the Cosmos and Ordering the World*: *The* Yijing (I-Ching *or Classic of Changes) and its Evolution in China*. Charlottesville, VA: University of Virginia Press.

Smith, Richard J. 2012. *The* I Ching: *A Biography*. Princeton, NJ and Oxford: Princeton University Press.

Spinney, Laura. 2018. "Did Human Sacrifice Help People Form Complex Societies? The Debate Over How Well Ritual Killings Maintained Social Order." *The Atlantic*. https://www.theatlantic.com/health/archive/2018/02/did-human-sacrifice-help-people-form-complex-societies/554327/ Accessed June 21, 2021.

Sullivan, Charles. 2009. "What's Wrong with the *I Ching*: Ambiguity, Obscurity, and Synchronicity." *Skeptical Inquirer* 33: 40–2.

Sung, Z. D. 1935. *The Text of Yi King (and Its Appendices): Chinese Original with English Translation*. Shanghai. (Recent reprint Taipei: Chinese Cultural Books Company 1983.)

Swetz, Frank J. 2008. *Legacy of the Luoshu: The 4,000 Year Search for the Meaning of the Magic Square of Order Three*. Wellesley, MA: A. K. Peters Ltd.

Takashima, Ken-ichi and Paul L-M. Serruys 2010. *Studies of Fascicle Three of Inscriptions from the Yin Ruins. Vol. I General Notes, Text and Translations*. Taipei: Institute of History and Philology, Academia Sinica.

Tiesler, Vera and Guilhem Olivier. 2020 ."Examining Heart Extractions in Ancient Mesoamerica: New Findings on Procedures and Meanings of Human Heart Sacrifices in Mesoamerica." *University of Chicago Press Journals*. https://www.eurekalert.org/pub_releases/2020-04/uocp-ehe042320.php. Accessed June 27, 2021.

Trovato, Paulo. 2017. *Everything You Always Wanted to Know About Lachmann's Method: A Non-standard Handbook of Genealogical Textual Criticism in the Age of Post-Structuralism, Cladistics, and Copy-Text*. Italy: ibreriauniversitaria.it edizioni

Unschuld, Paul U. 1985. *Medicine in China: A History of Ideas*. Berkeley, CA: University of California Press.

Unschuld, Paul U. 2003. *Huang Di Nei Jing Su Wen: Nature, Knowledge, Imagery in an Ancient Chinese Medical Text*. Berkeley, CA: University of California Press.

Waley, Arthur. 1937. *The Book of Songs: Translated from the Chinese by Arthur Waley*. Reprint of 1937 edition. New York: Grove Press.

Waddell, L. A. (Laurence Austine) 1895. *The Buddhism of Tibet, or Lamaism: With its Mystic Cults, Symbolism and Mythology, and in its Relation to Indian Buddhism*. London: W. H. Allen & Co.

Walsh, Lynda. 2013. *Scientists as Prophets: A Rhetorical Genealogy*. Oxford: Oxford University Press.

Wang, Robin. 2005. "Zhou Dunyi's Diagram of the Supreme Ultimate Explained ('Taijitu Shou'): A Construction of the Confucian Metaphysics." *Journal of the History of Ideas* 66: 307–23.

Wang, Robin R. 2012. *Yinyang: The Way of Heaven and Earth in Chinese Thought and Culture.* Cambridge: Cambridge University Press.

Watson, Burton, transl. 2007. *The Analects of Confucius.* New York: Columbia University Press.

Weston, Terry. 2010. *Psychic Cold Reading Forbidden Wisdom: Tips and Tricks for Psychics, Mediums, and Mentalists.* Swordworks Books Kindle.

Wilhelm, Richard, transl. 1962. *The Secret of the Golden Flower.* With a Commentary by C. G. Jung. Revised and augmented from 1931 edition. Princeton, NJ: Princeton University Press.

Wilhelm, Richard and Cary F. Baynes, trans, 1967. *The I Ching or Book of Changes: The Richard Wilhelm Translation Rendered into English by Cary F. Baynes.* Foreword by C. G. Jung. Third edition. Princeton, NJ: Princeton University Press.

Wu Xiaodong. 2011. In M. Schipper et al., 169.

Yau Shun-chiu and Chrystelle Marechal, eds. 2001. *Proceedings of the International Symposium of the Centennial of the Oracle-Bone Inscriptions Discovery.* Paris: Editions Languages Croisés.

Zhu Bokun 朱伯崑. 1995. *Yixue zhexue shi* 易学哲学史 (History of the Philosophy of the *Yi* Learning). Beijing: Huaxia chubanshe.

Index

Adler, Alfred 50
Adler, Joseph 7
'agglomerative/subordinative' 72
agonistic 47, 93, 221
Alexandria 21–22
animals
    appreciation of 176, 240n.1
    birds as omens 176–180
    butchering 192–195
    cows, sheep, oxen 189–190
    dangerous 196–197, 241n.6
    domestic 185–186, 190–191
    fish 195–196
    horses 175, 186–190
    hunting 152, 179–180, 191–192
    introduction 175
    and magic 197–198
    tortoises 137, 196–197, 198–199
    wild 180–183
Anthony, Carol 52
anti-parallelism 58
Argüelles, José 52
Aristotle 15, 27, 94, 100
Art of War 107, 201
astrology 18, 38, 41–42, 142, 212
auspiciousness 58–60, 63, 83
axial age/axiality 27–30, 221, 236n.5
Aztecs 159

bagua 209, 211
bamboo manuscript, Shanghai Museum 87, 224
bandits 111, 157
Baoshan 65, 112–113
Baynes, Cary F. *see* Wilhelm-Baynes
beheading 159, 164, 167, 197
bian 196
Bible 4–5, 93
'big data' 173
birds 176–180
blame 63–68
blood sacrifice 78, 199

Bouvet, Fr. Joachim 51, 212
Buddhism/Buddha 12, 17, 27, 29, 37, 94, 176, 209, 218
Buddhist mandalas 208
Burroughs, William 73
butchering 192–195

camels 175
Cassirer, Ernst 6
castration 188–190
Céline, Louis-Ferdinand 73
changeology 218
Cheng Yi 43, 49–51, 208, 211, 225
child sacrifice 173
China
    and animals 192, 194–195
    and axial ideas 26–29
    continuous mourning in 130
    and divination 35, 37, 39, 41, 43, 45, 57–58, 236n.3
    early hopes and fears 92
    early language 71, 75, 80, 87–88
    and esotericism 46–52
    facial expressions in 138
    health 112, 238n.1
    and hemerology 103
    hexagrams *see* hexagrams
    and hierarchy 145, 147
    and human sacrifice 159–161
    igniting philosophy in 30
    importance of text to readers 27
    introduction 3–5, 9–10, 12, 14–15
    and justification for insurrections 32
    and love 121
    and magical events 89
    and movement disorders 140
    and omens 98
    and polygamy 119–120
    servants in premodern 110–111
    and Song dynasty 209
    and travel 157
    virtuous government in 28

254 Index

and warfare 201
and women 117
and the *Yijing* 208
and yin-yang metaphysics 25, 211
Chinese Doubting Antiquity Movement 217
Christianity
   and figurism 51
   and infant sacrifice 160
   introduction 4
   and shame/guilt 66–67
   and weeping 132
Chunqiu (Spring and Autumn Annals) 28, 224, 236n.6
chuti 167
Ci Xi see Dazhuan
Cicero 36
Classic of Mountains and Seas 90, 175
Classic of Songs and the Spring and Autumn Annals 46
climate change 36
coin tossing 26, 35
Commentary on the Judgments 123
concubines 119–121, 123
Confucian Classics 90
Confucius/Confucianism
   and anomalous happenings 89–90
   and axial age 27
   and the *Dao* 145
   and disfigurement/mutilation 140
   and divination 11–12, 39, 43
   and esotericism 46–47
   and hierarchical societal structure 30
   and humility 152–153
   introduction/explanation 5, 12, 15, 17, 221
   and morality 65
   reflections on society 24–25
   respected more than read 94
   and shame/guilt 67
   and Sima Qian 208
   and simplicity 88–89
   and spirits of important events 28–29
context-dependent texts 24–26
Cook, Constance 64–65
Cook, Richard Sterling 52
core text 4, 10–11, 25, 51, 89, 207–208, 211, 221
cows 189–190

Croesus, King 203
curses 37, 42, 113, 129, 197

da ren 153
daily life
   accidents 113
   food and drink 113–114
   health 112–113
   home 110–112
   introduction 109
   water wells 114–115
   weather 115–116
   well-being 109–110
Dao De Jing 28–29, 114, 152
Dao Xue Study of the Way 209
Dao/Daoism 12, 37, 145, 181, 209
Daoist talismans 208
Dawkins, Richard 39, 185, 241n.4
daybooks 103
Dayeh, Islam 6
Dazhuan
   and magical/supernatural elements 68–69
   explanation 222
   fate/free will 81
   and hexagrams 25
   mythical individuals in 84
   and *Ten Wings* 26
   and trigrams 12–13
   and the *Yijing* 30, 82–83
deer 181
Di 4, 149
Di Yi 120
Díaz de Vivar, Rodrigo 203
ding 172
Diodorus 203
divination
   and ad hoc esotericism 48
   and animals 194, 198–199
   balanced view of 38–39
   and blame 63–68
   culture of 25
   and economics 40–41
   experiencing 42–43
   explanation of 35–38
   and the face 138
   favorable prognoses 56–60
   and health 112–113
   and hemerology 222

and human sacrifice 166
images for 79–80, 82
introduction 11, 18
learning from contemporary 41–42
locating correct response during 26
milfoil 145
and omens 98–99
other numbers 107
prognostic terms 55–56, 69
prophecy/science 39–40
recycled 100–101, 238n.2
ritualized 77
selection of texts for 13–14, 235n.3
sensations 142
and society 30–33, 145
three, seven as duration 104–106
time/work 103–104
unfavorable/negated prognoses 60–63
usually dialogic 93
and warfare 201
as word magic 68–69
DNA sequencing 155
domestic animals 185–186, 190–191
Dominicans 51
Doubting Antiquity movement 23, 47
dream interpretation 79, 238n.4
Duanci 84
Duke of Zhou Changes (Field) 21

earthquakes 142
Eastern Zhou 25, 65
Easy Classic 145–146
Ecclesiastes 132
eclipses 142
El Cid *see* Díaz de Vivar, Rodrigo
Elman, Benjamin A. 47
emotions
    bodily movements 136–140, 239n.2
    bodily sensations 142–143
    desolation/sterility 132–133
    disfigurement/mutilation 140–141
    expression of 129–130
    introduction 129
    mourning 130–131
    other images of 131–132
    positive, and happiness 133–134
    vocalizations 134–136
enchantment 198
enfeoffment 151–152, 240n.1

eren 141
esotericism
    and exotericism 47–48
    recognition of 45–47
    revival of 48
    Western readings of Chinese texts 51–52
    and *Xiangshu/Yili* 48–51
ethnic cleansing 164
execution 28, 124, 139, 145, 170, 172, 197, 240
exegesis 21, 26, 51

fei jiu 64
Fellowship with Men 204
Field, Stephen 5, 84–85
figurism 4, 51, 54, 222
Fingarette, Herbert 66
Fire in the Lake (FitzGerald) 33, 171
fish 195–196
FitzGerald, Frances 33, 171
Flad, Rowan K. 31–32
flaying 159, 192–193
fortune telling 42
Foucault, Michel 30
foxes 182–183
Frazier, Sir James 10
Freud, Sigmund 9–10
Friedman, Milton 40
fu 166
Fu Hao 115, 117–118, 239n.3
Fu Xi 12, 25, 43, 47, 84, 196–198, 207, 222
Fuyang text 123

Gaoci 84
Geaney, Jane 66–68
geese 175, 178
Genesis 1:1–5 (Douay version) 72
geng day 222
God 4, 67
gods 4, 9, 27, 37, 89–90, 149
Gould, Stephen Jay 39
grammar
    archaic text punctuation 73–74
    images for divination 79–80
    introduction 71
    judgment texts 76–78
    line texts and images 78–79
    parataxis 71–74

parsing 75–76
prognostication/prognosis 80–83
punctuating without rewriting 74–75
Great Commentary 81
Greece 15, 27, 88, 159, 201
Greek New Testament 22
gu 197–198
guang 60
gui 169
Guizong 106
Guodian manuscripts 24, 222

Hadot, Pierre 16–17
haemolacria 187
hallucinations 99
hallucinogens 99
Halys River 203
Han, the
  arcane philosophizing of 89
  and prognoses 80
  schools of interpretation 48–49
  Xiangshu school 74, 183–184, 208
  yin-yang 25, 37
haotao 136, 167
Harbsmeier, Christoph 72, 87
Harper, Donald 103
Harrington, L. Michael 50, 208, 211
haruspicy 99, 145, 194, 201
Hatcher, Bradford 15–16
Hawking, Stephen 39
Hayek, Friedrich 40
Heart Sutra 94
hemerology 58, 103, 222
heng 161
hengzhen 161
Hermetic Order of the Golden Dawn 48
hermeticism 48
hexagrams
  1 *Qian* 79
  3 *Tun* 186
  6 *Song* 58
  7 *Shi* Troops 201
  9 *Xiao Chu* 156
  10 *Lu* 196
  13 *Tong Ren* 204
  17 *Sui* 163
  18 *Gu* 197
  19 *lin* 167
  21 *Shi Ke* 138
  23 *Bo* 159, 192
  27 *Li* 131, 136
  31 *Xian* 142
  33 *Dun* 185
  34 *Da Zhuan* 190
  35 *Jin* 187
  36 *Mingyi* 177, 179
  37 *Jiaren* 122–123
  38 *Kui* 33
  39 *Ji An* 148
  45 *Gui* 179
  48 *Jing* 114–115, 132
  49 *Ge* 32, 90, 105, 170–172, 196
  50 'no blame' 64
  51 *Zhen* 135
  52 *Gen* 159, 193–195
  53 *Jian* 175, 177–179
  54 *Gui* 119, 133
  56 *Lu* 157
  58 *Dui* 170
  59 *Huan* 159, 188
  61 *Zhong Fu* 46
  63 *Ji Ji* 181–184, 241n.2
  64 *Wei Ji* 181–184, 241n.2
  aura of numinosity of 92
  changing lines 82–83, 238n.5
  chart 229, 230–231
  describing overall situation 69
  and divination 37, 42
  explanation 222
  finder 233
  and grammar 74
  introduction 10, 13–14, 17, 235n.1
  no evident context 25
  and psychedelic experiences 99–100
  texts 76–79, 222
  use of in *Zhouyi* 20–21
  used in diagnosis and treatment 113
  Xiangshu and *Yili* 49–52
  and yarrow sorting/coin tossing 26, 235n.3
hierarchy
  high-born women 150
  kings, nobles, commoners 145–150
  nobility 150–154
hieroglyphs 212
Hindu yantras 208
Hinduism 17
Homer 93

Hong Kong 119, 239n.4
horses 175, 186–190
Huang Di Nei Jing Su Wen 129
Hubei tomb 103
hui 61–63, 130
human sacrifice
    distress 165–168, 240n.3
    introduction 159–160
    mercy 168–170
    other violence 172
    procedures 164–165, 240n.2
    rationalization of 172–173, 240n.8
    ritual aspects 162–163
    tanning leather 170–172, 240n.7
    victim selection 163–164
    in the *Zhouyi* texts 160–162
hunting 152, 179–180, 191–192
hypotaxis 72

Iliad, the 28, 159
India 27, 160
inferior/superior man 190
inimical spirits 129
Inquisition 159
The Invisible Landscape: Mind,
    Hallucinogens, and the I Ching
    (McKenna/McKenna) 33
Iphigenia 159
Islam 6, 194

James, William 10
Jaspers, Karl 27, 223
ji 58–59, 161
jiu 61, 63–64, 66
Judaism 4, 9, 194
judgment texts *see* hexagrams, texts
Jung, Carl 9–10, 17, 29, 43, 75, 195, 218
Junzi 33, 82, 153, 223
Jupiter 106

Kalinowski, Marc 103
Kang, Marquis 187
Kerouac, Jack 73
Kongzi 5
Kun 196
Kunst, Richard 151, 156, 177

Laozi 15, 24, 27, 29, 147, 211, 218
Latin 22, 88

Lau, D. C. 6
Legge, James 7, 22, 46–47, 69, 85, 88, 90,
    217
Leibniz, Gottfried Wilhelm 207, 212
leopards 153, 172, 196
li 177
Li Jinchi 76
lin 61–62, 76, 130, 167
literati 4, 12, 37, 39, 50, 88, 145, 196, 207,
    223
Lofts, Steve G. 6
Lunyu, the
    and animals 176
    and Confucius 67, 89, 141
    explanation 223
    introduction 5
    and post-axial thought 28–29
    separate narrative anecdotes of 27
    and social position 145, 147, 152
    and women 123
Luo Shu 12, 197, 223
Lynn, Richard John 77, 123, 137–138, 172

Ma Wang Dui 22
McClatchie, Canon 217
McKenna, Terence and Dennis 33
McLuhan, Marshall 61, 237n.1
magic 8, 12, 25–28, 68, 89, 112, 155–156,
    197–198
manifestation 100, 238n.3
Mao Zedong 185
Marriage Law 1980 (China) 121
Mawangdui silk manuscript (MWD) 11,
    20, 64, 80, 194, 223
Mayans 159
Melzer, Arthur N. 45–47
memes 185, 241n.4
Mencius 24, 28, 160, 176
Meyer, Dirk 24
milfoil 145
misogyny 117, 239n.2
Moog, Hanna 52
Mu Jiang, Lady 93

Naked Lunch (Burroughs) 73
negations 60–63
Neo- Confucianism 208, 223
neo-liberalism 40
neophytes 23

New Age culture 41, 100
New Testament 94

occultism 38, 42, 48, 97
Oedipus complex 9–10
'oligarchy of the unknown' 41
omens
    animals as 175–178, 185
    explanation 223–224
    important in selecting women 120–121
    as internal sensations 142
    and mourning 132
    nature of 97–101
    and twitching 199
On the Road (Kerouac) 73
Ong, Walter 24, 72, 91–93
optical imagery 207–213
oracle bone inscriptions (OBI)
    and butchering 193
    and divination 31–32, 100, 103, 113, 117–118
    and hierarchy 145–146
    and high-born women 150
    and human sacrifice 160–161
    introduction/explanation 9, 224
    and spirits 66
    and tortoises 198
    and travel 155
Oracle of Delphi 38
orioles 131, 176–177
oxen 189–190

paratactic texts 74, 110, 224
Parkinson's disease 140
Pergamum 22
pheasants 177, 179–180
philology 6–7, 118, 217
Philosophy Between the Lines: The Lost History of Esoteric Writing (Melzer) 45
Philosophy of Symbolic Forms (Cassirer) 6
pigs 185–186, 190
Pines, Yuri 26
Plato 27, 94, 100
poison/poisoning 129, 139
Politics of Divination (Ramey) 33
polygamy 119–120
polysemy 20, 22, 71, 75, 88, 224

prognostication/prognosis 37–38, 55–63, 69, 80–83
propitiatory rituals 64–65
Proust, Marcel 21
pyromancy 146

qi 151
Qian 196
Qian Ning 5
Qing Dynasty 15, 22, 47, 77, 212

Radical Change (Lynn) 32
Ramey, Joshua 33, 40–41
'rejected knowledge' 42
Revolution (Molting) (Wilhelm/Baynes) 32
rhetoric
    Confucian simplicity 89–90
    early literacy 91–93
    and style of expression 87–88
    use of *Book of Changes* 93–94
    Zhouyi 90–91
Ricci, Matteo 51
ridgepoles 56, 111–112
Rome 159–160, 166
Rorschach ink blots 208
Ruism/Ruists
    compared to Confucianism 12
    and *Dao Xue* 209
    and divination 56
    and esotericism 46–47, 50
    explanation of 224
    and *Gen* 193, 195
    and hexagrams 77
    and human sacrifice 159–160, 165–166, 172
    and humility 152–153
    and language 88
    propriety in social interactions 67
    rise in the Warring States 10
    and social hierarchy 145
    and supernatural blame 85
    and Wilhelm-Baynes *I Ching* 17
    and women 37, 117
    and the *Yijing* 31
ruo 132
Rutt, Richard
    and birds 177
    and bodily movements 136–137

changes of prognostic terms 62–63, 237n.2
and emotion 131, 239n.1
and *gen* 193–194
important scholarship of 217
and *li* 177
parsing by function proposal 76
prognostication/prognosis 80
and rendering of 'meng' 23
and spirituality/philosophy 14–15
syntactical structure of *Zhouyi* 83–84, 238n.7
and travel 156
and twitching 199
and warfare 202–203
and weather 116
and Yue sacrifice 162

Sagan, Carl 39
Sapir-Whorf hypothesis 23–24
sati 160, 164
servants 110–111
sex 11, 31, 63, 105, 197–198
Shakespeare, William 21, 94
shamans 28, 37–38, 153–154, 196
Shan Hai Jing 90
Shang Dynasty 4–5, 28, 47, 149, 160, 171, 178, 186, 203
Shanghai Museum 22, 156, 224
Shangshu (Book of Documents) 90, 224, 238n.2
Shao Yong 39, 184, 209, 212, 225
Shaughnessy, Edward L. 23, 116, 138, 172, 177, 194, 197
sheep 189–190
shi 93, 203–204
Shici 84
Shiji Book of History 208
Shijing, the Songs of Chu 84, 88, 118
Shuogua 25–26, 69
Shuowen Jiezi 167
Sima 13
Sima Qian 47, 208
sin 66–67
Smith, Richard J. 207–208, 217
Socrates 11, 15, 17, 27
Song Dynasty 39, 47, 49, 78, 161, 208–209, 211
Song Zhu Xi 14

Spain 159
Spinney, Laura 173
spiritualism 18
Spring and Autumn Annals 88, 123–124, 145, 224
Stone Age 159
Strauss, Leo 45
Supreme Ultimate *tai qi* 211

Taiping rebellion (1850–1864) 32
Tarot 16, 18, 38–39, 41–42
Ten Commandments 4–5
Ten Wings
   authorship of 12–14
   and Confucian ideology 23
   and *Dazhuan/Shuogua* 211
   explanation 225
   fate/free will 81–82
   gloss on hexagram 61 *Zhong Fu* 46
   last two hexagrams 183–184
   and numerology 104
   obscuring plain language 88–89
   reading for wisdom 25–26
   text and line systems 69–70
   and trigrams 207–208
   and Warring States 207–208
'terror management theory' 99
thankas 212
Thirty-six Stratagems 107, 201
ti yi 167
Tian 4, 149
tian ming 4
tigers 137–138, 153, 172, 196
topos 91
tortoises 137, 196–197, 198–199
travel 155–158
trigrams 12, 25, 33, 69, 196–197, 207–208, 222
troops 201–202
Tuan 69

Varieties of Religious Experience (James) 10
Vietnam 194
Vietnam War 171
virtue 28, 236n.7

wailing 167–169, 240n.4
Waley, Arthur 6, 23

Walsh, Lynda 39–40
Wang Bi 14, 16, 74, 77, 121, 123, 138, 225
Wangshan 112–113
warfare 201–206
Warring States
   arcane philosophizing of 89
   and divination 37
   explanation of 13–14, 226
   and hemerology 103
   and philosophy of time 82
   and supernatural blame 65, 69
   and *Ten Wings* 207–208
   and yin-yang metaphysics 25
water buffalo 175
water wells 114–115
Watts, Alan 17
weather 115–116, 156
Webb, James 42
weeping 131–132, 168
Wen, King 25, 47, 203
Wen Wang 43, 226
Western Zhou Dynasty
   daily life 109
   and emotion 129
   and grammar 71, 75
   and hemerology 103–104
   and human sacrifice 159–160, 170
   introduction 3, 5, 15
   life and language of 25, 87
   much remains unknown 19
   and oracle bone divination 198
   and philology 217
   prognostic terms in divination 55
   regret/blame 67
   rise of 28
   and tanning/curing 32
   and warfare 204
wild animals 180–183
Wilhelm, Richard *see* Wilhelm-Baynes
Wilhelm-Baynes
   and animals 190, 193, 195, 198
   and bodily movements 137
   daily life 110, 116
   and emotions 132
   and esotericism 46
   grammatical approaches 74–75, 77
   and human sacrifice 166, 170–172
   important scholarship of 217–218
   introduction 7
   and omens 97
   presenting text as timeless 16–17
   prolix translation 88
   psychology/place of *Book of Changes* 10, 12
   and *Revolution (Molting)* 32–33
   text and line systems 69
   translation renderings 22–23
   visions of 29–30
   and warfare 204
Williams, Crispin 21
wine 114
witchcraft 37, 129, 139, 236n.2
Wittgenstein, Ludwig 10
women
   activities/household 122–124
   lives of 117–119, 239n.2
   marriage 119–122
wu 154
Wu Ding, King 12, 31, 106, 113, 117, 163, 203, 226
Wu, Emperor 207–208
wu jiu 60, 64, 84–85
Wu Wang 226
wu xing 211
Wu Zetian, Empress 117, 239n.1
wuhui 60

Xi Ci see Dazhuan
Xiangshu school 48–52, 70, 74, 182–184, 208, 222–223
xiao 116, 168
xiong 61
Xunzi 24, 36

Yanci 84
Yao 226
yarrow 14, 26, 74, 226
Yellow Turban Rebellion (184–205 BCE) 32
Yi 82, 145–146
Yi, Father 118
Yi River Commentary on the Book of Changes (Cheng Yi) 50
Yijing
   and ancient classics 88
   and animals 183
   and the axial age 27–30
   and *Dazhuan* 82–83, 237n.6

and divination 37, 43, 57, 69, 161
engaging with 19
and esotericism 46, 48–50
explanation 226
and *Ge* hexagram 171
grammatical approaches 75
introduction 4, 11, 13, 15
mythology of 25–26
and power interests 31–33
regarded as profound 94
and social hierarchy 145
text and line systems 69–70
and women 123
and *Xiangshu/Yili* schools 208, 211
and the *Zuozhuan* 93
Yili school 14, 48–52, 74, 208, 226
Yin Dynasty 117

yin-yang 25, 29, 37, 49, 51, 69, 184, 208–209, 211, 226
Yogi, Maharishi Mahesh 17
Yu the Great 104
Yue sacrifice 162

zheng 61
Zhou, Duke of 21, 25, 47, 84
Zhou Dunyi 208–209, 211
Zhou Gong, Duke 25, 43, 226–227
Zhu 212
Zhu Xi 43, 49–51, 67, 165–166, 208, 211, 218, 225
Zhuangzi 24–28, 90, 92, 131, 145, 147, 152, 199, 218
Zigong 176
Zodiac 106
Zuozhuan 28, 124, 145–146, 149

www.ingramcontent.com/pod-product-compliance
Lightning Source LLC
Chambersburg PA
CBHW071813300426
44116CB00009B/1295